GOD
IN A
CUP

GOD
IN A
CUP

The Obsessive Quest
for the Perfect Coffee

MICHAELE WEISSMAN

WILEY

JOHN WILEY & SONS, INC.

Published by John Wiley & Sons, Hoboken, New Jersey

Published simultaneously in Canada

For general information about our other products and services, please contact our Customer Care Department within the United States at (800) 762-2974, outside the United States at (317) 572-3993 or fax (317) 572-4002.

Wiley also publishes its books in a variety of electronic formats. Some content that appears in print may not be available in electronic books. For more information about Wiley products, visit our web site at www.wiley.com.

Library of Congress Cataloging-in-Publication Data

Weissman, Michaele.
  God in a cup : the obsessive quest for the perfect coffee / Michaele Weissman.
    p. cm.
  Includes index.
  ISBN 978-0-470-17358-9 (cloth : alk. paper)
  1. Coffee. 2. Coffee industry. I. Title.
  TX415.W387 2008
  641.3'373--dc22
                       2008001363

Printed in the United States of America

10 9 8 7 6 5 4 3 2 1

CONTENTS

To John Melngailis,

who brews my morning coffee

and shares the cup

ACKNOWLEDGMENTS

THIS BOOK IS A LOVE STORY. I WENT OUT ONE DAY TO DO some reporting, and I fell in love with specialty coffee and the people—especially the people—who populate this lively realm.

So many coffee guys have been so generous. A few have gone beyond what any reporter could expect. Peter Giuliano from Counter Culture Coffee and Geoff Watts from Intelligentsia Coffee & Tea let me tag along when I knew nothing. They worried about me when I was sick in Africa. They were my teachers, and now they are my friends, and so, I feel, are many who work at their companies. The gang at Stumptown in Portland—Duane Sorenson, Aleco Chigounis, Matt Lounsbury, and Stephen Vick, to name just a few—opened their doors wide and made me welcome. My gratitude to you all runs deep.

Many thanks as well to Ric Rhinehart, executive director of the Specialty Coffee Association of America, who served as reality tester, sounding board, and boon companion during my adventures in coffee world.

Specialty coffee attracts extraordinary people. Extraordinarily smart. Extraordinarily adventurous. Extraordinarily good company. The following people have shared all three—their smarts, their adventures, and their company. I learned so much from you and had such fun. Deepest thanks to Sarah Allen; Andrew Barnett; Lindsey Bolger; Willem Boot; Tim Castle; Nick Cho; Johnny and Zoraida Collins; Kim Cook; E. J. Dawson; Wendy de Jong; Libby Evans; Brent Fortune; Bob Fulmer; Shanna Germain; Daniele Giovannucci; Kyle Glanville; Dave Griswold; Don Holly; George Howell; Mark Inman; Nick Kirby; Tony Konecny; Ricardo Koyner; Wilford Lamastus; Ted Lingle; Shirin Moayyad; K. C. O'Keefe; Anne Ottaway; Heather Perry; Rachel, Daniel, Price, and Susan Peterson; Rick Peyser; Joel Pollack; David Roche; Stephen Rogers; Maria Ruiz; Tim Schilling; Menno Simons; Trish Skeie; Brett Smith; Paul Songer; Susie Spindler; Andi Trindle; Stephen Vick; Ryan Wilbur; and Doug Zell.

This book is living proof that fine people with high standards continue to devote themselves to book publishing.

Marly Rusoff of the Marly Rusoff agency flattered me by taking me as a client. When I transformed myself into a food writer, Marly sent me to her friend and fellow agent, Lisa Queen of Queen Literary. Lisa—so clear-thinking, so easy to work with, and so there when I came unglued. When my rowboat was going in circles, Lisa's colleague, agent, and editor Eleanor Jackson got me going straight.

My editor at Wiley, Linda Ingroia, named this book, nurtured this book, and pushed it toward completion. I can't imagine an editor who cares more about quality, accuracy, and literary grace. Her high standards marked my interactions with the entire Wiley team, including production editor Amy Zarkos, cover designer Suzanne Sunwoo, creative director Tai Blanche, interior designer Lee Goldstein, and publicity manager, David Greenberg and Michael Friedberg. My deepest, warmest thanks to all of you and to Dottie Jeffries for helping me be heard.

And then there are the people from my own little pod. Carol Hymowitz, fellow seeker, friend since our freshman year.

Marcia Adler, keeper of secrets, laughing companion in Shrinkville. Diana Altman, sister writer, whose family life is so entwined with mine. Liz Lerman, of fearless imagination, who knows more about making art than anyone else. Thank you, dear friends, for understanding.

My hometown pals Rhoda Baer, Cynthia Feiden-Warsh, Richard Warsh, Kathy Kretman, Alison Fenn, Gabe Skinner, and Briget Viksnins. You all saw me at my worst and at my best and helped me muddle through. And thanks to Ethan Warsh, who has the eye of a social scientist and the sensibility of an artist.

A special writerly thanks to Jeff Bailey, who urged me to pursue coffee, and Patsy Sims, who listened to me and said, "Michaele, that's your book." And to John Kafka, whose office I was lucky enough to land in. I could not have birthed this book without him.

Ah, and my family. How do I say thank you to my mother, Florence Weissman, wise and loving woman, who taught me the most important lesson a writer can learn—that secrets are revealed to those who listen. And to my children by birth and marriage, Ilze Melngailis, Sarma Melngailis, and Noah Melngailis—all of you have received my stories and now you are writing stories of your own. How proud I am of you and how grateful I am to have had you in my corner during this year of venturing forth. That goes for Steve Rosenstein, too, who adds so much to our family. And how do I say thank you to John, my partner and my friend. Still. Always.

One other person uniquely shared the mid-life burst of ambition out of which this book was born: My cousin Dale Tikoian, of blessed memory. Dale, I took you with me on my journey.

PROLOGUE

I FELL IN LOVE WITH COFFEE ON A SUNNY OCTOBER MORNING in 2005 while sipping a velvety cappuccino at an outdoor table in front of Murky Coffee, ground zero for coffee lovers in Washington, D.C., my hometown. I'd zipped downtown to Capitol Hill that morning to interview Murky's spiky-haired owner Nick Cho, then thirty-one, for an article on young coffee entrepreneurs I was writing for the *New York Times*. I'd been drinking coffee since my early twenties, buying whole beans and dutifully grinding them at home, but for all my efforts I might as well have been drinking hot water and Ritalin. Until I met Nick I don't think I had ever tasted coffee mindfully, or perceived it as a product grown, processed, and prepared by artisans. Coffee back then was notable for what it lacked. If it lacked bitterness, it was good.

In my reporting I had been tracking down the most respected small companies that roast the highest-rated coffees. The boutique end of the coffee business being what it is, that meant I was talking with a lot of entrepreneurs who were still in their thirties. These young guns took me by surprise. They were magnetic, anti-authoritarian, and rapturously in love with coffee. They were far more engaging than the high-tech entrepreneurs I had written about. When we talked, they poured all their mojo into explaining their world and their businesses, using every ounce of available juice to convince me that coffee is the culinary world's most enticing shore, a vast unexplored coast of limitless potential.

The coffee guys buy, roast, and sell what the industry refers to as *specialty coffee*. These are elite "craftsmen" coffees grown with special care by farmers using traditional agricultural techniques on farms located in Latin America, Africa and Asia— coffee grows in as many as fifty countries located in a mountainous band that circles the globe near the equator along common latitudinal lines.

The coffee guys shared their excitement about one super-high-quality coffee—Hacienda La Esmeralda Special. This much-ballyhooed bean from a small Panamanian coffee farm had won their hearts and their pocketbooks—boy oh boy, was it expensive. As I learned more about Esmeralda Special, it seemed to me that this coffee was emblematic, highlighting trends in the specialty business while showcasing the people who were driving the industry forward. In an era when so many strive for the ultimate something, Esmeralda Special had the razzle-dazzle of a superstar. Specialty coffee buyers described this precious bean as the most exotic and the most expensive coffee in the world.

Everything about Esmeralda Special was unexpected. Where it came from. What it tasted like. Even the look of the tree it grew on. Until this coffee from Panama made headlines, most coffee lovers outside and inside the specialty industry would have expected the priciest coffee on earth to grow on the side of a mountain in Kenya or on a volcano in Hawaii. But they would have been wrong. Hacienda La Esmeralda Special comes from Boquete, Panama, center of one of the world's smallest coffee-growing industries. Moreover, this precious coffee grows on a few acres most farmers would not bother to cultivate. Too steep. Too windy. That's what growers would have said until Esmeralda Special began commanding killer prices. In 2005 this coffee sold for $20 a pound green, and roughly twice that roasted—a record at the time. In 2006 it sold for $50 a pound green, fifty times the going rate, meaning customers in the United States were paying $100 a pound and more. In 2007 Esmeralda commanded $130 a pound green, meaning retail customers were paying in excess of $200 a pound. What coffee roaster would buy such a bean? And to whom could he possibly sell it?

The Esmeralda story is about an ugly duckling coffee that grew into a gorgeous swan. It's about scarcity, and the lust that scarcity engenders in those driven to possess what others can never have. It's about the greed that inevitably emerges when the possibility of making a great deal of money selling something rare and precious presents itself. And it is about a new generation of hip young coffee buyers who are madly, wildly, deeply in love with coffee in a way their elders in the coffee business find ever-so-slightly preposterous.

Thirtysomething guys in the specialty business, the main characters of this story, swoon for Esmeralda. They are smitten by its over-the-top nose and its cornucopia of fruity flavors. They are captivated by its mysterious origins. Their love is not rational and it's not all about business. But business interests do lurk in the background. Of course the young coffee guys are titillated by the price Esmeralda commands. And as entrepreneurs operating in the high end of the coffee business, they see Esmeralda as a point of entry for a new breed of coffee drinkers who will spend the money for coffee that is rare and fabulous.

These guys definitely have an agenda when it comes to raising the price of coffee. They believe charging more is key to the specialty industry's future. They reject the traditional buy-low-sell-high business model: that way of doing business squeezes the breath from coffee farmers and everyone else in the specialty world, they say. Their goal is to earn more money for everyone along the coffee chain. The new model—the Esmeralda model—demands that traders buy high and sell higher.

The young hotshots who led the bidding for Esmeralda call themselves coffee's Third Wave, and they think of themselves as coffee revolutionaries. This book tells the story of my travels with these Third Wave rebels in pursuit of perfect coffee. Together we tasted Hacienda La Esmeralda Special in Panama; observed the birth of a new specialty industry in Burundi; explored Ethiopia, coffee's fabled motherland; visited dozens of coffee farms; and met farmers living as their ancestors lived a thousand years ago and others who enjoy Hollywood-style luxuries. In Nicaragua I learned how coffee is "cupped," or tasted and ranked, by professionals, and I observed a famed international coffee competition. Back home, I got to know the high-end coffee scene in Durham, North Carolina; Chicago; Los Angeles; Portland, Oregon; and New York. I was awed and entertained by the skill and enthusiasm exhibited by young baristas taking part in barista competitions in every region of the country and many countries in the world. These competitions are a big deal. Thousands watched the World Barista Championship in Tokyo in August 2007, in person and online. Here at home, I visited the coffee guys' cooler-than-cool retail cafés where coffee is brewed in sleek, high-performance machines called Clovers that cost $11,000 apiece and skinny hipsters in Chuck Taylors serve up espresso drinks topped with latte art.

It was quite a ride.

In addition to my interest in coffee, I was motivated by curiosity about the coffee guys themselves. These young entrepreneurs were playing on a mighty big stage. Coffee, it turns out, is the second most often traded commodity, after oil, and the global coffee trade each year generates hundreds of billions of dollars worldwide.

Are these young guys up to revolutionizing this industry? Can they convince the public that there are real reasons to pay $12, $15, $20, or possibly $40 a pound for coffee beans? Is their focus on coffee quality and on bettering the lives of some of the earth's poorest farmers proof positive that their generation is different and better than those who came before? Or are they deluded egomaniacs who will overspend their businesses right down the tubes? Could it be that they are the real thing—members of an anomalous pool of talent that emerge occasionally to transform entire industries, from independent filmmaking to software?

Before I was ready to address the big questions, I had to know more about coffee as a beverage. Which brings me back to the memorable cappuccino prepared for me by Nick Cho. Unlike the other coffee guys I interviewed for my article, Nick Cho does not travel to end-o'-earth destinations in search of perfect coffee beans. He is not a coffee buyer or roaster; he is a café owner and barista who is in love with serving customers—his goal, he tells me, is to serve coffee so great that it redefines for his customers what coffee can be. Like a great chef, Nick has a way of making his work look effortless. In his plaid Bermudas and flip-flops, he owns the espresso machine the way Eric Clapton owns the guitar.

When Nick first offers to make me a coffee, I ask for decaf.

"Hey, just try a small real coffee," Nick says, with a knowing little smile. Then he gets busy preparing a double-shot, twelve-ounce cappuccino for me with whole milk and Counter Culture's Toscano espresso blend.

Standing before a LaMarzocco coffee machine, Nick, a regional barista champion, pours a single portion of milk into a stainless steel pitcher and then with focus and precision grinds and tamps the espresso. In use all morning, the espresso machine is hot and ready to go. Nick slips the portafilter that holds the coffee into its metal fitting and hits the button. Water heated precisely to 200°F is forced through the machinery at 8.5 bars (of atmospheric pressure). Dark brown espresso trickles through the grouphead into the preheated white porcelain cup.

As the shot trickles into the cup, Nick carefully angles the tip of the steam wand into the milk—if the wand enters too deeply it will produce fat air bubbles rather than a velvety foam. He keeps his fingers on the milk pitcher. As the stainless grows warm to the touch, he switches from frothing to swirling.

Twenty-five seconds have elapsed. The milk is ready and so is the espresso. Nick shuts off the power. He wipes and purges the steam wand.

Holding the cup in his left hand and the milk pitcher in his right, he turns to me. The espresso is topped with luscious, reddish brown foam called the crema. What happens next is pure theater. Nick swirls the pitcher. Holding it five inches away, he tilts the porcelain cup back in his left hand and pours. Milk, not foam, falls into the cup. Then he lowers the pitcher and wiggles it, coaxing velvety ribbons of foam onto the surface of the coffee. The foam undulates and folds back on itself. In the middle of the cup a pattern begins to appear.

Perfectly textured reddish brown espresso foam intermingles with the stiff froth of steam-blasted milk, and a brown outline of an evergreen appears in the center of the cup. The design—called a rosetta—lingers as I slowly drink my first real coffee.

Hemingway had it right. The first time, the earth moves.

The milk and coffee are as sweet as sugar and as thick as cream, but the effect is achieved magically, as he used neither of these ingredients. The milk and coffee together are as luxurious as cashmere and bring mouth memories of caramel, chocolate, and hazelnut.

"I've never tasted anything like this," I tell Nick.

"Most coffee is swill," he answers cheerfully. Later, I learn that baristas call this kind of an experience a Godshot moment, a rare but perfect example of their craft. I sip my little cup of nirvana sitting with Nick. He talks fast, speaking about the high-end coffee business. Of his dream of opening a luxurious coffee bar that would become a Washington, D.C., landmark—a swank yet inviting destination where customers would find it acceptable and worthwhile to pay $10 or more for a cup of perfectly brewed coffee that would be identified by estate or origin.

With that first cup of Murky coffee, a door opened and I slipped down the rabbit hole into coffee land. I got caught up in the story of specialty coffee, and you might say I haven't been home since.

THE COFFEE GUYS

PETER GIULIANO, COFFEE BUYER AND MINORITY OWNER OF Counter Culture Coffee, based in Durham, North Carolina, describes himself and the other Third Wave coffee guys driving the fast-growing specialty coffee industry as "a bunch of freakin' nutcase obsessives who have trouble hacking it in the real world.

"When I was studying music in college I had to figure out what was the most authentic expression of northern Mexican accordion music," he explains. "I spent years of my life figuring this out. Then I applied my attention to cocktails. In my house I had a thousand dollars invested in obscure kinds of alcohol. My friends would come over and I would make them a martini the way they were made in 1934."

Take Geoff Watts of Intelligentsia Coffee in Chicago or Duane Sorenson of Stumptown Coffee in Portland, Oregon. "You think these guys are normal?" Peter will ask, raising his eyebrows.

Peter has a point. The top tier of the specialty world is full of people who obsess about the details. These are individuals who will drive themselves past the point of reason to get it right, who will spend five years figuring out the perfect protocol for controlling the temperature gauge of their espresso machine. Guys who compare great coffee to great wine and are able to detect hundreds of flavors and aromas in a coffee from a small farm in Guatemala as great wine masters discern countless subtleties in an aged Burgundy.

Tasting—cupping is the term used in the coffee industry—ten or twenty coffees is never enough for guys like this. As Geoff Watts of Intelligentsia, a leading specialty coffee roaster/retailer, talking about his education in the industry, explains, "I wanted to cup two hundred coffees. I wanted to cup two thousand coffees. I wanted to know everything you could know about the nuances of flavor and aroma and then I wanted to know more."

Geoff and the other specialty guys would tell you that their devotion has been generously repaid. Considering his career and that of other industry leaders, Peter comments, "The beautiful thing about specialty coffee is that it rewards that obsessiveness. It uses all our talents. It fosters the development of lost kids like me."

Most Third Wave coffee guys you talk to will try to convince you that they invented specialty coffee, but they are wrong. As the organized high-end sector of the larger coffee industry, specialty coffee has been around since the early 1960s, and it has been evolving ever since.

Coffee itself has a long history in the United States. Ever since a band of enraged patriots tossed ninety thousand pounds of expensive tea into the Boston Harbor in 1773, coffee, after booze, has been the beverage of choice for Americans.

Early Americans drank coffee in convivial coffeehouses, and either roasted coffee beans at home or bought them from merchants and grocers, who sold freshly roasted coffee that their customers carried home in paper sacks. This coffee came from high-quality Arabica beans—the Arabica species originated in Ethiopia and was cultivated commercially in Yemen, from where it spread throughout the Islamic world in the fifteenth and sixteenth centuries. In the seventeenth century, coffee was smuggled into Europe. Shortly thereafter, European adventurers transported coffee to the New World.

Throughout the nineteenth century, most American homemakers purchased freshly roasted coffee. Grocers often roasted their own, and most towns and cities of any size were home to one or more coffee roasteries. In the first half of the twentieth century, however, coffee, like other foodstuffs, fell victim to the industrialization of the food supply. Consolidation. Technological innovations. Standardization. They all led to one outcome: heavily advertised national brands of coffee sold in supermarkets in vacuum-sealed cans. And after World War II came the lowest blow of them all: water-soluble instant coffee. By the time instant became the next new thing, American consumers were so acclimatized to bad coffee that they failed to notice the introduction of lower-quality beans from the far less expensive species called Robusta that price-conscious mass marketers had begun adding to their blends.

In his history of the coffee industry, Uncommon Grounds, economic historian Mark Pendergrast summed up decades of "progress" in the American coffee industry with this comment from an unnamed attendee at the 1959 National Coffee Association Convention: "There is hardly anything," said this fed-up coffee guy, "that some man cannot make a little worse and sell a little cheaper."

Just as casseroles made with canned string beans and ersatz cream of mushroom soup led to Julia Child and the foodie revolt in the 1960s, so did the ubiquity of Nescafé and other caffeinated insults lead to the birth of the specialty coffee industry.

The First Wave

Coffee guys aren't always the greatest historians, and there are many debates about what and who compose the First, Second, and Third Waves of the specialty coffee industry—all the young coffee dudes seem to believe without question, though, that they, the Third Wave, are the stars of the movie.

Coffee consultant Trish Skeie, who popularized the wave idea, described the First Wave as the people before and after World War II "who made bad coffee commonplace...who created low quality instant solubles...who blended away the nuance [in coffee]...and forced prices to an all time low."

The Second Wave

Trish has written that the Second Wave began in the late 1960s and extended into the mid-1990s. Among the Second Wave were a number of coffee-centric northern European immigrants who settled in California after World War II. These transplants carried with them old-world knowledge of coffee roasting, tasting, and sourcing.

Among this group was Alfred Peet of Peet's Coffee, who opened his first store in San Francisco in 1966, and Erna Knutsen, founder and president of Knutsen Coffee Ltd., based in northern California. It was Knutsen who coined the phrase "specialty coffee" to describe beans from specific "appellations." Like appellation wines, Erna said, specialty coffees are grown in distinct geographic microclimates and they possess unique flavor profiles.

Second Wave entrepreneurs such as Peet and Knutsen as well as Don Schoenholt of Gillies Coffee in New York; Ted Lingle of Lingle Brothers Coffee in Long Beach, California; Kevin Knox of Starbucks; and George Howell of Boston's Coffee Connection created the specialty coffee business in the United States. They introduced American coffee drinkers to high-quality coffees with discernible differences in taste from around the world. In 1982, a group of Second Wave guys founded the Specialty Coffee Association of America (SCAA). On their watch, specialty became the fastest-growing sector of the U.S. coffee industry, with sales in 2007 of more than $12 billion.

Starbucks emerged in this period, the brainchild of Second Wave guys. The first Starbucks store opened in Seattle in 1971, selling high-quality coffee, dark roasted by Alfred Peet. Soon the company had half a dozen stores and was roasting its own. The chain grew slowly until 1987, when it was bought by Howard Schultz. In 2006, with 12,500 stores worldwide and total sales of $7.8 billion, Starbucks reported its fifteenth consecutive year of 5 percent or more comparable-store sales growth. By 2007, however, over-rapid growth (including hundreds of new stores) had taken its toll—by year's end Starbucks' stock price had fallen sharply, and the company was closing stores and rethinking its business strategy.

The Third Wave

Trish believes the Third Wave emerged in the mid-1990s as a reaction to the Starbuck-driven industrialization of gourmet coffee. The Third Wave guys deplore the automation of café culture. Many of them are rebels who dress more like skateboarders than business executives, but you miss the point if you think they are laid back. They are fierce competitors who have built their businesses on their ability to outperform other cafés, especially Starbucks. Virtually all of the young coffee guys in the retail business own shops in neighborhoods where Starbucks operates. To stay in business, they have had to sell better coffee and make better drinks than Starbucks.

Third Wavers are members of what has been called the first global generation. The workplace they entered was one that had been transformed by technology and inexpensive overseas travel. Young guys in the Third Wave travel more and travel differently than their elders. They are comfortable toting backpacks, wearing sandals, and sleeping in hammocks. They don't mind journeying six hours in trucks with worn-out shocks.

The knowledge these young entrepreneurs gain "at origin" shapes their approach as coffee buyers and business people. To develop the potential of specialty coffee business in the United States, the Third Wave insists you have to focus on the production end, and you have to see the relationship between the producer and the consumer ends of the coffee chain. They are not the first coffee guys to realize farmers matter—far from it. But they are the first to travel constantly and communicate readily with farmers in remote locales. You have to go where coffee is grown, and you have to help farmers improve their product to meet specialty standards, say Third Wave coffee guys. And that is what they do.

The Third Wave guys entered the coffee industry toward the end of the 1990s, at a time of extreme financial crisis for coffee farmers.

Around the world some twenty to twenty-five million farmers, mostly smallholders with just a few acres of land or less, support themselves and their families growing coffee. In the past thirty years, these farmers have lived through a series of economic catastrophes, losing hundreds of millions of dollars. According to the World Bank, prices for coffee have averaged a 3 percent decline in real terms each year since the 1970s. Farmers who could once afford to send their children to school can now barely afford to feed themselves and their families. Many of the worst off face outright starvation.

A number of different events converged to cause these repeated upheavals. The coffee market, like other commodities markets, goes through boom and bust cycles. The boom-bust continuum in coffee is exacerbated by the many years coffee trees take to mature: Coffee prices go up. Coffee farmers plant more trees. By the time these trees mature, coffee prices are dropping, so a down market is flooded with excess product and prices don't just slip—they collapse.

Throughout much of the twentieth century, producing and consuming countries worked together to short-circuit the boom-bust boomerang. Under the terms of the International Coffee Agreement (ICA), coffee prices and coffee production were subject to a series of internationally agreed-upon quotas, price caps, and interventions. The ICA fell apart in the 1980s as world coffee prices were rising dramatically—Brazilian coffee farmers at the time were getting $1.40 or $1.50 a pound for their coffee, and many coffee farmers worldwide were certain the good times were here to stay. They were wrong. By the early 1990s, with the ICA no longer in place, prices fell to below $1 a pound.

Then in the late 1990s and early 2000s, Brazil and Vietnam flooded the international market with a glut of low-quality coffee, causing another monumental crash. High-quality coffee dropped to fifty cents a pound, far below what it cost farmers to produce. Coffee drinkers in consuming countries quickly became acclimated to lower prices.

It is hard to imagine a bleaker outlook than that facing millions of coffee farmers and their families. In parts of Africa and Asia, these farmers are among the world's poorest people. Conditions in some parts of Latin America are only marginally better.

Millions of smallholders around the world have been forced out of coffee entirely. In Central America tens of thousands of small farmers have replaced their coffee trees with flowers for the American and European market. In Kenya, where some of the world's most prized coffee is grown, coffee farmers are ripping out their coffee trees and replacing them with tea.

When farmers can no longer grow coffee, a way of life that has sustained families for generations is lost, setting off a cascade of miserable consequences, including accelerated urbanization in producing countries. Coffee lovers lose out too, for it is these smallholders, rather than the owners of large farms or plantations, who grow many of the world's best coffees.

For coffee farmers, the rapid growth of the specialty market presents one of the few hopeful prospects in this disheartening picture. Farmers who sell their coffee as specialty earn more for their crops. When farmers successfully access the specialty market, the extra money they are paid for growing higher-quality coffee can save them from drowning in a sea of debt. For growers in countries like Nicaragua, Guatemala, and Rwanda, the specialty label has delivered concrete, quantifiable dividends.

To sell their coffee as specialty, coffee growers need to meet very explicit criteria. Trained tasters following established rules make the determination. To be recognized as specialty, a coffee must be rated at least an 80 on a scale of 100, indicating that it possesses pleasing characteristics and no major defects.

In the past twenty years, demand for specialty coffee in North America, Europe, and parts of Asia has grown dramatically. In the United States, approximately 30 percent of the coffee consumed now falls under the specialty rubric. According to the Specialty Coffee Association of America (SCAA), in 2006 specialty coffee was sold in 15,500 cafés, 3,600 coffee kiosks, and 2,900 coffee carts, and by 1,900 roaster/retailers. Retailers include Starbucks, Peet's Coffee, Caribou Coffee, Green Mountain Coffee, Allegro Coffee (owned by Whole Foods), and many smaller companies. (In fact, Starbucks' U.S. business accounted for more than half of the $12 billion annual sales.)

The specialty coffee companies that I write about in this book are those at the top of the specialty coffee quality pyramid. These companies take pride in selling coffee that professional tasters and consumers recognize as better than Starbucks. With annual sales of less than $1 billion, the highest-quality specialty companies represent around 8 percent of the overall specialty coffee market in the United States. Their influence outweighs the numbers.

Dunkin' Donuts and other doughnut shops are not included in SCAA sales figures. McDonald's isn't included either, but both of these companies are clearly noticing what specialty purveyors are doing. In early 2008, McDonald's announced that it was taking on Starbucks by installing espresso machines in some of its stores and launching a line of specialty coffee drinks, with expectations of $1 billion in annual sales.

The small high-end companies are the trendsetters in the coffee industry. Insiders in the specialty industry get the joke. They know the most exacting specialty companies are run by a ragtag bunch of rule-benders. Still, there's no denying that the young dudes running elite roasting companies have seen what their elders missed: that specialty coffee has much more to offer in terms of culinary and economic value. The leaders of the Third Wave believe the sky is the limit—in their view there is no telling how huge specialty coffee can grow. Harnessing specialty coffee's expanding value for the benefit of all the stakeholders in the coffee business, especially farmers, is the mission of these young movers and shakers.

Independent coffee consultant Anne Ottaway, who played a central role in helping transform Rwanda into a respected specialty coffee producer, describes the guys who run the top specialty companies followed in this book—Peter Giuliano, Geoff Watts, and Duane Sorenson—as the Bill Gates, Paul Allen, and Steve Jobs of specialty coffee. "Twenty years from now we're going to look back and say, 'Isn't it amazing; we knew these giants when their companies were small.'"

Whatever happens in the future, there is no doubt that these three play a major role in driving the specialty coffee industry today. It is they who others in the industry look to for direction and leadership. Their coffees top all the Best Roasted and Best Coffee lists. And coffee geeks, nerds, fans, and hipsters who populate the coffee blogosphere follow their every move as if they were rock stars. In the coffee world, that's what they are. Stars.

Peter Giuliano, Counter Culture

"Until I found coffee it was unclear if I would ever find a place for me. I moved to Sicily in an effort to find some place I would fit in. My first wife and I moved to Japan. There was no place I fit in. I feel lucky to have landed in specialty coffee."

Today, Peter, thirty-seven, is an industry leader in the specialty coffee world and a part owner of the East Coast roasting company Counter Culture, based in Durham, North Carolina. Standing five feet nine, with black-framed eyeglasses and receding hairline, he is newly slender, having lost the pounds around the middle that spoke to his love of good food but belied his athleticism. Professorial and fair-minded, in 2004 Peter was the youngest person up to that time ever elected to the thirteen-member board of the SCAA. It's telling that he was part of an inner circle of SCAA leaders who helped to sort out the mess when someone in the office of the SCAA director embezzled $1 million. Peter and a few other coffee guys turned their lives inside out for a year to work on SCAA finances. Thanks to their efforts the wrongdoer is expected to go to jail and the organization, in turmoil for over a year, was able to move on.

A skilled storyteller with a Technicolor imagination, Peter is famous in the specialty world for his line of patter.

Duane, Geoff, and many others in the high-end specialty industry take their hats off to Peter for his ability to represent the industry and to speak and write beautifully about coffee. Peter is also famous for his on-the-road coffee stories: being driven out of town in Chiapas, Mexico, by a gun-slinging farmer with a grudge; waking up on a patio in Nicaragua after a night of partying, with a huge poisonous snake slithering toward his head; trudging fifteen hours on foot to a remote coffee-growing village in the shadow of Machu Picchu.

Peter grew up in Long Beach, California, in a big multigenerational Sicilian family—the kind that would gather for Sunday dinner every week to talk and laugh and argue about whose version of treasured family recipes was more authentic.

He spoke Italian with his grandparents, he honed his Spanish in restaurant kitchens, and even though it's not too useful in the coffee world, he says his Japanese isn't bad.

Peter's father shared his love of the outdoors with his sons: biking, hiking, surfing, golfing, tennis were part of the family repertoire. His mother, in love with folk music and indigenous cultures, taught him to sing and play music—he mastered half a dozen instruments, including the accordion.

When Peter was twelve, his parents moved the family to the bourgeois southern California enclave of Eldorado Hills. At first, Peter thought he'd be a preppie like the rich kids, but it soon became apparent that his mother wasn't going to pop for pricey pink shirts with little alligators. That's when his cousin Vinnie took him to a concert in Los Angeles to see the Circle Jerks, Black Flag, and X. "These were the ne plus ultra punk bands. That was it. I decided to be a punk," Peter remembers. "Of course I was way too young for this. But there was nowhere else for me to go. I couldn't do the New Jersey Italian thing. There weren't any other Italians in California. Punk saved me from really being lost. I had my tribe."

Peter got a job at a coffee shop the summer after he graduated from high school. "My friend and I used to hang out there and a guy didn't show up for a shift and someone tied an apron on me. There was a girl who worked in the café. She wore old-fashioned dresses and Doc Martens and I thought she was cool. She came up to me, I think she was playing me, and said, 'I love Estate Java.' Well, when I did some research, I discovered [that] there are four estates in Java that grow high-quality Arabicas. I just had to figure out this coffee thing so I could talk with her.

"I was always a factoid guy so all the details about coffee appealed to me and espresso appealed to my Italian American-ness and being a barista appealed to my love of showmanship. As I was making people's coffee drinks, I would entertain them with these outlandish stories about the coffees. I saw that people wanted a story along with their coffee. It was part of the whole experience. It still is," said Peter.

Peter studied musicology at San Diego State and worked at Pannikan, the café and coffee-roasting company. The business went through a number of iterations, and so did Peter's capacity to tolerate being a college student—although superbrainy, in love with learning, and the child of two teachers, Peter never got his college degree. Still, he has always seen himself as an educator. Working in coffee, he desperately wanted to spread the word, to teach. His early ambition was to train baristas and the people who sell coffee. By the time he was twenty-four, instead of teaching about coffee, he found himself working as the general manager of a coffee company with eight stores. "That's when I figured out that I suck as a manager.

"The founder wanted me to run a business. All I really wanted to do was be a coffee guy. I used to set up secret cuppings in the evening. My boss didn't want me spending my time studying coffee. So I would sneak back to the office in the evening, set up eight or nine coffees, and cup so I could learn more about the different coffees we were selling. One night the boss discovered me and he was so mad, he threw a clipboard at me," Peter said.

In 2000, Peter was thirty. He had been working in coffee for thirteen years and he had never had a job he really liked. At the time he was dating a woman named Alice, who would eventually become his second wife. Alice was moving to North Carolina to attend school. Peter hoped to follow her east. While running a roasting company called Café Moto, Peter had been fulfilling his "teaching jones" as an SCAA volunteer coffee trainer. He was active in the association, and he asked someone there whom he should call to see if he could get a job in North Carolina. The guy told him to call Fred Houk at Counter Culture. Peter called and Houk, who was looking to get out of the business, asked, "Peter, do you believe in fate?"

Houk and his partner Brett Smith, an MBA and business guy, hired Peter as Counter Culture's roaster and buyer. At the time, Counter Culture was a small regional wholesaler, bumping along with annual sales of around $1 million. Today Counter Culture is a fast-growing roaster, with 2007 sales of close to $7 million, and an increasingly high profile in the mid-Atlantic from New York City, where it is the dominant high-end coffee roaster, south through Atlanta to Durham. Peter is now a part owner.

Almost immediately after he'd settled in at Counter Culture, Peter began looking for a chance to "travel to origin" to see how coffee, the object of his passion for so many years, actually grew. "I had fantasized for years about going to visit a coffee farm. I remember trying to visualize what coffee farms would look like, smell like...."

"My interest in coffee drove me to become a farmer myself. At one point in California, I ripped out my front yard to plant a ten-foot-by-thirty-foot vegetable garden. I had chickens in a coop I had built by hand. I was making beer and vinegar and canning tomatoes in the kitchen.

"Vegetable gardening was a revelation for me. I had a new understanding of what lettuce was after growing it in my garden and tasting it that way—it had a more intense 'lettuce-ness.' I was growing old varieties, trying to understand what real tomatoes, carrots, eggs, chard tasted like. I figured I would get some big insight about coffee by tasting it and smelling it in the field. I remember wondering, would the juice of the fruit or the leaves taste like coffee?

"I had read some books about coffee production and farming techniques," Peter said, adding that it took a while before he understood how the coffee bean was separated from its surrounding fruit (called depulping) and then, still covered with sticky stuff called mucilage, the beans were left to ferment before being processed. "I didn't really understand what was involved. Maybe this is because the book I read was translated from German and was semi-unintelligible. There wasn't much accurate information out there in the 1990s."

Peter's first coffee-related trip was to a cooperative in Nicaragua. He traveled with a group that had been organized by an American environmental activist and his wife who went to Nicaragua to try to help the farmers in the coffee-growing village of San Ramon. The farmers in San Ramon were using agriculturally and environmentally sound practices, and Counter Culture was already buying from them, even though their coffee didn't taste all that great. Peter was hoping he could help the growers improve the quality of their coffee. He eventually accomplished this goal—San Ramon was a Cup of Excellence top-ten winner in 2007—although it took more years of trial and error than he expected.

In this first trip, as soon as he spotted his first coffee tree, Peter asked the driver to stop the car. "I got out and tasted the fruit and chewed the leaves and just hung out in the field for a long time. The cherry did not taste like coffee. It was juicy, like watermelon juice with jasmine flowers floating in it. It was intoxicatingly sweet and floral, with a definite melonlike characteristic," recalls Peter.

"Inside the cherry there was only about one millimeter of pulpy juicy fruit between the parchment layer and skin. It was a little slimy, like the fruit that clings to the pit of a plum, and it took a lot of force to separate it from the parchment that surrounded the actual coffee seed.

"That week I spent entire days picking with pickers, helping them depulp and then ferment the coffee. I didn't know at the time that there are myriad variations on fermentation, which is one of the factors that makes coffee from different locales taste so different. One morning I walked up the road to another farm and just watched the farmer work with his coffee for an hour. I started remembering details from things I had read and started asking the farmers questions. I had read that coffee was fermented underwater, but nobody I saw in Nicaragua was doing that. So I tried to figure that out—whether they were making a mistake or using a local technique." He had no idea at the time that virtually every coffee-growing region develops its own idiosyncratic processing techniques. In retrospect, Peter says, "I can see that I was a little too brash. I would challenge people all the time about cupping and agricultural techniques when I didn't know all that much myself."

Around the same time as Peter's trip to Nicaragua, two developments occurred that had a profound impact on his career and the careers of many Third Wave guys. First, some influential members of the SCAA figured out that roasters needed an organization of their own, and they set about creating what would become the Roasters Guild. More or less simultaneously, George Howell, of Boston's Coffee Connection, and some other experienced specialty coffee hands came up with the idea of staging specialty coffee competitions in Latin America—where winning coffees would be sold online in a series of auctions patterned after the famous coffee auction in Kenya. The competitions, which came to be known as Cup of Excellence, introduced small growers in Nicaragua, Guatemala, Honduras, El Salvador, and Colombia to the idea of specialty coffee, and provided Third Wave coffee guys like Peter with a chance to form relationships with farmers from these countries who were interested in improving the quality of their product.

It is doubtful that the specialty coffee industry would have taken off as it has if the Roasters Guild had not been formed. The guild galvanized the Third Wave generation. Created in 2001, its goal was to bring together a select group of coffee roasters and

Coffee 101

Coffee beans are dried pits from the red fruit—the cherry—that coffee trees produce. Coffee trees grow on farms and in forests. The higher the altitude, in general, the better the coffee. Coffee trees require fertilizer—organic or industrial—and pruning. They need a moderate amount of sun and rain at certain times in their growing cycle. Coffee cherries do not ripen at a uniform rate. In order to pick ripe red cherries, pickers must make repeated passes through coffee orchards.

Once picked, coffee cherries in Latin America are generally depulped mechanically to remove the skins and most of the fruit, and then they are subjected to a process called washing (which may or may not involve water), during which they ferment. Fermenting, or washing—the terms are used interchangeably—dissolves the sticky coating called mucilage that covers the hinged pair of coffee beans, and it alters the flavor of the coffee. Washing techniques vary from farmer to farmer, region to region, and can take one to three days or more. Washing stations are not terribly rediscover hand roasting techniques that had been lost after World War II. Up until then, young roasters in the United States were operating in the dark. There was no apprenticeship system in place. "Our knowledge of roasting was all conjecture. We didn't have much scientific understanding of the roasting process," Peter recalls. Peter quickly emerged as a leader of the Roasters Guild, says SCAA executive director Ric Rhinehart, now in his late forties. During that first meeting, the organizer, Don Holly, had to leave early. "I will never forget Peter stepping into that void. I say with total affection and respect that there was a Mickey Rooney-esque quality to the moment, as he stood up and earnestly declared what had to be done. It was like, 'Hey guys, if we all work together we can put on a musical.' Peter just jumped into

---

expensive to build, and villages, co-ops, and other small groups often have their own washing facilities.

After washing, coffee must be dried. Farmers around the world use a number of different drying technologies. Beans can be dried on racks, on cement patios, or in mechanical dryers that may be wood burning, gas burning, or fired with coffee parchment. Some of these machines use coffee tree prunings as fuel. Again, this process takes days. If it rains, mold and mildew can ruin or degrade the coffee.

After drying, coffee must be milled. During this process a papery parchment skin covering the coffee is stripped from the bean. Next, coffee beans are sorted by size and quality. This can be done by hand or by machine. Once the beans are sorted, they are packed in clean bags and stored in a dry place. After resting for a month or two, the beans are ready for sampling. At every step along the production process, the coffee loses weight, so that the final milled product is approximately 20 percent of the original. During the roasting process, coffee shrinks another 15 percent or so.

the breach and got a lot of rotten tomatoes thrown at him, but he harnessed enough energy to get other people to help him move the Roasters Guild forward."

"At that first retreat, a guy came up to me dressed in a track suit and soccer jersey and introduced himself," Peter recalls. It was Geoff Watts from Intelligentsia Coffee. "He was only twenty-seven or so, but he was so into coffee. We talked about our companies and we asked each other lots of questions. I remember getting that feeling one gets when you meet someone you are comfortable with."

Geoff Watts, Intelligentsia Coffee

Today Intelligentsia, with 2007 sales near $12 million, is the largest and arguably the most influential of the elite specialty roasting companies. It boasts roasting plants in Chicago and Los Angeles, retail stores in both cities, and an active wholesale business centered in the Midwest and Los Angeles that reaches out across the entire country.

And Geoff Watts, thirty-four, with rosy cheeks, heavy dark brows, and unruly black curls, is famous in the specialty world for spending more days a year on the road than anyone else in the industry, sacrificing comfort, tranquility, and at times sanity itself in the quest for great coffee. His company, Intelligentsia, buys more highly ranked coffee than any other elite roaster, but it pays for that privilege. Geoff is famous for spending big bucks on coffee and on travel. In any given year, he spends as much as nine months overseas, with travel expenses and roaming fees on his cell phone costing his company a fortune.

If Geoff wants a particular coffee, he will pay whatever it takes to beat out the competition, whether his company can recoup the full cost or not. Many people in the specialty coffee business think this amounts to sheer recklessness, but while

Geoff may be a spender, few would deny that his tireless work and profound knowledge of coffee has been a major factor in Intelligentsia's growth. For this reason and others, Doug Zell, Intelligentsia's founder and CEO, supports Geoff no matter what and Geoff, the best-known specialty coffee buyer in the world, is the guy whom others in the industry admire, talk about, envy, and sometimes love to hate.

Doug Zell is as hard-driving as the Japanese bullet train—you would never stand in his way, expecting him to change course. Doug's discourse has that locomotive energy too. When he talks, he speaks in perfect sentences and he covers every topic at top speed. Talking about the small cafés that were driven out of business in the early 1990s when Starbucks appeared on the scene, for example, Doug said, "I would argue that these smaller players drove themselves out of business by poor execution." He then went on to explain why every aspect of coffee execution in his stores is superior to Starbucks. "My baristas are trained in a three-month certificate-granting program, they make all our espresso drinks by hand, and they pour beautiful latte art. There simply is no comparison," he says.

Geoff approaches questions differently. He develops his thoughts slowly, somewhat circuitously, as he threads many related ideas together and then finally zeroes in on his point. Talking to him on the phone about his buying trips to Latin America or East Africa, I learned to type fast and relax.

Asked to comment on the growing consumer interest in coffee that is certified organic, for example, Geoff talks for twenty minutes with no pauses for questions. He begins by telling me that coffee trees in Africa produce one-third as much fruit as coffee trees in Latin America, and then he analyzes why that is. "Poverty," he says, "is the greatest problem in coffee." He describes how poverty in coffee-growing regions leads to increased pollution: "A guy doesn't have a nice stove, so instead he burns ten times the amount of wood, or he can't afford to repair the exhaust on his truck, so he pours pollutants into the air."

The monologue continues with Geoff explaining to me how coffee is grown. He tells me which chemical fertilizers are acceptable and which are not. He describes farmers who use sustainable but nonorganic farming practices, and he describes farmers whose farms are theoretically organic yet are compromising the environment.

Geoff goes on to address coffee agronomy, coffee sustainability, coffee chemistry, coffee economics. My notes from Geoff are a library full of comprehensive knowledge about the coffee industry. He and Peter were my coffee college. But Geoff's not the guy to call for a sound bite.

Like his language, much about Geoff is not immediately accessible. A complicated guy who admits he has a hard time connecting to people, Geoff isn't easy to know. It's only when he shoves his unruly mess of hair under a baseball cap, enabling you to see the crystalline eyes, bluer than blue, do you start to fathom what's there. Sadness. Brilliance. Will.

Maybe the sadness is constitutional or maybe it comes from his father dying of a brain tumor when Geoff was only eleven years old. His dad was a business guy, not rich, but well insured, and the problems that followed his father's death weren't financial. Geoff's mother fell apart when her husband died and stayed that way for a long time, leaving Geoff and his younger brother to bring themselves up. Geoff did fine in school; in fact, he was driven to do his schoolwork perfectly. But his wild side surfaced early. Not old enough to possess a driver's license, he'd nevertheless take his mother's car and drive into Chicago, where he'd hang out at clubs, listen to music, and dabble in dangerous stuff.

His father had left a trust to pay for Geoff's and his brother's education. Drawn to California, Geoff studied philosophy, linguistics, and German at Berkeley. In 1992, he spent half a year studying German literature in Vienna, Austria, falling in love with the dark, smoky Viennese coffeehouses where so much of the city's intellectual life had played out.

Geoff liked the rich, viscous Viennese coffee, a semi-extracted cross between espresso and drip coffee, almost as much as he liked the ceremony and ritual associated with it. In the café he frequented, formally attired waiters served small cups of coffee—three ounces, not much bigger than an espresso—in porcelain cups on silver trays, each with a white linen napkin, a glass of water, and a biscuit.

Geoff returned to Berkeley in the fall of 1992. The coffee scene in Northern California was starting to heat up. Alfred Peet had been roasting and selling specialty coffee in Berkeley near the university for decades, but now small microroasters, each with its own roasting machine and its own approach to roasting, were setting up shop. "Until then, coffee had seemed pretty faceless to me. When all these small roasters opened, I realized there was more to good coffee than the freshness of the beans and the talent of the barista," recalls Geoff.

After graduating in 1995, Geoff drove across the country in his Honda Civic with his two dogs for company. He returned to Chicago to be with his girlfriend who was in school there, thinking that when she graduated they would both return to California. Instead they broke up. Not knowing what else to do, he took a job walking dogs. At night he played the drums in two different bands, one doing jazz rock improvisation, the other West African percussion.

Walking the dogs one morning, he saw an ad for a soon-to-open specialty coffee company. The idea of getting in "on the ground floor" appealed to him. When Doug Zell and his wife and business partner Emily Mange first interviewed Geoff for a job with Intelligentsia, they weren't sure Geoff would fit in their company. He was the last person they hired. Geoff's never been much of a dresser, though he likes nice things.

"They were concerned about my being kind of a California hippie dude. I had hair down my back and I was into meditation and that sort of stuff. A couple of years later when I first got on a basketball court with Doug, and the two of us wanted to win so bad, we didn't care what we did, we were roughhousing, pushing each other. Emily was shocked. She didn't think of me as a competitive person." Geoff recalls.

Intelligentsia opened its first café and roastery on Broadway in the fast-gentrifying Lake View neighborhood in Chicago in 1995—the roasting machine was located inside the café. Geoff worked as a barista at first, although soon, taking note of Geoff's zeal, Doug taught Geoff how to roast coffee. Then customers started complaining about the sourish odor from the roaster. (Coffee does not smell delicious until it is fully roasted.) For a while, Geoff roasted at night and worked the coffee bar during the day. "I'd sleep on coffee bags and then get up and open shop," he recalls. After that he ran the wholesale operation—meaning he was the wholesale operation.

In 1998, Geoff reached a crossroads. He had to make up his mind. Should he stay with Intelligentsia? Return to California, go back to school, maybe study philosophy or microbiology? He sat down with Doug and Emily. "I told them if they were willing to give me a stake in the company, if they thought they needed me, I would love to continue as an owner, rather than employee. They thought about it and decided to give me sweat equity," says Geoff. He still had a little money from his father's trust, which enabled him to invest around $20,000 in Intelligentsia. In exchange, he became a 15 percent owner. Later he was named vice president.

Around the time that Geoff became a part owner, he started to cup coffees intensively. "We'd been doing tastings all along, but then I got the idea to take a fleet of eight little Krups home brewers and brew up eight different coffees, weighing the samples on a little digital scale to make sure I was using the same amount of coffee in each pot. That's how we would compare coffees, which was totally ridiculous because home brewers are inconsistent. But our thinking was we wanted to taste the coffees as our customers will taste them."

They were buying coffees from four or five importers. One of their importers, Tim Castle, a very knowledgeable trader, visited Intelligentsia and taught the partners how to conduct a formal cupping.

"When we needed coffee we would call Tim Castle, or Royal, or Volcafe or another one of our importers who provided us with coffee and say we need a great Guatemalan or Costa Rican or Kenyan, and they would assemble samples and send them to us. Importers liked working with us. We were digging into coffee, generating feedback about the coffees they were sending us. Still, we were dependent on the luck of the draw.

"When importers sent us samples, they were blended from 40,000-pound batches—that's how much coffee is in a single container, the kind that is shipped from origin in large ships. That could be the total output of a single large farm or a month's worth of harvests from many small farms. We couldn't taste samples from a particular farm or a particular day or week; all the samples were bulked.

"I started to understand we were standing on the wrong side of the counter, that there were hundreds and thousands of coffees out there and we never got to see them. Slowly it dawned on me that the only way to look behind the curtain was to go to origin where coffee was grown."

Doug Zell and Emily Mange made their first trip to origin in 2000. They came back with stories and pictures. Geoff couldn't wait to go. Some months later he had his chance. Kenneth Davids, who had written three books on coffee, organized a tour of coffee farms in Guatemala, and Geoff signed up. He went to learn, not to buy coffee.

"I was there to see what was going on. For a roaster who has never been to origin, the first trip is a pilgrimage. Working with coffee you become obsessed, so making that first pilgrimage is like visiting your wife's childhood home to understand how she got to be who she is. Finally standing next to a tree and picking a coffee cherry—it's that romantic, that full of emotional urgency."

Once he saw how coffee was grown, he says, "I started to think about the differences among coffees. Just spending a few days driving around Guatemala you could see there are extremely different areas in terms of climates and soils. Driving west to San Marcos, the weather is misty, there's red clay soil, very high altitude, it's lush and wet. Go in the other direction to Huehuetenango, there are jutting cliffs and the weather is drier and cooler. In one little country, so much diversity. At that point I started feeling like I am getting gypped; there is so much to know about coffee that I don't have access to in Chicago."

Geoff's coffee education continued back in the United States. The first Roasters Guild retreat was held in a lodge in Forest Grove, Oregon in 2001. Nearly one hundred people showed up, including Geoff. The attendees were divided equally among experienced hands and young guys new to the business. "At that first meeting we did a lot of cupping," Geoff recalls. "I remember Ric Rhinehart leading a cupping. At that point I had been cupping for two years, but always by myself. Participating in cupping with a lot of people, that was a big moment. It's much different when you think in your own vacuum, or you taste coffees and discuss them with a lot of cuppers, each with his or her own opinion, and you have to reason through why did he give this coffee an 88 and I gave it an 83.

"Cupping together got a lot of us thinking about sensory experience in a broader way. How do you take a sensory experience and quantify it and how do you take a fleeting experience and find a way to describe it with words? One man's 'caramel' is another man's 'maple' or 'honey-nut.' It was interesting to think about. I got interested in this whole idea of trying to describe, how you convey the experience of taste in a handful of words."

Geoff remembers meeting Peter and a lot of other coffee guys who have became his friends. "Looking back, I realize how impactful this meeting was. One hundred roasters playing with all these machines, sharing ideas, incredible spirit, I don't know that anyone understood how lasting [an] effect it would have."

Peter and Geoff spent 2002, 2003, and 2004 traveling to origin, separately, and together, and with other colleagues, some as young as they, some a bit older. The two were trying to figure out how specialty markets in producing countries worked, devising strategies that they hoped would help them influence the way farmers processed their coffees, pouring themselves into learning and teaching at the Roasters Guild, accepting assignments as judges at Cup of Excellence competitions, and taking on the roles of Coffee Corps volunteers paid by U.S. AID to teach coffee farmers how to cup their own coffee. All their volunteer work dovetailed with their paid work. It was a grueling way of life—one that you had to be young to tolerate. Hard work, endless travel, and few comforts, punctuated by long nights of partying, drinking, dancing, and, well, you figure it out. These were young guys and they had to blow off steam now and then.

Peter and Geoff were two very different guys, but they shared a similar point of view: they were building their companies by building the specialty coffee industry here in the United States and overseas. Both were ambitious, driven, and hungry in their own ways for recognition, but they were also altruistic, putting in hundreds of hours annually on pro bono work. Their paths crossed frequently and their time together deepened their friendship. It was not uncommon for one of them to throw his arm around the other's shoulder, as I saw in Rwanda.

"My brother," Geoff said.

"My brother," Pete answered.

Like brothers, they are competitive. Each wants to beat the other to the punch, to get his hands on the best coffee. Geoff is a natural extremist. "He's fearless as a buyer. He'll confront anyone," says Peter, who will tell you he relies more on judgment than raw nerve.

Each guy thinks his own way of doing business is superior. Still, over the years, Geoff's and Peter's views of the specialty coffee business have been forged collaboratively, and to some degree they still are.

Duane Sorenson, Stumptown

Nobody in specialty coffee would call Duane Sorenson, founder and CEO of Portland, Oregon's Stumptown Coffee, a collaborative guy. In a business run by naughty boys, the pot-smoking workaholic—two words you don't often see side by side—Duane is the naughtiest of them all. And he wants everyone to know that he runs a business that is "new and cool and outside the lines." Which is why he offers a visiting journalist (me) who is without question on the far side of forty an illegal substance when, frazzled, she arrives at his office at 2:00 p.m. on a bright May afternoon to interview him. The office, around the corner from Stumptown's Division Street café, is located in a two-story converted craftsman, of a type that is so common inside Portland city limits.

"Want some coffee?" asks Duane, thirty-five, with a beefy build, a round face, long messy black hair, and blue eyes—unexpected given his dark hair and brows.

"I am already overcaffeinated," I answer.

"Then how about a hit on my big bad bong?" he asks.

"How about herb tea?" I respond.

Someone gets me an herb tea. When it arrives, I take the tea bag out of the cup. I don't want to mess up Duane's desk and I place the tea bag on some paper napkins in a spot that looks safe to me. Duane watches me intently, saying nothing. He doesn't hand me an ash tray or a cup, but when I put the tea bag down in its little nest of paper napkins, he picks the whole mess up and puts it in another spot that seems more suitable to him. I get the feeling that Duane is not only a pothead and a maniacally driven entrepreneur, but he also has the soul of a German housewife. Later in our interview he tells me that his wife, Jereme (pronounced like Jeremy), is a fabulous mother, but her housekeeping doesn't meet his standards. He tells me that at home he often does the housework.

In eight years, Duane has built a do-everything-by-hand, perfectionist $7 million-a-year roasting/wholesale/retail specialty business, with five cafés in Portland and two new cafés in Seattle, that many consider the most uncompromising, cutting-edge specialty coffee company in the United States and perhaps the world. Purist Stumptown takes pride in not marketing itself. It's a company you have to be hip to know about. A company for insiders.

Duane will readily tell you that his company buys the world's best and most expensive coffees and possesses the most expensive stock of coffee in the world. No price is too high for him to pay for great coffee. In its buying practices Stumptown is similar to Intelligentsia, but Intelligentsia is almost twice as large. Duane and company respect Intelligentsia and they especially respect Geoff. With a few exceptions, Duane looks down on everyone else in the business. He and Peter used to be friends—Duane learned quite a bit from Peter and from Geoff when he first started traveling to origin—but the relationship has frayed.

Stumptown, Duane will tell you, roasts coffee so perfect that not everyone deserves to buy it or sell it. The company won't ship its coffee by air to wholesale customers because Duane does not feel he can maintain quality control at long distance. "You wanna sell our coffee in your café?" the Stumptown team asks and then proceeds to grill potential customers about their brewing and cleaning practices.

Duane didn't get his coffee snobbery or any other snobbery from his parents. He grew up in Puyallup, Washington, outside of Tacoma. His family life was "weird," he says. His father, Duane Sr., was a sausage maker who went bankrupt a couple of times. "We were dirt poor. We lost our house, everything. We saw our father go nuts. He'd sit there rocking all night in a chair, pulling out his hair." His parents were "very, very religious, Pentecostal, speaking in tongues, hopping and hollering, going to hell, that kind of stuff," Duane says. He has one sister, Tonya, seven years older, "a good sweet person," who works for Stumptown as the company's CFO.

Duane's parents sent him and his sister to evangelical schools. He got his first school spanking in kindergarten. "I pushed my sister's boyfriend into this lake. I don't know if I was jealous or protective or what, but the principal made me lay on the desk and he smacked my ass with a stick." After that, you could count on Duane being the most rebellious kid in the class. He got kicked out of one school after another for bad behavior. "I was getting into trouble. I would talk to kids about rock and roll, stuff they didn't approve of." (Rock and roll is still one of Duane's passions. He doesn't play an instrument but is a big supporter of Portland's live music scene, and he has a huge record collection.) Once he'd been booted, none of the religious schools would take him back. "The last one I went to, I was shipped all the way to Seattle from Tacoma every day—an hour and a half each way."

When it got to the point where there were no religious schools he hadn't been thrown out of, Duane went to public school, which he liked a lot better. He did poorly in academics, but well in sports, especially wrestling. In the eighth grade he met Jereme, his wife, who is pretty and smart and not noticeably insubordinate. With a few times off for (Duane's) bad behavior—they separated for some months last year—Duane and Jereme have been together ever since. They have two young children, of whom Duane says he is very, very protective.

Duane has always been a rebel, but never a slacker. "I was six or seven when I started working. In the summer, my sister and I had to pick beans and berries to pay for our school clothes." Talking about that experience, Duane and Tonya laugh about the misery of it, the sunburned ears and necks, but Duane takes pride in what he calls his "weird work ethic."

He started working in his father's sausage kitchen when he was eleven. He liked the culinary part of the job. "My daddy made me and my sister taste everything"—sauerkraut, horseradish, fennel, herbs and spices—but he had no desire to be a sausage maker. "It's cold, wet work, hard work," he says.

He wanted to be a business owner. In his fantasies, he wasn't a cowboy or an Indian. "I would be out throwing rocks, spacing out because of my strange upbringing. I was always thinking about being a businessman. I had certain stories I would make up about being a businessman or a shop owner."

Another dream had to do, improbably, with a love of design. "In sixth grade if someone asked me what I was going to do when I grew up, I would say I wanted to be an interior designer. I have always been very passionate about design. I don't know where that comes from. Not my family. When I escape from Stumptown, I escape into design magazines."

His interest in design permeates Stumptown. Aesthetically, all six of the Portland retail stores are very different, their styles reflecting the neighborhoods where they are located. The cafés run the gamut from the old-couch-you-can-sink-into hominess of Stumptown's first store on Division Street to the superswish, dark wood urban elegance of the latest store in the Ace Hotel that has four superhigh-tech, one-perfect-cup-at-a-time Clover brewing machines. Guests at the hotel benefit from Stumptown room service.

In high school, Duane started working in a coffee bar called Shockabra in Tacoma. He told *Barista Magazine* that he took the job "to play music and be around the kind of people I like to be around. They're the kind of people I'm hiring right now at Stumptown." What he meant were people who were young and hip and outside the system.

Mindful of his father's catastrophic experience with debt, Duane grew Stumptown using the profits from his retail operation to underwrite the cost of expansion. Until recently, he and a crew did much of the construction themselves. He claims his move into Seattle has been accomplished with characteristic fiscal restraint, though for the first time Stumptown has borrowed to underwrite the cost of constructing two new stores and a roasting plant, built by a professional crew under Duane's vigilant eye.

Duane chose Seattle to expand in because of its proximity and similarity to Portland. He understands the coffee culture in Seattle, the espresso-centric hometown of Starbucks, where the rising and falling fortunes of coffee shops are followed the way sports teams are followed in other towns.

For Duane a big part of the attraction of specialty coffee is its us-against-them, we're-the-cool-people ethos. "Next to quality, the most important thing to me is holding onto the culture of the company," he told *Barista Magazine*. "I've always been attracted to that—indie cred, cutting-edge, weirdos. Those were the fuckers I was hanging out with in high school, the art kids, the mechanics, the kids who played records and were putting bands together in their basements...."

Duane's mentality is tribal. The people inside his tribe are different to him from the people outside. Employees who are hip and also live up to his demanding work ethic are family, and he lavishes them with full benefits—including health care, free meals, free booze, company outings, even annual recording sessions for musicians. Other people—squares, bores, those who don't care about the environment (Portland is the country's most environmentally conscious city) or coffee quality or rock and roll—are outside his tribe, and not worth his time.

Up until 2004 or so, Duane bought most of his coffee from a handful of high-quality importers and didn't spend all that much time traveling. As Stumptown prospered, however, Duane revamped the company's buying strategy. In line with this change, he began traveling to origin one week out of every month to buy coffee. Running a growing company while traveling and having a family was too much even for Duane. In 2007, he hired Stumptown's first overseas buyer, Aleco Chigounis, though he still continues to do some traveling.

Duane's no slouch as a taster, and he's not a guy to let a great coffee get away. Not surprising, then, that when Hacienda La Esmeralda Special, that darling of the high-end coffee world, made its first appearance in 2004, Duane flipped. In 2004, and every year since, he has purchased part of the auction lot, joining the successful high bidders who drove the price of this coffee into the stratosphere.

Duane, nothing if not irreverent, describes Esmeralda as tasting like Juicy Fruit gum. He has bought as much of this coffee in Panama as he can get his hands on. With the greed of a true connoisseur, he wants more.

And he actually found some more.

Many people in specialty coffee have traveled the world looking for new supplies of Hacienda La Esmeralda. In search of the mysterious birthplace of these fabled beans, an Indiana Jones–style expedition was undertaken in the wilds of Ethiopia. But Duane, who seems to have a preternatural gift for landing in the right place at the right time, may be the only man on earth who stumbled onto this treasured bean by accident and knew enough to recognize what he saw, even though he wasn't looking for it.

This lucky find took place in the highlands of Costa Rica. Duane was driving around the countryside visiting coffee farms with Francisco Mena, a well-known Costa Rican coffee guy. "We pulled over to take a leak. I looked up and there were these trees that didn't look like Typica. I tasted the cherry. 'Man, this tastes like Juicy Fruit,' I said.

'No. No. It's not possible,' Francisco said.

'I said taste this, man,'

"We looked around and noticed trees that looked an awful lot like Geisha—Esmeralda's varietal name—were scattered around the forest." Turns out they were Geisha. The trees had been planted in the 1960s, same as in Panama. Francisco contacted the owner and made arrangements for Stumptown to purchase that coffee. Duane paid the pickers, who were instructed to keep this coffee separate, and he insisted that the coffee go to a certain mill for processing.

The processing had to be perfect because the coffee in question cost more per pound than the average coffee picker earned in a month.

Duane paused in his storytelling and his round face lit up in a fat-cat, cream-licking grin. "People were running all over the world looking for this coffee and we stumbled across it in Costa Rica taking a leak."

GOD IN A CUP

YOU CAN'T UNDERSTAND LOVE WITH YOUR MIND.
You have to use your heart and your senses. While the average person might taste Panama's Hacienda La Esmeralda Special, the crown jewel of the coffee world, and say, "Hmmm. Good coffee," for the coffee buyers and growers who spend hours and hours a day contemplating the one thousand volatile compounds that comprise the aroma wafting from a four-ounce cup of coffee, the experience is quite different. These guys train their senses the way pianists train their hands—they practice, practice, practice. To more sensitively perceive the flavors and aromas in a single coffee, they follow formal training protocols during which they sniff little glass vials filled with various essences and try to identify their contents. For coffee tasters like these the flavor definition "sweet and woodsy" is far too vague. They want to be able to identify birch bark. Or a specific grass. They want to be able to differentiate the aromatic differences between wet and dry coffee grounds. Reaching this level of sensory acuity requires years of serious effort.

When Geoff Watts, the green buyer for Intelligentsia, tasted Esmeralda Special, the coffee was so aromatic, he said he felt as if streams of light were pouring out of it. But Geoff's comment is not the one everyone in the coffee world remembers. The remark that got the specialty industry's attention came from Don Holly, quality control manager for Green Mountain Coffee in Vermont, a respected coffee guy who lectures on coffee history and economics. When Don tasted Esmeralda for the first time at the 2006 Best of Panama coffee competition, he said the coffee was so transporting that when he tasted it he saw the face of God in the cup.

Don was in Panama that week to work on a project funded by the Coffee Quality Institute, the nonprofit arm of the SCAA. Lindsey Bolger, Green Mountain's specialty coffee buyer, was serving as a judge at the competition. "Lindsey was the face of Green Mountain at the competition, and I had told her that I would stay in the background.

"At the final cupping," Don continues, "there were eight coffees on a table; I was walking around the table trying each one of them and there was one that just sang sirens to Odysseus. I was almost not believing how extraordinary this coffee was."

All the judges went bonkers over this unknown coffee. Don was standing in the back of the room. "I made the comment…that when I tasted this coffee I saw the face of god in a cup. [It turns out that] a reporter from Reuters was standing right next to me, and he overheard what I said. 'What did you say?' he asked, scribbling in his notebook. I replied, 'I am the least religious person here and when I tasted this coffee I saw the face of God in a cup.'" The remark was sent out on the Reuters wire, and it was picked up and repeated in numerous print, broadcast, and online stories all over the world.

In 2006, the year that Holly attended the competition, Esmeralda Special scored an extraordinary 94.6 out of a possible 100.

From the first moment Holly and the other judges leaned over the small white porcelain "cupping" bowls and sniffed, this coffee demanded their attention. At a national competition, judges cup or taste six or more coffees at a time. Grown in similar terrain from similar varieties, national coffees almost always resemble one another. But Esmeralda was different.

Esmeralda Special hit the judges over their heads with a crazy perfume bath of floral and citrus. Within this heady brew they detected fragrances no one had ever smelled in Panamanian coffee: ginger, blackberry, ripe mango, citrus blossom, and exotic bergamot, a citrus oil used to flavor Earl Grey tea. Many commented that Esmeralda was bursting with the kind of good acidity—coffee buyers call it brightness— that is rare in Latin America, but common in the best coffees from East Africa. In fact, some said Esmeralda tasted more like a great Ethiopian than a Panamanian coffee.

Discerning judges sensed that Esmeralda was something unfamiliar—a wild child, a changeling. They wondered if geography and climate, and all the factors that wine makers call terroir, were responsible. Did Esmeralda's unique taste result from the high elevation and cold, windy, yet sunny climate on the hillside where it was grown? Could the skill of the farmer be credited for this standout coffee?

All of these were certainly in play. Esmeralda Special was grown by an experienced father-son farming team in a high corner of Boquete, Panama, known as Jaramillo. Price Peterson is an American-born neurochemistry professor turned dairy and coffee farmer who settled in Boquete with his family in the 1970s and has been farming there ever since. In 1996, around the time Price's youngest son, Daniel, a recent college grad, got interested in coffee farming, Price, already a substantial landowner, purchased Jaramillo Farm.

When Price and Daniel explored the new property, they discovered odd-looking trees about which they knew little growing wild here and there on the property. Tall and spindly, like the kind of Christmas tree you buy when all the nice fat ones are gone, Geisha appeared to be hardy, but it produced less fruit than other coffee varieties. Daniel at the time was studying all the trees on the property and rethinking what coffee varieties he ought to plant where. He sorted through a lot of different options and decided to cultivate this tall thin tree on a particular windy hillside where other coffee trees had perished.

Coffee trees take at least five years to mature. In 2004, the Petersons harvested their first Geisha crop from this hillside. There were just three thousand pounds of coffee from several distinct areas. These Daniel separated into microlots. Daniel cupped the beans in the family's cupping room, which is paneled with beautiful cherry-colored wood cut from their own trees. While he was impressed by Esmeralda's fruity nose, he feared that the judges might consider its flavor profile so different from anything else grown in Panama that it was the product of a defect and disqualify it from consideration. But after conferring with his family and others in the industry, Daniel decided to take a chance. He selected what he thought was the most flavorful microlot and entered it into competition. He named the beans from this sample Esmeralda Special.

The rest is history. Esmeralda Special quickly became one of the biggest things to happen in the rarefied upper reaches of the specialty world. Though some criticized its tealike lack of body, specialty buyers with highly trained palates flipped. The coffee's oddball qualities made it a connoisseur's dream. Specialty guys began talking up Esmeralda Special on their websites and blogs.

Soon the press got wind of the story. By 2006 high-end retail customers in the United States, Canada, and Japan were spending crazy amounts of money for a pound of this rare little bean.

Buyers of green (unroasted) coffee, coffee roasters, café owners, coffee geeks, coffee bloggers, and foodies worldwide all were eager to get their hands on Esmeralda Special. The fact that there was almost none to be had fueled the craze. While a few other Boquete farmers had discovered these distinctive-looking trees growing on their property, the number of trees was small and, outside of Boquete farms, no one knew where else to look. The origin of this varietal was unknown.

Price Peterson and some others in the specialty business immediately starting digging into coffee archives for answers. Eventually a coherent story describing the probable origins of this coffee emerged. In the 1930s, a British diplomat stationed in Ethiopia, the country where coffee first appeared, had collected samples of coffees growing wild in Ethiopian forests. Among the coffees he chose was one apparently from the Gesha region that somewhere along the line got labeled "Geisha." This coffee was thought to be disease resistant. Beans from the diplomat's collection were sent to coffee research laboratories in Kenya, Tanzania, and Costa Rica, where they were planted in 1953.

In the 1960s, Francisco Serracin, an employee of the Panamanian Ministry of Agriculture, sought coffee plants that were resistant to leaf rust, a crop-destroying disease. Serracin, also a coffee farmer, asked agriculture officials in Costa Rica for samples of disease-resistant trees. Agronomists from the Costa Rican coffee research lab sent a number of coffee plants, including those labeled Geisha, to growers in Panama.

In general, coffee quality increases with altitude. The original Geisha trees were planted at fairly low altitude—1,400 meters, around 4,500 feet. At that elevation, the tree produced relatively little fruit and the flavor of its beans was nothing special. Like a tennis player who could excel on grass but only gets to play on clay, Geisha did not have a chance to show what it could do until it was cultivated at higher elevations (close to 6,000 feet).

The fact that Geisha was part of an exchange that included coffees from Ethiopia tantalized coffee cognoscenti. Biologically speaking, all coffee comes from Ethiopia. Most of the coffees we drink today are the distant descendants of two varieties of coffee that were stolen from Ethiopia and taken to Yemen, before being sneaked out of that country about five hundred years ago. From these two heirloom varieties—Bourbon and Typica—agronomists created many hybrids, some more successful than others. There are no indigenous coffee varietals in the New World or in Asia. In Ethiopia, however, thousands—some Ethiopians say as many as one hundred thousand—of unique coffee cultivars may have evolved since the plant appeared in the forest tens of thousands of years ago. Hundreds, maybe thousands, of these varieties still grow wild in Ethiopian forests, though no one knows the impact of recent, rapid deforestation on Ethiopia's coffee diversity. Some agriculturalists suggest that every Ethiopian town at coffee-growing elevation may have its own distinct variety of coffee, but no one really knows for sure. The majority of farmers in this growing region live without electricity, motor vehicles, paved roads, cell phones, running water, or information about modern agronomy. And coffee researchers don't spend much time traveling to these regions.

Despite the lack of hard evidence at the time, a few coffee guys came up with a pretty convincing theory: if every Ethiopian town has its own strain of coffee, they said, Geisha was probably a misspelling of Gesha, a coffee-growing town in the mountains of southern Ethiopia.

Adding to the romantic charm of the Geisha/Gesha theory was a bit of geographical happenstance: Gesha is located near Kefa, the town from which coffee is said to get its name—the town where legend has it, a young goatherd discovered coffee a thousand years ago. According to this oft-told tale, after watching his goats dance and jump like sugar-crazed five-year-olds, the young herdsman connected his animals' manic liveliness to their habit of eating those small green beans inside of rotting cherries.

Those with a romantic streak—and show me a coffee guy who isn't a romantic—couldn't help feeling that there was something ordained in the Geisha/Gesha connection.

The vision of Ethiopia with its untapped potential coffee wealth has long enticed young coffee guys. When Hacienda La Esmeralda Special—aka Geisha—appeared, the timing couldn't have been better; after thirty years of communist rule and civil strife, Ethiopia had a new government and was slowly opening its door to outsiders. Specialty guys could hardly wait to visit coffee's motherland and go searching for the amazing Geisha.

In November 2006, a well-known coffee consultant named Willem Boot organized an expedition to Ethiopia to do just that. Willem, a Dutch guy now based in California, had fallen hard for Geisha, so hard he had become a coffee farmer himself, planting Geisha trees on land in Panama he had bought as an investment. Willem had learned that there are at least three towns named Gesha near towns known as Kefa or Kafa. He hoped to visit all of them, looking for tall, skinny coffee trees with Geisha's distinctive long, narrow leaves.

Under his banner, a three-car caravan of westerners and Ethiopians did indeed carry out an assault on Gesha, Gesha, and Gesha, searching for specialty coffee's goose that laid the golden egg. The expedition turned out to be a grueling foray into the realm of human discomfort worthy of the reality show *Survivor*.

The participants traveled to a remote highland redoubt in south-west Ethiopia where the roads, pitted, rocky, and nearly unnavigable to begin with, got a lot worse when torrential rain began to fall and didn't stop. One day the adventurers hiked for six hours in a downpour in mud so deep that their shoes got sucked off their feet and one of the Ethiopian participants, an older man, hurt his leg. Later they were run out of town by an angry local official who accused them of plotting to steal Ethiopia's precious coffee resource. The party spent a night in what they thought must have been the most squalid hotel in Africa—no bathroom, just a fetid open pit.

The story of this miserable expedition circulated widely in coffee world and grew wilder and wilder in the telling. Geoff Watts reported that he had heard that one guy on the Gesha trip went mad and had had to be sedated and spirited out of the country. Another story shared by Geoff raised the possibility that an agronomist friend of Willem's from Panama named Graciano Cruz had snuck back to Gesha by himself, went into the forest, and stole Geisha plants to take back to Panama. In one version of this story the authorities were said to have thrown Graciano in jail and then tossed him out of the country with orders never to come back. Hot stuff. But none of it true. Graciano never went on any Gesha expedition. Visa problems kept him in Addis Ababa, where he spent a week jumping through Ethiopian bureaucratic hoops. No one went crazy. No one stole plants. Most importantly, no one found the fabled Geisha tree in Gesha or anywhere else.

The expedition was a total failure. But the enticing thought that Hacienda La Esmeralda Special originated and might still be growing somewhere in Ethiopia highlighted what coffee guys had always known: Ethiopia is coffee's citadel. It's Jerusalem the Golden.

Hoping to understand coffee's Ethiopian derivation, I would soon follow Peter Giuliano and Geoff Watts to Africa. But that momentous journey would take place following my first "trip to origin"—to Nicaragua. This is where my real coffee education would begin when I attended a Cup of Excellence coffee competition, and I met Peter and Geoff in person for the first time.

GRANADA, NICARAGUA

GRANADA, NICARAGUA, IS A TATTERED COLONIAL CITY located one hour south of Managua. When night falls, it gets so dark that you can barely make out the outlines of Granada's sixteenth-century Spanish palaces and grand buildings, some crumbling, some newly restored thanks to the "gringo" hunger for tropical real estate.

In May 2006, I fly to Granada for Nicaragua's Cup of Excellence competition, widely recognized as having had a beneficial impact on the country's specialty coffee industry.

My taxi driver careens into the city square and stops directly in front of the Hotel Alhambra's broad veranda where hotel guests lounging in rattan easy chairs look out into the darkness. With its thick stucco walls, overhead fans, leafy interior courtyard and broad patio, the Alhambra looks like a place I've seen in more than one movie.

The next morning, forty or fifty hotel guests, almost all of them associated with the Cup of Excellence coffee competition, are crammed into patio tables ingesting fried eggs, toast, and the kind of over-roasted burnt-rubber coffee that people in coffee-producing countries drink because exporters don't want to "waste" the good stuff. I am in Granada not only to observe but also to write a story on young coffee guys for the *New York Times*—one reason I grab a chair at the table with two of them. Stephen Vick, the espresso trainer from Stumptown Coffee in Portland, Oregon, is tall, fair, and confident. The other guy, wearing a skullcap despite the heat and carrying a skateboard and fancy photography equipment, is E. J. Dawson, a cupper from Intelligentsia. E. J. tells me he had skateboarded out into the square before breakfast to photograph the homeless people who live there. E. J. and Stephen order fruit juice.

"I'll get my caffeine fix at the cupping," Stephen says. "Even when you're sipping and spitting, not swallowing, you get buzzed. The caffeine invades your body by osmosis."

When I learn that he works for Intelligentsia, I ask E. J. when Geoff Watts would be arriving. "You never know about Geoff," E. J. answers cryptically.

"Isn't he cupping?" I ask.

"Not officially. But he's supposed to arrive on Thursday and Friday so he can taste all the coffees," E. J. says.

I say, "I hope he shows up because my editor at the *New York Times* expects me to write about him."

"Geoff will show up eventually," E. J. answers.

At 9:00 a.m. a throng of animated English and Spanish speakers gather in the hotel's shaded interior courtyard, anticipating the beginning of the competition. The Cup of Excellence (COE) program was created in the hopes of raising the profile of Latin American coffees, and to pour desperately needed cash into the coffers of farmers who devote themselves to cultivating quality. Each year national competitions are held in eight Central and South American countries. (In 2007, Rwanda held a successful

Golden Cup Competition patterned on COE, and it is expected that more such events will be held in Africa in coming years.)

The pre-event hubbub has a certain Oscar-night excitement, because coffee is a big deal—the major cash-producing export—in Nicaragua. Representatives from the coffee industry's many stakeholders and supporters, including the government of Nicaragua, the U.S. Embassy, U.S. AID, and other development organizations and foundations, view COE as a "must-show" event.

Nicaragua is one of the poorest countries in Latin America. Many aid organizations, including U.S. AID, fund projects designed to increase the value of the country's coffee exports and improve the lives of coffee-farming families. Often programs that promote development in Central America and elsewhere cost a great deal of money and accomplish little in the way of quantifiable results. Cup of Excellence is an exception. Despite being chronically underfunded, the program has data supporting the view that it is accomplishing its goals. At COE's behest, McKinsey & Company, the consulting firm, undertook an evaluation of the Cup of Excellence competition in Nicaragua. In 2006, McKinsey researchers released their report, in which they concluded that Cup of Excellence in Nicaragua had

- motivated farmers to improve the quality of their coffee,
- helped to improve the reputation of Nicaraguan specialty coffee, and
- strengthened and deepened the specialty market in Nicaragua.

McKinsey said that Cup of Excellence in 2006 helped the mass of Nicaraguan producers, cooperatives, and exporters earn an additional $1.1 million in profit that they would not have had were it not for the publicity and other ancillary benefits generated by the competition. This figure did not include the $229,000 in premiums top winners of the competition earned when their coffees were auctioned online. Comparing these benefits to the cost of the program—around $140,000 per year—McKinsey concluded that the Nicaragua contest yielded benefits nine times greater than the cost of the program.

Not everyone in the specialty world agrees that Cup of Excellence is the right program to help coffee farmers. Mark Inman, thirty-nine, a founder and principal of Taylor Maid Farms organic coffee roastery in Sebastopol, California, says the competition doesn't teach farmers anything. It's a "beauty pageant for homeless women," he adds, meaning that it's misguided, not what's needed.

Inman believes COE approaches quality from the wrong direction. "If you want to motivate a farmer, don't start with the contents of the cup. Start with his agricultural practices. Start with the dirt. You can't build great wine from crappy soil. Same thing with coffee," he says, adding that funds to pay agronomists would be far more helpful in the long run than prize money falling from the sky. The money is enticing, but, says Mark, "most farmers have no idea why they win one year and lose the next. They see it as the function of luck."

Further to his point, at a fiesta in honor of COE judges and past COE winners a few nights later, I interviewed several growers, one of whom expressed outrage that after coming in among the top ten one year, the following year he failed to place in the top twenty-five.

There's no denying the lure of the prize money. For farmers the major draw of Cup of Excellence is the auction and the promise of extra cash. Top COE winners earn as much as $60,000. These are one-time cash bonanzas; most farmers who win one year do not win again. Still, for those who come out on top, the benefits can be world-changing. It's hard to imagine what $20,000 or $40,000 or $60,000 can mean to an impoverished coffee farmer. One year the top winner in Honduras was so poor that he couldn't afford a bus ticket. He had to hitch a ride to the auction. His Cup of Excellence earnings enabled him to get out of debt, purchase another small plot of land, and buy drying racks to prevent his coffee from rotting on the ground. In 2005 one of the top winners in Nicaragua, a small, spirited woman, used half her earnings to build a guest house; now her coffee plantation is an ecotourism destination, and she has a diversified revenue stream. Not all the growers "get it," of course. One bought a Hummer. Another gave all her winnings to her church.

More than raining cash on a lucky few, the point of the Cup of Excellence program is to familiarize Latin American farmers with the benefits of raising the quality of their coffee to meet specialty market standards. Equally important, COE introduces specialty buyers to small growers producing outstanding coffee. Peter, Geoff, Duane, and many other discerning buyers from coffee-consuming countries in North America and Europe as well as Japan monitor all the COE contests. Many of them have established long-term buying relationships with winning farmers.

Shortly after 9:00 a.m. the twenty men and seven women on the 2006 Cup of Excellence judging panel are seated on metal folding chairs facing the podium in the Alhambra's meeting room. Later that day, the Granada temperature and humidity would flirt with 100°F and 100 percent unbearable. The meeting room was cool except when the power died, which only happened once or twice a day. The judges had been asked to dress up—in Nicaragua starching and ironing are national pastimes and hot weather is no excuse for looking sloppy. The young guys from the United States serving on the panel don't agree; most, except Peter Giuliano, wear shorts, T-shirts with logos or slang, and flip-flops. Peter is a bit more sensitive to dress codes, influenced, perhaps, by his Old-World upbringing by Sicilian grandparents and his interest in other cultures.

The judges come from all over the world—the United States, Canada, Holland, Germany, Lithuania, Norway, Russia, Taiwan, and Japan are represented. Stephen Vick, twenty-nine, is the youngest judge. Unlike a lot of young American baristas and coffee guys, Stephen is university educated. Trained as a computer engineer, he'd lost his one and only engineering job in the aftermath of 9/11 and hadn't looked back. California-based Erna Knutsen, eighty-two, founder of Knutsen Coffee and one of the pioneers in the post–World War II specialty industry, is the oldest. Erna is a bit wobbly on her feet. Her friend and fellow judge, Becky McKinnon, chairperson of Canada's third largest coffee roaster/retailer, Timothy's World Coffee, provides a ready arm to help steady her. Adding luster to the panel is Kentaro Maruyama, thirty-five, owner of Japan's Maruyama Coffee. In addition to running his own business, Kentaro buys for a small group of high-quality roasters in Japan. Many in the specialty world consider Kentaro to be the world's most discerning coffee cupper—certainly he is the most loved. Cheerful, with an unexpected talent for mimicry, Kentaro takes pride in attending every Cup of Excellence competition in every country every year. "That dude rocks!" is how Duane Sorenson later sums him up.

Cupping requires sensory acuity, experience, a strong back (you can spend hours leaning over chest-high cupping tables), and concentration. People in the specialty world argue endlessly about whether cupping is an art or a science, a debate that comes down to questions of standardization: When a dozen professional coffee cuppers smell and taste the same coffee, do they all experience the same thing? If they do not experience the same thing, how can they collectively make judgments about quality? And what about scoring?

Cup of Excellence director Susie Spindler raises her voice to get the judges' attention. Crowded into a corner of the discussion room are auditors from PricewaterhouseCoopers. Cup of Excellence competitions are conducted blind: coffees are numerically coded, so no one knows which farmer grew what coffee. In an industry that is infamous for corruption, this transparency is very important.

Slender with curly hair framing her face, Susie, in her early fifties, shouts to get the panel's attention. "Okay, you guys, we need to get started." She tells the cuppers that they will be judging sixty-four Nicaraguan coffees—the best of five hundred submitted to the competition.

Paul Songer, also in his fifties, quiet-spoken with white hair and decades of experience as a university-trained sensory analyst and coffee consultant, serves as the head judge.

"When you come across coffee with defects, make sure you point them out to me on the table so we can discuss what you are tasting," Paul urges.

"Watch out for phenol too," Susie chimes in. Phenol is a mysterious chemical defect that shows up in individual beans in some coffees. Exactly what causes phenol is something of a mystery. Just one phenol-tainted bean in a roasting sample of sixty or seventy can result in the coffee's immediate disqualification.

"Some people think phenol tastes like chlorine in a swimming pool," says Paul, "but I'm not sure that captures it."

"More like a Band-Aid floating in the coffee," opines Peter Giuliano.

The doors separating the discussion room and the cupping room are flung open. At the back of the cupping room, a team of technicians are at work. They are charged with grinding, measuring, weighing, and preparing the coffee samples to ensure uniformity—without uniformity the judges cannot fairly compare coffees to one another. On each cupping table the technicians have placed four small white porcelain cups containing samples of each of the ten coffees to be judged in the first flight—forty small cups in all. The cupping protocol mandates that the judges taste all four samples of each coffee because defects can appear in one cup, but not all. Temperature is also an important factor—the judges, like Goldilocks, are required to taste the coffees when hot, middling, and cool.

Before they do any tasting, however, they do a lot of smelling. They begin marking up their score sheets immediately, noting the aroma of the beans when dry and the fragrance when wet. They sniff the dry coffee in each cup before the technicians pour near boiling (200°F) water over the samples. Then they sniff the wet grounds and wait as coffee particles float to the surface, creating a crust of coffee grounds. When little gas bubbles appear in the crust, the senior judge at each table gives the signal and the panelists pick up their spoons and move the wet grounds to the side, which most judges do with a particular flourish. When the surface is broken, invisible gases are released that are particularly aromatic. Noses dipping down to take in this aroma often land in the drink: a slightly parboiled nose is a cupping room norm. After the sniff and the break and the sniff, someone skims off the grounds that have not drifted to the bottom and the tasting begins.

Entering the cupping chamber at that moment after a chat with Susie, I am hit by a wall of warm, moist air—all that boiling water—and a cacophony of snuffling and snorting. The room is large, with high ceilings and stucco walls that send the sound bouncing back at me. Ranking sheets in hand, the judges in their blue Cup of Excellence aprons circle the tables, bending before each cup. They tip their silver spoons into the brown liquid, suck in small amounts of coffee, and noisily aerate it in their mouths, allowing coffee molecules to travel to the throat and back into the portion of their nasal cavities where the supersensitive olfactory membrane resides. Shooting the coffee up through the mouth with these staccato sips is hugely important, as noses are much more sensitive sensory receptors than tongues. After smelling and tasting the coffee, the judges spit into red plastic cups and make their first markings on their score sheets.

With more than two dozen cuppers in the room, the noise is deafening. I feel like I am in the waiting room of an ear, nose, and throat doctor during flu season.

"You think this is noisy?" comments George Howell, sixty, owner of Terroir Coffee in Acton, Massachusetts. In Brazil, where being a noisy slurper has a certain macho panache, "you need earplugs in the cupping room," he says with a grin. George is well respected in the specialty coffee world. His reputation is based on his accomplishments as an innovator. At his first company, the Boston-based Coffee Connection that he later sold to Starbucks, he was one of the first coffee guys to champion light roasts when everyone else was touting dark, and he invented the frappuccino—made with coffee, evaporated milk, and ice—and sold the recipe to Starbucks. Recently, George has been beating the drum for cryogenically frozen coffee and nonreactive Mylar bags instead of jute for coffee shipping and storing. Mostly, though, George is famous for being persnickety and uncompromising—the ultimate purist in an industry that celebrates purists.

The cuppers move around their cupping tables. Kentaro, his face rimmed by Buster Brown bangs, cups with a still, Zen-like countenance. He is one of the smallest people in the room; he is also one of the loudest. The insistent "whoiop, whoiop" sounds as he aspirates coffee sound like an avian mating call.

The coffees cool, and as they do they lose their flavor—part of coffee's beauty is its evanescence—while the judges make their final scribbles on their score sheets. Grabbing bottles of water to clear their palates, the panelists head back to the discussion room, clipboards and pencils in hand, water bottles at the ready.

Paul Songer stands before an easel equipped with 24-by-36-inch sketch paper, a black marker in his hand. Nervous chattering sweeps across the room. Coffees that score under 83 would be out of the competition; those with an 84 or better would be recupped in the finals.

Paul leads the discussion, allotting fifteen minutes or more for the panel to talk about each coffee. He encourages every judge, including the members of the Nicaraguan national cupping panel whose scores are not included in the tally, to share their thoughts. This painstaking process helps the panel coalesce as a group, and helps sharpen the cuppers' skills.

The first two coffees are eliminated from the finals with scores of 82 and 83. The next is more popular. One panelist says it has a nice aftertaste and a subtle floral flavor.

"It tastes of rye bread," says Joost Leopold, a Dutch cupper and former perfume tester.

"Extremely clean," says Peter.

"Lemon blossom," says Becky McKinnon.

Paul does the math. This coffee earns a respectable 87.

The fifth coffee is controversial.

"I really liked this coffee," says George Howell. "It is really clean, really sweet, balanced, elegant."

"A hint of pineapple," someone says.

"I disagree," says Peter. "I knew George would love this coffee, but I think it lacks character and one cup on my table was astringent."

Number five sneaks into the finals with an 85.

Number six. "This coffee smells great but it was not suffi-ciently developed," Kentaro answers when called on by Paul—at least that's what people believe he said. Though Kentaro is popular and respected, Kentaro's English is not always comprehensible.

"Nice floral finish," someone else says. "Long, long finish, huge acidity," Paul adds, noting that the scores add up to 86.

Number seven. "Dry and chalky." "Dead as a doornail." 78.

Number eight. Some love this coffee. "Rosewater, pear, creamy." But more hate it.

"Motor oil," says Stephen Vick.

"Dry, unpleasant finish," says E. J.

"Bimodal," Paul says, noting that the coffee has high scores and low scores and few in between. Result: a score of 83.5, and it is out.

Number nine. This coffee earns an 85.9 and triggers a few unusual responses. "Root beer." "Wintergreen." "Bubble gum."

Number ten. "A no-brainer," Paul says. "Peanutty"—as in peanut fungus. "Salty." "Earthy." "Good-bye," says Paul.

The cuppers head back to the cupping room for their next flight. I decide to try cupping this round. "Cupping is about paying attention," George tells me. "It's like trying to remember the num-bers on the license plate of a passing car." Carmen Vellejos, the highly respected head of the Nicaraguan national cupping team who'd been born on a coffee plantation and later trained as a cup-per at a U.S. AID-sponsored cupping school, tells me she thinks of each new coffee as a person she doesn't know, whose qualities, strengths, and defects she has to find out quickly.

George sets me up at a cupping table.

I don't know how to aerate the coffee—you have to suck it into your mouth between your teeth—so I sip and swallow instead of snorting and spitting. The first coffee is easy, but each coffee after that gets increasingly difficult to analyze. They all taste the same to me.

Mostly I taste chocolate. The taste of citrus hits me now and then. Once I note the herbaceous and woodsy taste of twigs. After imbibing all ten coffees I circle the table again. Now I am lost. I can't tell one coffee from another. I watch the cuppers intently doing their work, marking their sheets, conferring with one another. I can't believe that they can get so much from four ounces of brown liquid. I feel like a woman faking an orgasm: I know what I am supposed to be feeling, but it just isn't happening for me.

I had met Peter Giuliano, who is in his mid-thirties, when I arrived at the hotel the evening before. We'd had a beer on the patio. He was easy to talk to and obviously knew a ton about coffee, so when the cupping breaks for lunch, I make a beeline for the table where Peter and Paul Songer are sitting. I ask them to explain why I am having trouble perceiving the range of qualities in the coffees on the cupping table. Paul makes it clear that it takes several years to train a coffee cupper, and even then, the ability to capture nuances in the cup continues to develop. The two provide me with a quick tasting tutorial. They explain that the capacity of our smelling apparatuses outstrip the talents of the taste buds on our tongues. These perceive just five flavors: sweet, sour, salty, bitter, and savory or meaty.

- *Sweet.* As mammals, we are hardwired to prefer sweet tastes to all others—milk, of course, is sweet, as is fruit and some vegetables. In coffee, sweetness is related to the ripeness of the coffee cherry when it is picked.
- *Sour.* When coffee cherries are picked green or when they get wet during their drying phase and the fruit ferments, the resulting beans can exhibit an unpleasant vinegary sourness that is undesirable in coffee. (This accidental fermentation is distinct from the fermenting that is often

a part of coffee processing after coffee cherries have been depulped and their fruit removed.) But some sourness in coffee can be an asset; our sour receptors, for example, perceive the kind of good acidity coffee guys call brightness.

■ *Salty.* A salty flavor in coffee comes from the soil and generally occurs when coffee is dried on the ground. It is always considered a defect.

■ *Bitter.* Some bitterness in coffee comes from caffeine but most comes from trigonneline—both of these are alkaloids, a class of organic molecules that have a pharmacological effect on humans. Other alkaloids include chocolate, nicotine, and cocaine. Tasters consider a small amount of alkaloid-related bitterness in a coffee a plus. Some bitterness in coffee can be traced to compounds that emerge during roasting and are caused by browning reactions.

■ *Savory.* Experts believe savoriness or meatiness in coffee is related to the yeast activity that occurs during fermentation as coffee is processed. Meatiness in coffee can be a positive or a negative.

Flavor is the combination of tastes perceived by the tongue and aromatics perceived in the nasal cavity, Peter tells me. "The interplay of these two is what makes coffee so irresistible," he says, noting that "coffee has more aromatics than any other food." Number two on the aromatics list is red wine.

Turns out most of what professional cuppers and laypeople experience when they "taste" coffee isn't a taste at all: it's fragrance. Cuppers detect thousands of different aromas and fragrances in coffee. All of these, however, are by-products of just three kinds of chemical reactions that occur naturally in coffee or when coffee is roasted.

- *Enzyme by-products* stem from how the plant keeps itself alive. These produce both the floral, citrusy, and fruity aromas that we love and the oniony, vegetal ones most people don't enjoy in coffee.

- *Sugar browning by-products* are aromatic compounds that occur during roasting as sugars in the coffee are browned. These release the sweet, caramel-like, nutty, toasty aromas most of us love and the grainy ones we find less pleasing.

- *Dry-distillation by-products* are related to the burning of plant fibers during roasting. We experience these as spicy, smoky, and woody aromas. Some we like, some we don't.

Peter explains that, in order to cup well, you have to practice. "Sensory awareness is like a muscle that you develop. I'm convinced anyone can learn," Peter says.

Paul isn't so sure that practice alone can make a cupper—"It seems to me some cuppers have palates that are just dead on arrival," Paul says. He adds, "No matter how much they train, they don't taste or smell what most people taste and smell. So while I agree that training and practice count, I also think the palate you are born with matters."

"There's one other thing," Peter adds, looking at me. "Age counts too. The younger you are, the more acute your senses of taste and smell. Cuppers lose acuity with age."

I raise an eyebrow in his direction.

During the course of the competition, Paul and the other Cup of Excellence regulars mention again and again how impressed they are by the quality of the coffees they are tasting. Nicaraguan coffee, they say, has improved remarkably in the past few years. Which was good news and bad news for the judges. Just as it's easier to write a scathing review of a movie, it is much simpler to weed out poor coffee than to judge many high-quality coffees against one another. On Thursday morning the judges learn that they have given thirty-nine coffees scores of 84 and above. In the final round of cupping they will have to recup all 39 to come up with the 25 official winners. The judges groan when they learn this news. But they set to the work of cupping and discussing.

The most poetic descriptions of the week come from Becky McKinnon of Timothy's.

"Lovely." "Soft mouth." "Plums." "Plum juice, clean and sweet." "Juicy pulp rolling down your chin." "Slightly nutty taste hiding beneath the sweetness of the fruit." These are some of her comments about one of the coffees.

George comments on one of the coffees, asking, "How did a Siberian tiger get into Nicaragua?"

"I got tears in my eyes," Joost, the Dutchman, says, explaining why he gave one coffee a 100.

"It got rounder and rounder," Betsy says about another. "Like Debussy."

"Deep chocolate all the way through," Paul says.

"Lemon blossom citrus...sweet roundness...viscous syrup body...crisp red apple...velvety soft texture...creamy, buttery."

By the afternoon the judges' backs and necks ache from bending over and the strain of concentrating so hard, and ingesting all that caffeine through their capillaries is starting to take its toll.

Only Kentaro seems unperturbed. Solidly built and still as a yogi, Kentaro moves up and down the table sucking in, trilling, spitting. His concentration is unshakeable. He had been born in the mountains of Japan, into a family that had worked as artisan potters and weavers for generations. He has said that as a child he would grow agitated when eating shrimp, overcome by the astringency of one or two that had gone slightly bad—spoilage others in his family did not perceive. At his own shop, every cup of coffee is brewed individually in a French press, and no adulterants—no milk, no sugar, no nothing—are allowed.

A groan sweeps across the cupping room after a favorite is eliminated when phenol is detected.

"Damn," says Stephen Vick. "Double damn. I worshipped that coffee."

By noon on Friday the competition is over. Ten coffees, still identified only by their numerical codes, are identified as the top winners. The growers of these would be honored that evening at an awards ceremony. The other finalists in the competition will, like the top winners, be entered in the auction which is to take place in a month. All the coffees that did not make it into the finals will be sold through the usual specialty sales channels.

Geoff Watts, thirty-two, finally shows up at the competition late on Thursday, looking scruffy after weeks on the road. He greets a few people and then disappears. On Friday, he joins the morning cupping, looking as though he'd slept in his clothes. He doesn't look like the most important specialty coffee buyer in the world. But by that evening, at the awards ceremony in Granada's five-hundred-year-old Convent of San Francisco, there is Geoff, all cleaned up: smooth-shaven, rosy-cheeked with thick black eyebrows, arresting blue eyes, and a freshly laundered guyaberra.

Nicaraguans, Americans, and assorted other nationalities, highborn, lowborn, government officials, development guys, coffee cooperative honchos, growers, mill owners, and exporters throng the steamy old church. Most of the local people are dressed to the nines. It is hotter than hell and everyone is waving their paper programs in an effort to create a breeze.

Rows and rows of folding chairs have been set up in the nave of the church. The awards ceremony begins late and goes on for hours. Susie Spindler is the emcee. The speechifying takes place in two languages. As the speeches drag, many prefer milling about the open loggia that runs the length of the church to sitting.

As darkness falls, Geoff joins the crowd swirling about in the relative cool of the loggia. Geoff greets a coffee grower, Norman Canales, son of the 2004 Cup of Excellence first-place winner, George Canales, who was the first organic grower to win in Nicaragua. Norman and his brothers Milton and Donald also grow organic coffee recognized by Cup of Excellence. Intelligentsia buys from the whole family.

Norman gives Geoff an exuberant hug. "My friend," Norman says. "My friend," he says again, patting Geoff's back.

Norman later tells me that his family thanks God for Cup of Excellence, which enabled Geoff Watts and Intelligentsia to find them and which dramatically increased the price they get for their coffee. "We consider Geoff to be our guardian angel," he says.

I chat with a sleek-haired woman in white linen—small, fortyish, aristocratic—who tells me about the Marxist Sandinista regime that took power in Nicaragua in 1979, and the anti-Marxist insurgency and resulting civil war that ripped her country apart from 1981 to 1990. Some of the farmers here tonight, she says, work land that was seized and redistributed by the Sandinistas. The cooperatives that play such a large part in Nicaragua's coffee trade, she says, were also a product of Sandinista collectivization. I am surprised when she says that she had supported the Sandinistas—though her family did not. "Terrible wrongs were committed by both sides," she adds.

As Susie Spindler announces the names of the growers of the top ten coffees, one by one the men and women make their way to the podium to receive their plaques. In June their coffee will be auctioned off online. Often it is poor smallholders possessing just a few hectares of land high in the mountains in areas without electricity who grow the best coffee. Coffee guys endlessly debate why this is so. Many believe farmers with relatively small numbers of trees lavish loving care on each plant. Quality is also related to altitude—traditionally, wealthy farmers preferred living lower down, closer to town and transport for their crops. Whatever the reasons, the belief appears to hold and only one of the winning growers comes from Nicaragua's upper class.

Then Susie announces the name of the top winner. He is Jose Noel Talavera from the region of Depilto. The tinny, staticy sound system blares "Anchors Away" as Senor Talavera, a slender, dark-skinned man with a moustache, wearing a magenta shirt and black jeans, with a cell phone tucked on his belt, makes his way to the podium. Susie reads the judges' description of his coffee, which earned a score of 91.6. The judges detected "a solid structure" in this coffee, "the essence of lemon and citrus blossom," and "a sweet softness" and mouthfeel that reminded them of "rounded honey."

Senor Talavera's hands shake as he addresses the crowd in Spanish. Peter Giuliano translates for me. "Dear Nicaragua," he says, "I want to say hello and tell the small producers how important it is that we work inside our cooperatives to grow the best-quality coffee. If we devote ourselves in this way, striving to grow better and better coffee, we and our children and all our country can move forward together."

I carry my bags downstairs the next morning before breakfast. I am tagging along with Peter and Geoff while they visit a small coffee co-op in the mountains above Matagalpa called Las Brumas. The Las Brumas farmers—forty or so in number—are past Cup of Excellence winners, and Geoff has been buying their coffee for three years. The morning is hot and humid and the guys, who had been celebrating the night before at La Nuit, the local reggaeton club, look a little bleary.

Geoff is going to Las Brumas to offer the farmers there a new pricing strategy that would increase what he pays for the highest-quality beans. Also on Geoff's Las Brumas agenda: a "come to Jesus" meeting with Cecocafen, the mega-cooperative that acts as the Las Brumas farmers' banker and agent. Several nesting layers of cooperatives represent Nicaraguan coffee farmers; this highly bureaucratic co-op-within-a-larger-co-op structure is the legacy of the socialist Sandinista regime.

Geoff's romantic enthusiasm for the entire cooperative system has waned over the years. He no longer believes that cooperatives necessarily protect the interest of poor farmers. In his opinion many, perhaps most, coffee cooperatives are poorly run. Elected officials within the co-ops rarely have the training, temperament, or sophistication to manage large sums of money—some officials, he believes, are outright corrupt. Geoff attributes many of the most difficult problems he faces in Latin America and in East Africa to the inability or unwillingness of co-op officials to operate efficiently and transparently.

Geoff says he is pretty sure Cecocafen is subverting his efforts to reward farmers' individual initiative. Cecocafen said that the Las Brumas samples that were to have gone to this year's Cup of Excellence competition were lost, preventing farmers from competing and earning the recognition and possible monetary reward that he thinks they deserve. This is just one of the reasons Geoff is angry at the Cecocafen leadership, and he is traveling to Las Brumas to deliver an ultimatum. Either they shape up, or he will suggest that the Las Brumas farmers find other representation.

As our driver plays pothole hopscotch on the mostly unpaved road to Matagalpa, hot air whooshes through the open windows of the truck. Peter, Geoff, K. C. O'Keefe, a consultant working for Intelligentsia, and Nick Hoskyns, a development worker and specialist in coffee co-ops, spend all four hours of the journey talking intently, describing their evolving understanding of specialty coffee and helping Geoff sharpen his strategy for the coming meeting.

Peter and Geoff are competitors, so it strikes me as odd that Peter should be privy to information about Intelligentsia's struggles with Las Brumas and Cecocafen. But as I get to know them better I realize that the two have grown up together in the industry, and they face many problems in common. The understanding they've acquired of specialty coffee is a result of traveling together, buying coffee together, and endless conversations on the subject. The differences between their companies and the differences in their natures have helped to smooth over the awkwardness of being simultaneous competitors and friends.

In the car that day, Geoff and Peter explain how their mutual love of specialty coffee inspired their friendship: "We felt as if we had discovered a secret that nobody else, not even chefs, understood," Geoff recalls.

For these two, the Cup of Excellence competitions, launched in 2001, were life-changing experiences. The competitions introduced Peter and Geoff to many of the best coffee farms and coffee-growing areas in Latin America and enabled them to cup with local tasters who had grown up on the very farms the coffee samples came from. This exposure opened up many lines of inquiry that had previously been beyond roasters' ken, such as the differences among coffee varietals, the impact of processing methods, the importance of altitude and climate—all sorts of issues that had an impact on taste. "We could ask them why this coffee tasted this way and that coffee tasted a different way," says Geoff. "It was amazing."

Their contact with national cuppers was facilitated by the U.S. government's development organization, U.S. AID, building cupping laboratories in Nicaragua and other coffee-producing countries. U.S. AID got this idea from one of the SCAA's founders, Paul Katzeff. U.S. AID pays to build the labs, and the SCAA's non-profit arm, the Coffee Quality Institute, provides the teachers through its Coffee Corps program. Many—but not all—young coffee guys are on the left side of the American political divide and, having seen more of the world than most, few have anything good to say about the vast U.S. AID bureaucracy or the impact of American foreign policy in Latin America, Africa, or Asia. Still, you won't easily find a coffee guy who criticizes the U.S. AID cupping labs. Most specialty guys say this program has been hugely—and cheaply—successful. From 2001 on, Peter and Geoff and many other skilled cuppers from coffee-consuming countries have spent a week or two at a time teaching young people from coffee-growing regions how to cup coffee in the U.S. AID labs. Some of the graduates of these programs, like Carmen Vellejos, the head of the Nicaraguan cupping panel, possessed tremendous talent and helped midwife their countries' emerging specialty industries. Today hundreds of trained cuppers in Central and South America work as well-paid coffee professionals.

Teaching cupping when the labs first got started proved to be an important win-win for Peter and Geoff, because U.S. AID picked up their travel expenses. "Our company wasn't rich. At the time a $700 plane ticket was a big deal for us," Peter recalls, adding that in the early days he would wrap his coffee-buying trips around his teaching assignments in order to save money.

Those national cupping laboratories were the brainchild of one of the most colorful guys in specialty coffee: sixty-eight-year-old former hippie, coffee roaster, and longtime social activist, Paul Katzeff. One of the "second wave" guys who founded the specialty coffee industry in the United States, Paul helped organize the SCAA in the 1980s, and he later was one of the movers and shakers behind Fair Trade certification in the United States. Paul and his wife own Thanksgiving Coffee, a company based in Mendocino, California. Invited by the Sandinistas, Paul visited Nicaragua in 1985 during the height of the revolution. It was his first trip to origin, and he was appalled by the poverty and suffering he saw. Bored with life as a businessman, he decided to merge his coffee business with social activism, seeking justice for coffee farmers.

"Paul Katzeff's a total wild man," Peter explains with a laugh full of simultaneous admiration and exasperation. "He's a guy who blows hot and cold. He's made amazing contributions to the industry, but he's a nutcase. His most notorious escapade happened when he and a band of followers burst into an SCAA board meeting banging drums and shouting about Salvadoran death squads. Then they poured watered-down red paint—symbolizing the blood on our hands—on the hotel steps.

"Geoff and I traveled with Paul in Nicaragua and in Africa and we learned a lot from him," Peter adds. He notes that this was before Paul decided that Peter and Geoff were the devil incarnate.

Peter's sense of Paul's opinion of them is apt. When I later meet Paul in California and mention that I had traveled with Peter and Geoff, Paul screamed at me, "I hate those guys. I hate those guys. They're a bunch of coffee Nazis."

Paul's a small, weather-beaten guy—handsome, when not having a choleric fit. Later, when he calms down, we talk. He is eager to tell me all that he had contributed to the specialty coffee industry. He makes it clear that he despises being shoved to the sidelines by young coffee guys he considers to be limited in their understanding, cramped in their politics, and less talented than he.

Ironically, one of Paul's major contributions drove the specialty industry in a direction he now despises. Paul is one of the people who introduced the idea that coffee should be separated into small lots and the achievements of individual farmers who grow particularly good coffee should be recognized. Paul promoted this idea as a way to encourage Nicaraguan coffee farmers to focus on quality.

To do this, Paul believed you had to be able to prove that a particular farmer grew a particular lot of coffee, which meant separating coffee by lots, keeping track of these lots as the coffee was processed, and then cupping them individually. When the coffee was cupped, talented farmers would be singled out as craftsmen who had hand-produced something of beauty and value. Paul thought that the additional money high-quality "craftsmen" coffee brought in would add to the common good by benefiting the cooperative of which the farmer was part. But when he promoted this idea, he let the genie of individuality out of the bottle.

This system, introduced in Latin America, later spread to other coffee-growing regions. Until farmers began separating their coffees into small lots, there was no way to single out the achievement of farmers who took pride in their work, fed their soil, diligently pruned their trees, picked only ripe cherries, and, in general, worked harder than their neighbors. In fact, under the commodity system in which coffees are aggregated—meaning that hundreds of small lots produced on different farms are dumped into one container—the hardest-working farmers suffered from the shortcomings of their neighbors. A relatively small amount of coffee tainted by "blacks"—overripe and rotten cherries—or by poor processing could ruin an entire container with 37,500 pounds of coffee inside, and make it far less valuable.

Separating coffee into small lots was quickly adopted as a practice by Peter and Geoff, but not in the way Paul had hoped. The young buyers thought farmers who worked harder ought to be paid a premium for all their effort. "We did separation to find excellence," Peter recalls. "We started to hyper-reward excellence—that made Paul angry. He wanted coffee to get better and everyone to benefit." Paul worried that if the best coffees were sold separately, what was left would no longer qualify as specialty. Often this was not the case, but sometimes it was. Some have accused Geoff, in particular, of having few scruples, of grabbing up the best coffee for Intelligentsia and leaving farmers to sell the bulk of their coffee on the commodities market. Geoff doesn't deny that he has sometimes been greedy. "At first," he admits, "I didn't fully understand the importance of developing long-term relationships with farmers." As his business has developed as well as his understanding of the importance of continuity, he says he makes it a practice to buy farmers' highest ranked coffees—those with scores of 90 and above—and those with more moderate scores. Intelligentsia markets these lots separately for different prices. "Now I see that you have to take the long view," Geoff says. His statement does not mollify all his critics. More recently, this charge of loving and leaving the farmer after skimming off the best has been leveled against Stumptown's Duane Sorenson and his coffee buyer, Aleco Chigounis, who brag that Stumptown owns the most expensive supply of coffee in the world.

Like it or not, separating coffee by lots is now standard specialty practice all over the world. Specialty buyers insist that coffee beans from specific small farms and from sectors of larger farms be separated out and tracked as they are picked, processed, bagged, and sold. Small lots are then cupped separately. High-end buyers pay premiums for this treatment because separating coffee in this way costs farmers time and money. In some cases, these premiums are huge: in 2007 Duane Sorenson paid premiums of $25 a pound for some Ethiopian coffees. In other cases, the quality premium may fail to cover extra labor costs and other expenses.

Back in 2001, Peter and Geoff had no idea how all this would develop. In fact, they didn't know much except that they were desperate to get their hands on great coffee. "We were bewildered by all we had to learn as coffee buyers, and we were making it up as we went along," remembers Peter. "When you are faking it, you work extra hard. You don't want to be exposed as a fraud. That drove a lot of us at this time."

"We based our travels on what we thought our predecessors had done—guys like Allegro's Kevin Knox and Tim Castle, the California-based coffee broker. Castle was a celebrity; he had written a book and he was untouchable to guys like us. Castle wrote with knowledge about Antigua, Guatemala. We thought 'Jeez, we better get our butts to Antigua.'" But when they got there they realized that no one had made inroads among the farmers or begun to explain what was needed to sell coffee as specialty. "Because the cupping labs were emerging, that was a thing we could focus on. So we would go and cup and taste great coffees and then we would go out and visit the farms where the coffees were grown and try to develop a relationship with the farmer and then we would have to go back. Geoff and I were the only small roasters doing this. We had a little rivalry going, I suppose, and we would try to outdo each other traveling," recalls Peter.

"Some of what they did was a matter of intestinal fortitude," chimes in K. C. O'Keefe. K. C., thirty-one, is an Intelligentsia consultant (now full-time employee) who owns a specialty coffee company in Peru called Jungle Tech. "These were young guys. Instead of going to the top floor of InterContinental Hotel to get wined and dined, they would get in a truck with a miller or somebody from a co-op and ride for hours to visit a farm and actually see for themselves what was happening there. Up until then the importer and exporter had the industry by the balls, but when buyers started traveling out to coffee farms, the industry started to change," K. C. explains, because buyers could finally understand some of the intricacies of coffee growing and coffee trading.

Geoff and Peter spent a lot of time during their first years as buyers trying to follow the money trail. Who was profiting from the coffee? Where was the value being made? The farmer? The miller? The overseas exporter who sold coffee? The U.S. importers who dealt with the exporter and managed the finances and logistics of the sale? As small roasters Peter and Geoff were completely bewildered by the confusing cast of characters, all of whom had their hands on the coffee at some time and all of whom managed to extract some of the coffee's value. "During these years it became a challenge to figure out where the money went," Geoff recalls.

It rapidly became clear to them that farmers were getting screwed.

"The coffee business functions on the discoverer's model devised by Spanish explorers five hundred years ago," says K. C. "In coffee-producing countries, white explorers came along, and they 'discovered' great coffee. They'd buy it up cheap. Their attitude was don't tell the farmers that they've got a treasure here."

Geoff and Peter realized the game was rigged. "We had to care about the growers because they had no other advocates," Geoff explains. What seemed especially unjust was the tiny differential farmers were paid for growing a superior product. Grape growers in the wine industry and olive growers in the olive oil industry were paid a fat premium for producing gourmet-quality products. This was not the case in the coffee industry, where coffee prices had been falling in real terms since 1970. "In coffee the price and quality scale is so truncated," says Geoff. "Even today, farmers growing the best earn only pennies more than farmers growing commodity-grade coffee. They might get, say, twenty-eight cents more a pound, which doesn't come close to covering the costs of production."

Their eagerness to help coffee farmers is, while admirable, contrary to generally accepted business practice, which is based on the assumption that the interests of buyers and vendors can converge but are not the same. So like most moral stances, Peter and Geoff's devout loyalty to farmers sometimes produces unexpected consequences.

The two buyers spent huge amounts of time trying to figure out how to get more money into farmers' pockets. "We would strategize about how to do this. Say an importer is offering me really good coffee at $1.10 a pound. I could say to the importer, this price isn't appropriate for coffee of this quality. I need to pay more. But if I say that to the importer, he'll charge me more and he'll put the money in his own pocket," says Peter. "He has no incentive to give more to the farmer." The only importer talking about giving more to the farmer back then was a guy named Dave Griswold from Portland, Oregon, whose company, Sustainable Harvest, put a cap on its own profits, ensuring that the premium that people like Geoff and Peter pay for coffee goes directly to farmers and farming communities, rather than enriching Sustainable Harvest's bottom line.

Clearly some other pricing approach was needed. While Geoff and Peter were trying to figure all this out, the bottom was dropping out of the international coffee market and prices were collapsing.

"We could have reduced our costs by 50 percent from 1999 to 2004 when the coffee market was at its nadir and prices were lurking around seventy or eighty cents a pound. I never took advantage of the low-price era and neither did Geoff," Peter says. "I know how companies work. Prices like that are like heroin, and companies get addicted to them. It was at this time that Fair Trade pricing was emerging—I have my arguments with Fair Trade, because it speaks to labor standards, not quality, but when prices were at their lowest, Fair Trade worked to get more money into the hands of growers."

Neither Peter nor Geoff had studied economics, but in their efforts to figure out how to do business at origin they spent a lot of time wrestling with stunningly complicated economic issues: how markets function, the impact of globalization, the devaluing of commodities, economic cycles, and the legacy of colonialism. Eventually they determined that their business dealings with coffee farmers and coffee industry middlemen had to be based on three fundamental principles that were spelled out by Intelligentsia:

- Buyers should have the chance to deal directly with the farmers whose coffee they are buying.
- Farmers should be paid a premium for growing superior coffee.
- Contracts to buy coffee should be completely transparent, so that everyone along the chain, from the farmer to the miller to the exporter to the importer to the roaster, knows exactly how much each is earning. (Dave Griswold's company, Sustainable Harvest, actually posts this information on the Internet.)

Counter Culture and Intelligentsia base their coffee-buying and coffee-marketing strategies on these principles, but it hasn't been easy. Demanding transparency in a coffee contract is a bit like demanding love and loyalty in a marriage contract—sure, it's a good idea, but how do you get there when the people involved have wildly different notions of how to behave and what to expect, and how do you enforce it?

And given nature's unpredictability, what can roasters reasonably demand from coffee growers in terms of quality improvements and consistency? Peter says that over time he has realized that "farmers have to take risks to improve quality. You can't make the standards so high they just opt out. What are we aiming for, anyway? Are we paying a huge bonus for excellence or are we paying an across-the-board high price, with a bonus for extraordinary excellence? These are questions we had to figure out, and none of it was easy."

Geoff formed his first successful "direct trade" relationship with a farmer named Mauricio Rosales, owner of Finca La Maravilla in Huehuetenango, Guatemala. "This was where we introduced our direct trade system that built price and quality differentiation into the system," he says. Rosales was given a base price 25 percent higher than Fair Trade, plus a series of bonuses for coffees that cupped above 85. (The emphasis on cupping scores underlines the importance of training local cuppers. Direct Trade coffees are cupped by both buyer and seller, and the system only works if both agree on the score.)

The relationship with Finca La Maravilla was uncharacteristically easy to manage, Geoff explains. "Working with one guy is way easier than working with a cooperative. Senor Rosales, he is like a big teddy bear. Just the nicest, warmest guy. He'd lived with his parents and never owned his own farm before he purchased Maravilla. When he bought his own farm, he put a lot of money into upgrading it. All his neighbors thought he was a fool. He told me other guys made a joke of it. He'd say, 'I am spending money because I think it will pay off,' but they didn't get it. That day when we sat around the table and worked out the details of our Direct Trade agreement, everyone was crying. Now he could turn to his neighbors. 'You see, you guys, I am not a fool. You are the fools for not believing in the idea of specialty.'"

Geoff was bowled over by the difference he could make in a farmer's life. "It was amazing to see the impact you could have," Geoff recalls.

Geoff signed the La Maravilla contract in 2003. Since then much of Intelligentsia's coffee has been bought directly from farmers. Geoff feels tremendous ownership regarding this approach, and Intelligentsia has trademarked the term Direct Trade, though Intelligentsia has not decided if or how it will enforce its copyright. Because copyright or no, Intelligentsia is not the only company buying direct. Counter Culture has been doing it for as long as Intelligentsia has. Peet's, Starbucks, and the specialty division of Green Mountain have also been buying direct for a long time, although they do not necessarily have the same desire to pay farmers a premium that Geoff has. George Howell now buys much of his coffee for his new company, Terroir, direct. Stumptown began buying direct in 2004 or 2005; up until then Duane told K. C. O'Keefe that he was "staying in his own neighborhood," meaning he preferred to remain in Portland and build his business, a decision that seems to have paid off.

In the past couple of years a dozen or more small roasters have begun traveling and buying at least some of their coffees directly from farmers. This way of purchasing coffee is grueling, time consuming, and expensive, and Peter and Geoff can't help being irked when, as Peter puts it, "some guy who knows shit about coffee buys himself a plane ticket to Guatemala, visits one farm, takes a few pictures with pickers that he posts on the Web, and claims bragging rights" for supporting coffee farmers. In 2007, one such roaster was outed online for stamping the name of a farm he had never visited, nor bought from, on sacks of roasted coffee.

No one knows better than Peter that forging a relationship with farmers takes time, patience, and wisdom. Speaking Spanish, as Peter does, helps, but you can't expect to rely on Spanish when explaining to pickers that they need to pick the ripest, reddest cherry. Many pickers understand Spanish poorly at best; among themselves, they speak their own indigenous languages.

Peter remembers Geoff's and his first effort to form relationships with farmers—not in Nicaragua, but in Mexico—as a fiasco. "We were trying to convince the Mexican farmers to upgrade their method and do some lot separations. They were really resistant. What we were asking would require a lot more work. They would have to have a special warehouse, rather than pool all their coffee. They would have to stop production and send samples to us to cup. Of course, they would be paid more, but payment was down the line. We signed an agreement with three different communities connected by one cooperative. We had it all worked out. It took us days to hammer out the contract, but then at the last minute the cooperative decided it was way too much work to do all this, and they bailed.

"On that same trip, one of the farmers we were dealing with had a longstanding beef with another guy. He showed up and started shouting he was going to kill the guy and then he started shooting, and Geoff, whose Spanish at the time wasn't very good, didn't understand what was going on. He kept saying, 'What? What?' I was afraid if I translated that would be provocative, and it all turned into one comic, terrifying mess. That might have been one of the things that scared the farmers away too." After that Geoff and Peter looked elsewhere.

Peter forged his first successful direct relationships with farmers in the village of San Ramon, in Nicaragua. A Peace Corps couple from Durham (where Counter Culture is located) had bought some land in San Ramon with the idea of creating a model organic farm for the region—the farm, run by Nicaraguans, is set up as a nonprofit. When Peter visited in 2001 on his first trip to origin, he realized more was at stake than a do-good project. The coffee had potential. In the following years, Peter visited San Ramon often, as did others on his staff.

"We worked with the San Ramon farmers on improving coffee quality. I introduced them to technologies I had seen used on other coffee farms in other countries. I suggested they float their cherry to separate out inferior fruit. In coffee, density generally equates to quality. Many farmers in regions with adequate water use some sort of water tank or trough to float their coffee—high-quality cherry sinks to the bottom, while damaged and defective fruit rises to the surface and is easily separated from the rest. When I started buying coffee from Aida Batile's Finca Mauritania in El Salvador—Aida was the number one Cup of Excellence winner in El Salvador two years in a row, an unprecedented achievement—I took pictures of her picking technique, laminated these pictures, and attached them to the baskets used by pickers in San Ramon. As a result, they started picking much riper cherry and the coffee quality jumped," explains Peter, adding that farmers who almost never drink their own coffee just didn't understand the impact picking only the ripest cherry can have. As the specialty movement has grown, this message, urging farmers to pick ripe cherries, is the lesson that buyers most often deliver. Agronomists, too, who work with coffee farmers, make special efforts to emphasize the importance of picking ripe red cherries. It is the single thing farmers can do to most affect the taste of their product.

Peter also encouraged the farmers to replace their inferior Catimore cultivar. Catimore plants were bred to produce a high yield. Farmers love these easy-to-maintain trees—roasters disdain the taste. "Tearing up these trees was like ripping out their own eyelashes," Peter recalls, "but it totally paid off because in 2007, the coffee from San Ramon made it into the top ten of the Nicaraguan Cup of Excellence. Their coffee went for $6.30 a pound. Of course I bought all 21 bags for $20,000. I couldn't let that coffee go to anyone else. These farmers have been so diligent," says Peter.

A fiesta—paid for by Intelligentsia—is already under way at Las Brumas when we arrive. Las Brumas is 4,400 feet above sea level, and there is no electricity, so a generator has been set up. Girls in flouncy skirts are grilling meat. There is music. A little dancing. After eating and schmoozing, thirty-five coffee growers and their families crowd into a small outbuilding to listen to Geoff; those who can't fit inside stand outside at the open windows. It's Geoff's seventh visit to Las Brumas in three years.

Geoff begins his presentation speaking Spanish, but quickly switches to English with the consultant, K. C. O'Keefe, translating. He begins by recalling how he first came to the town after cupping the village's coffee and being mesmerized by its enticing flavor. "I had to know more about this wonderful coffee and the people who grew it," he says.

Then he tells the farmers that for Las Brumas and Intelligentsia to continue to do well, "we need to grow more connected. Through our relationship, we can make Las Brumas coffee taste even better," he says. Rising prices were enabling the farmers of Las Brumas to send some of their children to high school. By working with Intelligentsia, Geoff says, "You will be able to send all the children to school and make other important improvements as well."

He urges the growers to pick the ripest red cherry and to make sure that their washing stations are covered with tile (easier to keep clean than cement) and kept sanitary. "Dirty washing stations produce a dirty-tasting coffee," he says.

Then Geoff releases his bombshell. From now on, not all farmers in the village will be paid the same price per pound for their coffee. Instead, he would pay $1.60 a pound for what he called AA grade coffee that earned a cupping score of 84 to 87 (on a scale of 100); $1.85 per pound for what he called AAA coffees that earned scores of 88 to 93; for extraordinary coffee that scored 94 and above, he would pay an unheard-of $3.00 a pound.

Furthermore, he declares, these rates would never decline; they would only increase.

Change does not come easily, and the response to Geoff's unprecedented offer—no other roaster is offering such prices on a sustained basis—is muted and fearful. The one-for-all-and-all-for-one cooperative ethos is deeply ingrained in the farmers. The notion of one farmer earning more for his coffee than his neighbor is extremely unsettling. The farmers have many questions.

Many focus on the amount of money Cecocafen would skim off the top—Cecocafen represents fifteen hundred producers from eleven large cooperatives. "None," Geoff answers. Cecocafen would be paid separately, earning twenty-six cents a pound for acting as the farmers' banker and representative and for preparing the beans for export.

The crowd stirs, but no one speaks. Never before in the history of this village had financial information like this been shared with ordinary people. Not by the co-op. Not by the government. Though Geoff had fought and would continue to fight with Cecocafen in an effort to get more information to the farmers, it turns out the growers had no idea how much the cooperative charged Geoff for their coffee, or what kind of profit margin the cooperative earned. There was no transparency whatsoever between the farmers and the cooperative that was supposed to be representing their interests. To Geoff's horror, he realized that the growers did not even know the relationship of quintals to pounds—they did all their arithmetic in quintals. He had to clarify that one quintal equals one hundred pounds.

Finally, the village's bearded doctor, who has consumed more than a few free beers, asks, "Why should Cecocafen take any money from Las Brumas growers?"

Geoff tells the farmers Cecocafen should be paid for the work it does acting as banker and agent, financing the farmers' crop and helping to prepare it for market. "But if you think Cecocafen does not do a good job representing you, you can fire the co-op and hire an agent to represent you. Cecocafen works for you," Watts tells the crowd. Though he has visited Las Brumas repeatedly, Geoff does not fully comprehend how unprepared these farmers, who had never questioned authority, were to grapple with these questions. Only much later did he begin to comprehend the depth of the farmers' fear and the power of their dependence on Cecocafen.

The doctor, whose name is Javier Rodriquez Catillo, asks more questions. How could Las Brumas farmers be sure that the judging of their coffees—on which their pay would depend—would be fair, impartial, and consistent? Was this not yet another scheme for cheating the poor?

"The cupping will be blind," Geoff tells the farmers. "There will be no cheating. I really do believe in this process," he says. So far as transparency in judging is concerned, Geoff promised that he will build a cupping lab in the village and teach Las Brumas growers to judge their own beans.

The sun is beginning to set. Geoff urges the farmers to continue talking among themselves about his offer. Nothing was settled, but he would be back in the fall, and he was relying on the good will felt toward him and Intelligentsia to convince farmers to go along with this new way of selling their coffee.

The next day, Sunday, he and K. C. O'Keefe meet with officials from Cecocafen for four hours at the co-op's headquarters. The co-op's new president applauds the idea of customers paying more for coffee, and she is eager to take credit for the new pricing plan. Still, she is unable to say whether the union would indeed be willing to oversee a program so at odds with the cooperative's philosophy. It was possible. It was not possible. The meeting went on and on. Geoff's and K. C.'s ire flared, but to what avail? As they board the truck belonging to the cooperative for the long drive to Managua, they have no idea what would happen next. All they know is that they will return in the fall.

RWANDA, BURUNDI, ETHIOPIA

LOVE COLORS HOW YOU PERCEIVE THE WORLD—WHAT strikes you as essential and what seems secondary. When Peter and Geoff visited Ethiopia for the first time in 2005, they didn't focus on the poverty or the exploding population or the wearying disorganization. They saw an African country ruled by Africans; a country never successfully colonized by white people; a country with diverse and rich cultures, haunting music, spicy food; a country with the most beautiful women on earth. And then there was the coffee. The glorious coffee. The endless, untapped potential of the coffee.

They were bewitched by the fragrance of coffee that permeates the air in villages and in the capital. At Addis Ababa's sleek new airport, women in traditional long dress sit on the floor before open braziers making coffee and serving it to travelers in tiny porcelain cups. Ethiopia is one of the few coffee producers where ordinary people love coffee and drink it every day, though their thick black brew—the beans are roasted on an open fire to the point of charring, ground fine, then boiled—is quite different from European-style coffee.

More than anything they were swept away by Yirgacheffe, the small town where some of Ethiopia's brightest, most fragrant coffee grows. They traveled with their pal, importer Tim Chapdelaine, thirty-seven, assistant general manager of Volcafe Specialty Coffee, who was leading eight of his best customers on a five-day coffee tour of Ethiopia.

The five-hour drive from Addis Ababa to Yirgacheffe takes Peter, Geoff, Tim, and their colleagues through the Great Rift Valley that splits the Ethiopian highlands in two. It is here where thirty years ago, the anthropologist Richard Leakey discovered the skeleton of Lucy, one of humankind's earliest hominid ancestors. Looking out the window at the savannah, Peter was struck by the thought that he was traveling through the place where the human species evolved. He noticed that the acacia trees scattered across the grassland were around five feet tall. "Three million years ago, when our hominid forebears first stood on their hind legs, they could peer over these trees and keep track of their prey," Peter said, recalling this moment. "Holy shit, this is the environment I was evolved to be in! I wanted to get out of the car and go hunt an animal for dinner."

As the coffee guys approached Yirgacheffe, the vegetation grew more verdant and the number of flower-filled villages along the road increased. In some of these, they saw round stick houses with thatched roofs. Elsewhere the locals lived in small rectangular houses with bright blue or green exteriors and designs painted on the front walls. Outside each village: a tidy graveyard with stone crypts, some topped by Coptic crosses, others by little minarets, depending on the religion of the village.

After five hours bouncing around in trucks, the coffee buyers arrived at their destination: Yirgacheffe. They jumped out of their cars and began to look around the coffee cooperative located high in the hills. Finally, they were in the presence of what they had been seeking: the forest where coffee of near-perfect quality grew in joyous profusion.

Peter recalled: "Walking down the roads—our truck got stuck in the mud—we were smelling the smells of the forest. The birds were singing and the children were laughing and running from hut to hut. The monkeys were screeching and the wind was rustling. I was swept away and grinning from ear to ear and my hair was standing up on my neck. Part of the thrill was feeling like I had finally arrived at a place I had been trying to get to for years, part of it was this odd feeling I had that I was home—that this was a place to which I was mystically connected."

"In Yirgacheffe, you feel as if you are walking in the biblical Eden," Geoff said. "There is an abundance of water, an abundance of sun, an abundance of life. The trees are intensely green and dripping with moisture. The coffee growing in the forest [reflecting these conditions] seems so happy. Everything is lush, the air smells good, people's skin is wet, and they wear these soul-piercing smiles."

Visiting this spot, Peter and Geoff understood why Yirgacheffe had been chosen as the site of Ethiopia's first coffee-washing station sixty years ago. With such an abundance of water, this was the obvious place to introduce the water-based processing technology that had done so much to improve Latin American coffees. Washing ferments and then removes the sticky mucilage that coats the hinged pair of coffee beans tucked inside the coffee cherry. Successful coffee washing generally requires trained workers, clean washing stations, enough water, and one to three days of constant monitoring. In Yirgacheffe, all this effort resulted in what the specialty coffee world agrees is a revelation: a near-perfect coffee with intense flavor and a superclean finish.

In the 1970s and 1980s when washed coffees from Yirgacheffe first appeared on the international market, they created a sensation in Europe and elsewhere—the Geishas of their day. Dealers in high-quality coffee immediately recognized that washing, benefited Ethiopian coffees as it had coffees from Latin America, America, bringing out and underlining the innate qualities of Yirgacheffe beans. It gave the coffee a refined mouthfeel and finish that you just didn't find at the time in African coffees that were processed "naturally," which meant they were left to dry on trees, or they were picked and dried on the ground. Soon washing stations were being built everywhere in Ethiopia where sufficient water existed.

Peter and Geoff were delighted to discover that coffee trees grew wild in Yirgacheffe, like pine trees in New England. Yirgacheffe farmers tend their trees in the forest or in semiforested areas. Walking through coffee forests in Golgolcha and Harfusa cooperatives, Peter and Geoff were amazed to see half a dozen varieties of coffee trees growing hither and thither in the forest, each with its own idiosyncratic shape, height, leaf size, and leaf color. None of these varieties were familiar to the buyers. Looking at all these different kinds of trees, Peter later said, something shifted in his understanding of coffee. He had already started to question the common wisdom of the time that said microclimate and processing trumped all else when it came to cup quality. Still, until he visited Ethiopia his understanding of coffee's amazing diversity had not yet evolved. Only when he saw all the different kinds of coffee trees growing in Ethiopia did he understand that the species Coffea Arabica produces varieties of coffee as different from one another as concord grapes are from champagne grapes or Muscat grapes. Observing so many new kinds of coffee trees and correlating these with the coffees he was tasting in Ethiopia, he began to awaken to the importance and variability of Coffea Arabica's genetic structure.

This biology lesson was reinforced by what he and Geoff and their colleagues learned during an on-the-road lunch stop at an Italian café in a town called Awassa—thanks to Mussolini, who invaded in 1941, you can usually get a plate of spaghetti anywhere you go in Ethiopia. The café in Awassa had better spaghetti than most and foreign travelers invariably stop there. Waiting for his meal, Peter chatted up another white guy. Turned out he was a Swiss botanist who was in Ethiopia cataloguing the different varieties of coffee growing there. The botanist invited the whole group to visit his lab after lunch. At the facility, he explained that he was going into the forest, finding coffee trees that were thriving, taking samples, testing them, and preserving the tissue for future grafting. The idea was to build a library of varietals. He was working on a grant from Nestlé, the Swiss food conglomerate. Nestlé apparently had the go-ahead from the Ethiopian government to do this work.

The botanist told the coffee guys that he believed there were between twenty-five hundred and thirty-five hundred varieties of coffee growing wild in Ethiopia. Peter was blown away by this statistic. Later he would hear other numbers. Some would tell him that there are ten thousand varietals of coffee growing in Ethiopia. An Ethiopian would say there were one hundred thousand varieties. The particular number was almost irrelevant. What mattered was the understanding birthed at that moment of an almost unimaginable coffee wealth in Ethiopia. Recognizing this abundance transformed everything for Peter. It opened his eyes to coffee's seemingly limitless genetic and culinary diversity.

In the weeks and months after he visited Ethiopia, Peter could not stop thinking about what he had seen there. None of the other coffee-growing countries he had visited in Latin America, elsewhere in Africa, or in Asia had as big an impact on him. He saw Ethiopia as a vast DNA dictionary containing all the possible forms of animal and vegetable life. He saw this diversity in the beautiful faces of Ethiopians from different tribes and regions. Some Ethiopians looked as if they came from Africa, others looked as if they came from the Arab Peninsula, Asia, ancient Persia—the country we know as Iran—and Europe. Peter saw the entire genetic database of humanity on their faces. Ethiopian music was like that too. In the music clubs in Addis Peter heard musical possibilities that were developed all over the world—American rhythm and blues, Japanese tonalities, Ghanaian high life, Latin salsa rhythms.

And the coffee. "In Ethiopia, I looked around coffee farms and I felt like Alice in Wonderland," Peter commented. "I was overcome by the endless variety. That's when it started to hit me, this intangible thing, the richness of this place, the richness of this genetic soup.

"If you are a coffee professional and you taste Ethiopian coffee long enough you find you can taste everything you have ever tasted in coffee and a lot more," Peter said. "Ethiopian coffees are so diverse that it is, in a way, overwhelming: it's not just about the blueberry flavor in Harar or the tealike flavor in Yirgacheffe; these coffees are way more complicated than that. At every table you can taste something you have never tasted before. In this land where coffee evolved we can jump into the DNA swimming pool and begin to comprehend, to taste and experience the unknowable bounty that is in coffee."

In February 2007, two years after their first trip to Ethiopia, Geoff and Peter were planning to attend the East Africa Fine Coffee Association (EAFCA) conference in Addis Ababa. They said that anyone who was anyone in specialty coffee would be there. Prior to the conference, Peter and Geoff's friend, the irrepressible coffee importer Tim Chapdelaine from Volcafe Specialty Coffee, who organized the guys' first trip to Ethiopia, sent out the word that he was putting together another of his excursions to familiarize coffee buyers with new markets. This expedition was to Rwanda and Burundi. Peter and Geoff said if I signed on to Tim's expedition and I attended the EAFCA conference, I would get to see three very different East African coffee-growing countries.

Rwanda is one of specialty coffee's success stories thanks to Dan Clay, a Michigan State professor and development specialist. Clay was working in Rwanda's coffee sector when the genocide began in 1995. He and his family fled for their lives. Rwanda's coffee industry was wiped out. Clay, however, was determined to help the country rebuild. It was he who dreamed up Project PEARL, a U.S. AID–funded coffee project that helped some 400,000 smallholders owning, on average, just 165 trees upgrade to the specialty market. PEARL's leader, Tim Schilling, is a development specialist with a PhD in agronomy and tremendous enthusiasm for coffee. He and Clay enlisted the help of some of the most respected people in the specialty business, including Peter, Duane, and Geoff. Rwandan coffee had certain natural advantages. Heirloom Typica and Bourbon varieties predominated. Weather and altitude were excellent, as was the condition of the red volcanic soil. According to U.S. AID, by 2004, coffee prices had risen in Rwanda by 91 percent. In subsequent years, the upswing continued. Of course, many problems persist. Still, in recognition of progress made, in 2008 Rwanda will be the first African country to host a Cup of Excellence competition.

Not surprisingly, Burundi would like to re-create the success of Rwanda's coffee sector. Burundi and Rwanda are very similar: both countries are small, about the size of Maryland; both freed themselves from their Belgian overseers in 1962; and coffee is the most important cash crop for both. The per capita annual income in Burundi is roughly $84 a year, the lowest per capita income in the world, half that of Rwanda. Burundi is, in some regards, the poorest country on earth, though the ability of the majority of the population to grow food for their own consumption alters the meaning of that statistic a little. As a result of political violence and HIV/AIDS, life expectancy in Rwanda and Burundi has fallen from around 50 to around 40 since the early 1990s.

Given all these countries' historic, social, and economic catastrophes, the physical beauty of both takes you by surprise. Burundi and Rwanda are sunny, temperate places with plenty of rain in the growing season and undulating green hills that at their highest shoot up toward nine thousand feet. The hillsides are gracefully terraced and farmed—whip-wielding Belgian overseers saw to that. When you drive through the countryside, the view reminds you of a remote Shangri-la, somewhere far from the strife of interior Africa.

As notable as the beauty is the steady stream of barefoot people walking along the highway. Barefoot women carry bundles on their heads. Barefoot men pull oxcarts up hills. No unused or open land separates one village from another. The countryside is made up of village after village. There is no break in the population density.

The main roads in both countries are paved and pleasant, resembling two-lane country roads in remote corners of Europe. The good roads are the useful legacy of a brutal colonial past. Up in the highlands where coffee is grown, the roads, as in Ethiopia, are steep, unpaved, rutted truck killers. Heading across Rwanda we see few trucks, few motorcycles or scooters, and almost no private cars. Bikes are common. Tim Schilling arranged for a famed American bicycle designer to create a sturdy bike costing just $100 that farmers use to carry huge sacks of coffee cherry to washing stations. Counter Culture, Stumptown, Intelligentsia, and some other high-quality coffee roasters have signed on to buy bikes for Rwandan coffee farmers.

On our last day in Rwanda we drive to Butare, near the Burundi border. The city of Butare is Rwanda's Cambridge, someone riding in the truck says. Maybe Geoff. Seven thousand students are enrolled in the university here. "I love this town," Geoff says. "Somehow I feel less stressed when I am here."

We spend the night at the Hotel Ibis, located in a back courtyard on the main drag of Butare. My room is large and dim with beat-up wooden furniture that gives the place an air of a Salvation Army outpost. That aside, it's clean and there is a bathtub, hot water, and electric power. When I walk out of my room in the morning, three skinny men—hard to estimate their age, maybe thirty, maybe forty—wearing rags are ripping up cracked cement in the courtyard pretty much by hand and replacing it with new cement. Their only tool: a small trowel-like implement. I see men all over Rwanda, Burundi, and Ethiopia working like this—with virtually no tools or labor-saving devices. Human labor is the most plentiful resource in this part of the world. In Rwanda, the per capita income is about $200 a year; that's a daily wage for manual workers of, say, eighty cents. Ten cents an hour. In Kigali, Rwanda's capital, I'd been sick with a stomach thing and had to go to the hospital to see a doctor. The hospital was plain, but, as my grandmother would have said, so clean you could eat off the floor. The care was competent and kind. The bill for a private patient to be seen by a doctor, for lab work, and for medicine: about $15. My hunch is that few laborers and few of their children in this part of the world are seeing doctors, certainly not as private patients.

Peter and Geoff drive out to the countryside at 7:00 a.m. to visit a washing station. "These farmers would feel terrible if they heard that I was within a hundred miles of them and didn't visit," Peter tells me, explaining why he is going to tear himself out of bed at 6:00 a.m. They return from the countryside while I am having tea and toast for breakfast—the stomach thing. They were sympathetic. No one is exempt from getting sick on the road. Peter tells me that he returns home ill from many of his long trips. We hang out, watching the action as cars and trucks travel up and down Butare's main street. We are waiting for the two trucks that will take our party to the border. The street is dusty and the wooden frame buildings are ramshackle. The place has a buzz, though. Lots of street action. A sense of something happening, though it is hard to say what that might be.

Pete and Geoff stand with an arm thrown over each other's shoulders for a photo. "Pete and I are interchangeable," Geoff says, meaning they have the same devotion to coffee and coffee farmers. "He's the only guy in the business I would trust to do my job," Geoff adds: who can he hire to replace himself is a question that Geoff, chronically exhausted from nine months a year of travel and a hard-driving lifestyle, often asks. The problem is that he can never imagine anyone sufficiently dedicated and intelligent. Except Peter. And Peter already has a job and a company and an equity position.

Eventually the trucks arrive and we head out to Burundi. A person in one of the pickups creating a mini traffic jam in downtown Butare stares out his window at us. "Fuck you, American," he says to no one in particular as we pull out and head for the border.

In the truck with Tim, Geoff, Peter, and me is Anne Ottaway, a U.S. consultant who played a very large role in the Rwandan coffee development project. The World Bank has asked her to assess the coffee industry in Burundi, which was nationalized in 1979. She sees a lot of potential in Burundi, and it is she who encouraged Tim, Peter, and Geoff to include Burundi on their itinerary.

Rwanda and Burundi are twin countries, but you have to cross no man's land to get from one to the other. It's hot and dusty at the Rwandan border. We get out of our vehicle, wait around, hand our passports to a person in a little booth. Nothing happens and we all look at each other nervously. Bad things have happened at this border—bad things happen at East African borders all the time—and you can't help feeling exposed, as if you are a player in a dangerous game. Then a guy in a black wool suit comes and takes our passports. Turns out he's the Burundian minister of agriculture, Nestor Niyungeko. We get back in the trucks, drive a quarter of a mile, come to another border crossing, get out of the vehicles, look for our visas, and realize we don't have them. Where are our passports and our visas? These questions come at us in Kirundi, the most common local Burundian language, and in French. A lot of guys in uniforms carrying guns watch us fumble around. Now it's hot and dusty and tense.

Then Minister Niyungeko appears. He has our passports and visas and it should all be fine, but this is a country where it seems nonviolent solutions to political problems are an idea someone thought up about fifteen minutes ago. We are here to celebrate the denationalization of the Burundi coffee industry. We surmise that some government functionaries or their cousins or friends who have been getting rich from Burundian coffee aren't going to get rich anymore. It doesn't take a genius to figure out some guys aren't going to be thrilled by our visit.

Suddenly we hear the screeching of brakes. The scene is straight out of a thriller. Racing cars. Sirens. Lights flashing. Cars racing toward the border from the Burundian side. Peter counts sixteen vehicles. This is our official greeting party from Bujumbura, the capital. A contingent of government officials, businesspeople, and reporters descends on us, including a very large videographer whose sole job, it turns out, is to follow us around during our stay because, you see, Peter, Geoff, Tim, and Anne are rock stars in Burundi. They are the very first coffee people to appear in Burundi since the process of privatization was contemplated. Some of those cars are full of Burundi's first private coffee exporters, and they descend on Peter and Geoff with the excitement of children contemplating chocolate ice cream. They want some. Now.

"Come this way!" they shout at Peter and Geoff. "Drive in our car! Drive in our car!"

"No fucking way," Peter mutters to himself. "I'm not getting anywhere near those guys." Peter's uncharacteristic surliness is born of experience. He doesn't want to be squeezed to buy coffee he hasn't cupped and doesn't know. He is here for fact-finding for the World Bank and not, at this time, for buying. Buying Burundian coffee down the road is neither ruled in nor ruled out. It all depends on the coffee.

Before anyone goes anywhere we must be officially greeted. The Minister of Finance, Denise Sinankawa—a small round woman wearing a long magenta robe wrapped like a sari (the color signifies an important occasion), plenty of gold jewelry, and a stylish handbag I hope is a fake—is the official greeter.

She says a few words and we are swamped by Burundians wanting to shake our hands, take our picture, find out who we are. We all introduce ourselves. It's hot in the sun. Above us, on a small hillside, sits a small Byzantine-style church covered in tile. The scent of eucalyptus fills the air. Black and white magpies perched in the trees watch the crazy scene below as a dozen and a half vehicles—government people, media, exporters, soldiers, and us—tear away.

We are heading high into the hills to the site of the first washing station built in Burundi, back in 1953. Along the way, we pass little kids harvesting sweet potatoes. Cows munch grass on the hillside. The increasing altitude makes my ears pop. We pass a boy pushing a bicycle loaded with firewood up the mountain and men cutting the soil with hoes. Near the side of the road, a grandpa minds two small children while working a foot-pedaled sewing machine set up outdoors. Along the road we see many broad-leaved false banana trees with audacious pink-purple fruit.

Red tile roofs top the small houses in this area. The road is made of red-clay bricks.

We turn down a dirt road and soon we are at the washing station, which is set in a verdant valley with a small stream running through it. On both sides of us, green trees rise up. We jump out of the trucks and head toward the sound of drumming. In the field in front of the dilapidated mill with a rusted corrugated metal roof, an outdoor performance area has been marked off.

A crowd of twelve hundred coffee farmers and their families has gathered around a troupe of musicians who are drumming a welcome for us. Burundian drummers are famous throughout Africa. Dressed in long white and red toga-style robes splashed with green, the drummers shout out the words *muzungu* (white person) and *amashi* (celebrate). They use the flat of their hands to exuberantly slap their tall wooden drums. They sing and they dance as well as drum. They are airborne. They are joyful.

Some women in the crowd of bystanders are dressed in bright green costumes with orange head wraps; more wear Western castoffs, used clothes sent to Africa from the United States and Europe. The men wear dusty bits of gray and brown. Every day of their lives, these farmers have been beaten down by landlords, government bureaucrats, and soldiers—you can see it on their faces. Coffee prices rise and fall, war breaks out, there is killing, so much killing, and it is all beyond their power to control. They watch today's hullabaloo with exhaustion, skepticism, no great excitement. The children are excited. The drummers are excited. The officials in their black woolen suits and white shirts are excited. And the finance minister in her magenta robe, she is the very essence of lively interest and excitement.

Boys climb tall skinny trees, ascending twenty or thirty feet, to get a better look. The drummers follow the welcome song with another in which the entire process of coffee farming is mimed from planting the seed and pruning the tree to fertilizing, harvesting, drying, washing, getting paid, and finally drinking coffee.

When the performance ends, we are taken on a guided tour of the washing station. Half a dozen men in black suits lead the way. I follow Geoff, and the crowd follows us up the hill. We cross over the stream on a shaky wooden bridge. The translator, a handsome Burundian who works for the state radio and speaks elegant, resonant French, looks down at the little footbridge and tells me we are crossing over into a new era in Burundian coffee.

We enter the washing station. Geoff looks at an old machine for removing pulp. Fermenting is done dry, rather than wet. Geoff tells me the station is one of the most decrepit he has ever seen. In the storage room Geoff detects a sour odor and wrinkles his nose. "It smells of ferment," he says. Not a good sign.

A member of the official greeting delegation, a grower, tells me that growers like her are hoping the government will sell or give the existing washing stations to growers' cooperatives. Privatization has just begun, and no one knows exactly what is going to happen next.

A cool wind whips through the trees as we return to the field where the drumming ceremony took place. A delegate chosen to speak for the farmers steps forward, holding a large ledger. I am standing just a few feet from him and I can see he has written his address on greenish-yellow graph paper in blue fountain pen ink, his small, careful penmanship a lovely relic of French pedagogy. He has a worn, intelligent face and wears a slope-shouldered jacket several sizes too big, and an unusually large mauve necktie. The way he wears his oversized clothes reminds me of Harpo Marx. And like Harpo, the farmer possesses an amazing dignity and expressiveness that transcends cultural differences.

He reads his speech, imploring the government to return to coffee growers what it seized thirty years ago—control of their own product and their own industry. "Farmers themselves should be granted control of the nation's 133 coffee-washing stations because it is they who do the work at these stations, and they who deserve to profit from their own labor. This is a matter of simple justice," he says in French, pausing for his words to be translated into English. "Farmers are eager to establish channels that will allow them to communicate directly with those who would buy their coffee. So let our guests know: we are ready to strengthen our ties to them." To these ends, he reports, "The thousands of farmers who use this washing station are working to create a cooperative and elect representatives that will speak for us, fairly and honestly."

The crowd is silent. The moment feels serious, freighted, historic. Then Minister Sinankawa steps forward. "Coffee is crucial to the economy of Burundi," she says, "because it brings hard currency into the country. Moreover, eight hundred thousand households depend on coffee for their livelihood. Since the end of colonialism," she continues, "the government has been in control of the coffee industry, but the government did not do a good job. Now a new era has begun and we believe coffee production should belong to the farmers."

This is what the crowd has been waiting to hear. Huge applause interrupts her remarks.

The minister continues. "The government needs to restructure coffee marketing from bottom to top." Then she turns to Peter and Geoff. "Please come back and help us get more skills in marketing."

This announced change seems to be big news, because the Burundian media springs into action, filming and taking pictures and scribbling notes.

As usual, it is Geoff who steps forward to speak—I don't know if this is because Intelligentsia buys twice the amount of coffee that Counter Culture does or because Geoff is fearless.

"We are excited about the changes taking place in Burundi," Geoff tells the crowd. "It is the right decision that control of the washing stations should be in the hand of producers. As roasters we crave working with farmers," Geoff says to big applause.

"We believe the most effective way for farmers to advance is through high quality. By improving your quality, you can improve your price." At the mention of rising prices, the applause grows even louder.

Reporters swarm around Geoff and Peter as a warm steady rain starts to fall. We race to our trucks and promptly get stuck in a gridlock of official vehicles and ancient trucks.

In the truck Peter says that he is stunned by the minister's speech—stunned by the lack of rhetoric and cant that usually accompanies such speeches.

A lot is at stake, Peter says, because Burundi has tremendous potential: its coffee trees are of the treasured Kenyan SL-28 coffee variety—one of the most valued coffee varieties in the world—and the country has other advantages, including high altitude and plenty of water.

On our way to our hotel we stop in Ngozi to tour a dry mill where the papery parchment covering washed coffee beans is removed. The modern mill, built ten years ago by private investors, is located inside a large brick building. The mill is certified organic. Milling usually takes place in factories after farmers have sold their coffee. It is the last complicated process that coffee undergoes before roasting. Coffee mills are generally owned by large cooperatives, independent businesspeople, or coffee exporters who mill and then sell coffee beans to overseas buyers.

Inside the factory, the air is warm. Huge German-made machines roar and tiny bits of lung-clogging parchment swirl; we're handed paper face masks as protection.

As we tour the huge, noisy, bewildering factory with its fifty-foot-high catwalk, Peter says, "There's provenance issues here. No provisions have been made for keeping track of what coffee belongs to what farmer." The factory was designed to process undifferentiated commodity coffee and can handle four tons of fully washed beans per hour.

Peter sniffs the air. To me it smells of body odor. "Ferment," he says. Dampness is rotting some of the beans.

This dry mill has potential to produce specialty coffee, Peter says, "but the operators would have to cut back their production. That's the problem with specialty: it involves hand processing of specific small lots." It is interesting that in a country where most of the work is done by hand, this large, modern milling factory requiring little hand labor has been built. Clearly some investors inside Burundi have high hopes that privatization will greatly benefit the country's coffee industry.

Geoff feels the beans as they shoot out of the milling machine. "The production processes are running too hot," he says. Beans are heating up, and heat can alter taste.

Despite the problems, Peter says he sees a lot of potential here.

The coffee mill has a twenty-first-century feel. When we walk outside, however, we return to the preindustrial age. Here women and children sitting under a brightly colored canopy are sorting the cleaned coffee beans by hand, carefully separating them according to size and quality. Handsorting is a hallmark of the very best East African coffees. In other countries, sorting is done fully or partially by machines.

Somebody in our party makes a joke about child labor. Something to the effect of you'd think they'd hide the child workers before we came. This is an issue we run into in every coffee-growing region we visit in Africa: children working with their parents. Poor families need the pennies children earn. And what alternative do parents have? Where schools exist, they are not free. Parents are required to pay fees far beyond what the poorest can afford. Rather than leaving their children alone, poor parents prefer to have their children at their side—working, yes, but safe.

Peter shoots pictures of the women and children sorting a small mountain of milled coffee beans—the beans look more gray than green to me. He holds the digital camera screen so the children can see. They find the images of themselves comical and enthralling. They stare at the tiny screen. It's a television. A movie screen. They pose and vamp. More pictures. More pictures. They want to see more pictures of themselves. They circle Peter. He's a magnet, and they are sticking to him.

It's raining, cold, and damp when we arrive at our hotel, which is out in Ngoma, the heart of Burundi's coffee region. Coffee-growing areas are never very hot, and now the temperature must have dropped ten degrees. I am shivering as I wash my face and prepare for the banquet for our delegation and the Burundians, paid for by the World Bank.

Our hotel is made up of a lot of low buildings; some, like our rooms, are attached to one another motel-style. Other buildings, like the canopy-covered outdoor bar, are freestanding. The dinner is served in a banquet/meeting room. We choose our food from a buffet—simple fare like fish, beef, rice, and plantains—but a butler and maid in colonial-era black uniforms bring our drinks and clear the dishes.

The Burundians thank Geoff for recognizing the overheating in the mill. This information is valuable. There is so much the buyers can teach them, they say.

Geoff says, "Peter and I want to buy coffee from you. We are happy to help." He urges the Burundians to focus their attention on the specialty market and avoid the commodities market.

"Burundi has one grand advantage," he says. "Lots of people, and a small number of trees per farmer. This is how the best coffee is produced. You have to teach people to be very careful. Create an industry of craftsmanship, not volume.

"As roasters, we want traceability when we buy coffee. We want to know who the farmer is and how much he earned. We believe that, along the entire chain, we can all make money."

Anne Ottaway, who is sitting next to me, whispers, "Geoff is a coffee prophet..."

Then Peter speaks. "We work for different businesses, but we represent a group of roasters who have an interest in high-quality coffee. The coffee industry in the U.S. is changing. You asked for tools from us to change your industry; most important is the taste of the cup. *La tasse.* This is what the market wants. Coffee is not a tree, a seed, or an industry; it's a beverage. A cupper understands this better than anyone...

"Now that your doors are open, you'll see a lot of us. I have this final word of advice," he says. "Preserve the character of Burundi coffee. You have a special combination of your environment, excellent varieties, good processes, your people. All this makes your coffee different from any other. Don't listen to others who want to make your coffee like anyone else's."

In the back of the room there are a couple of electronic games—one is a virtual car-racing game and the other a terminator game. As the party breaks up, Geoff asks that the games be turned on. He challenges everyone to play. But the games are out of order. Then the guys go to a bar, which is not out of order. I go to my room. Outside it is rainy and cold. Inside, it's just cold. I pull on a sweatshirt and go to sleep.

The next morning we are on the road again. We are heading for Bujumbura—Burundi's pestilent capital city—and our flight to Addis Ababa. First, though, we have a meeting at the heavily secured U.S. Embassy with Ambassador Patricia Moeller, who is a Republican businessperson of a certain age. She is about five feet two with blondish hair, wearing a hot pink suit, pale fishnet stockings, and cream-colored heels, and has ramrod straight posture.

"I'm a Southern girl," she says, introducing herself. "Just terribly, terribly proud to be serving the American president."

The ambassador has been on the job for a year—before 2006 Bujumbura, beset by civil war since the late 1990s, was too dangerous and the embassy was shuttered. The U.S. government is strongly supportive of the current Burundi president, a former leader of the insurgency who seems to favor reform. Ambassador Moeller points out, though, that assassination is common—three Burundi leaders in thirty years have been killed in office—and violence sporadically breaks out between Burundi's Hutu and Tutsi populations. Conditions could degenerate at any moment, she admits.

It turns out the ambassador is a former investment banker. She asks a lot of questions about coffee.

Geoff answers. Up until this moment, I hadn't noticed what he is wearing. He's just Geoff to me. But in the ambassador's genteel presence, I see him through a new lens. He is unshaven. His clothes are wrinkled; it looks as though he slept in them. And he is wearing a baseball cap backwards. Not that the rest of us look ready for a fashion shoot, but we are more or less presentable— Peter is wearing a pressed shirt, khakis, and real shoes.

Geoff looks like a guy who bunks at a homeless shelter, but he talks coffee brilliantly, explaining to the ambassador what it takes to launch a successful specialty industry, delineating what Burundi lacks. "...And then, of course, there is the problem of the shitty roads," he says, and there is a moment of silence as we all suck in our breaths to see what will happen because Geoff cursed in front of the ambassador. But the lady doesn't blink.

It's not a warm and fuzzy visit. The ambassador is sharp as hell, but her formality has put us all ever so slightly on edge and we all breathe a sigh when we get out of there. We race to the airport to catch our flight to Ethiopia. Again the minister of agriculture shows up with our visas just in time. It looks as if we will all be able to leave on our flight as scheduled, but the airport is in total chaos, and the local people who shove us into this line and that seem particularly paranoid. Armed soldiers patrol the airport. In the waiting area, young gate attendants done up in pale blue uniforms, with orchid-colored beads woven into their braided hair and matching lipstick, are about as friendly as Los Angeles traffic cops. Geoff's skill at making eye contact with the ladies fails him and for a while it looks as if, for no reason we can discern, airport officials won't let Geoff and Tim on the old Boeing 707 that is supposed to take us to Addis by way of Kampala. But eventually, we are all allowed on board. Then the plane sits on the tarmac. After thirty or forty minutes, Anne, who is sitting behind me, taps me on the shoulder.

"Look out the window," she says.

I am sitting next to Peter. He raises the shade, and we both turn to look. We can't hear much, but we see a brass band. A red carpet has been rolled out, and 150 gold-spangled soldiers goose-step in formation as a crowd of one hundred well-dressed onlookers take their places on a reviewing stand. The crowd appears to cheer as a rotund gentleman and lady dressed in white step out of the airport and onto the red carpet—he in a military uniform, she in carpet-tickling formal robes. The scene reminds me of descriptions I have read of Louis XIV departing Versailles. The pilot announces that the Burundian president and first lady are flying with us this afternoon—Ambassador Moeller had told us during our embassy visit that he'd just sold the presidential jet to raise cash. She'd also revealed that politically and militarily, the situation in Burundi is a bit tense because the president has just dismissed his top military advisor. She also mentioned shooting down airplanes is the preferred method of murdering political enemies in this part of the world. In 1994, Burundi's president was killed alongside the president of Rwanda when the plane they were traveling in was shot down. Some 300,000 Burundians died in ethnic violence following that attack.

Peter and I turn back from the window. We look at each other. "Good thing the president and first lady are keeping a low profile," he says.

Never underestimate the allure of hot water. And WiFi access. And room service. We're all really looking forward to a well-appointed hotel. The Sheraton and the Hilton both offer reduced rates for people attending the East African Fine Coffee Association (EAFCA) conference. Geoff had told me to book at the Hilton because the Hilton bar is the place in Addis where everyone hangs out. That's where he is staying. The room was close to $200 a night, which strikes me as odd in a country where people earn $100 a year, but the guys explain that's how it is: in Ethiopia and other very poor coffee-growing countries you stay at the Ritz—and pay top dollar—or you stay in a hovel. Outside of the major cities, they tell me hovels are sometimes the only choice, though so far on our trip our accommodations have ranged from good to tolerable. I book the Hilton. Peter thinks he is staying at the Sheraton. He thinks Tim made a reservation for him, but Tim, who handled the logistics for our visits to Rwanda and Burundi, says he didn't make hotel reservations in Ethiopia. "Don't worry," Tim says to Peter, "you can share a room with me."

We're all sitting in the Addis airport waiting for hotel shuttles to pick us up. There are huge banners in the lounge welcoming all five thousand attendees to the EAFCA conference. We're all weary, Peter especially so. He's been on the road for more than a month, and he doesn't look happy about the prospect of sharing a room. The functionary checking people's names against his list of hotel guests before they are allowed to board the Sheraton shuttle tells Tim he is not registered at the hotel.

Tim calls the Sheraton. He talks to the desk at great length. He comes back and tells us that Duane Sorensen, the founder of Stumptown, who is a friend of Tim, Geoff, and Peter, has taken Tim's hotel reservation. None of the coffee people in our party is surprised by this news. Anne says that Duane is a brilliant coffee guy, but he's not a team player. Tim does some more checking. After a long time on the telephone, he reverses himself and says he has been wrong, and Duane didn't take his reservation. Tim and Peter find somewhere to crash.

Like some modern-day Acropolis, the United Nations Conference Center in Addis Ababa sits on the top of the city's largest hill. Fully loaded with every form of advanced technology and communications, plus simultaneous translation capabilities, the building appears to possess almost no relationship to its surrounding. Or to the broken-down taxicabs—many deficient in brakes—that ferry attendees back and forth from their hotels. It is convenient, though; huge convention space enables vendors from all over the world to set up shop. Dorman's, the large Kenyan coffee exporter, is dispensing free cappuccinos. Here and there you can cadge a cookie to accompany your cappuccino. There's a huge auditorium seating hundreds. Though the weather in Addis is almost always temperate, sunny, and dry—the Ethiopians say Addis is the site of the Garden of Eden—the AC in the conference center is shiver inducing. (I can't help wondering how it can be that in Africa, I am so often cold.)

Thousands throng the hall the first day of the conference: growers and growers' reps from all over Africa, middlemen, academics, representatives of nongovernmental organizations (NGOs), financial people, coffee buyers.

Dub Hay, senior vice president of Starbucks, delivers the keynote speech. Hay does not refer to the huge legal fight being waged between Starbucks and Ethiopia. Recently, Ethiopia has been making an effort to trademark its coffee-growing regions, an idea Starbucks vehemently opposes. Ethiopia, encouraged by Oxfam, the international development organization, has accused Starbucks of gross exploitation. By opposing the trademark initiative, Oxfam says Starbucks has stolen $88 million from Ethiopia's fifteen million coffee farmers and coffee workers.

Instead, Hay talks about his company's profarmer initiatives in Africa, which are similar to the kinds of programs Intelligentsia and Counter Culture fund, only larger. Starbucks, he asserts, pays premium prices for quality coffee. It brands and sells African coffees in its thirteen thousand stores worldwide, builds schools, clinics, and bridges to support coffee communities, provides millions in investment grants, digs wells, and is taking steps to protect and create clean drinking water by adding another $1 million to the pot.

To combat what it deems as Starbucks' corporate theft, Oxfam has organized campaigns and fundraisers on campuses all over the United States, but listening to Hay speak, I wonder what the coffee guys—who have no reason to love Starbucks—think of the brouhaha. I am surprised when they tell me they think Oxfam's charges are absurd.

Tremendous animus toward Starbucks, on the part of Ethiopia's British and American legal and policy advisors, fuels this fight. I learn this when I sit next to a couple of these folks at breakfast. Starbucks, they say, is a bully that needs to be tamed. However, several people with no pecuniary interest in this conflict tell me that Ethiopia's trademark campaign is based on a misreading of American law, and that the Ethiopian lawsuit against Starbucks is based on mythical math.

It appears that the charge that Starbucks has "stolen" $88 million from Ethiopian farmers, a charge also leveled in the documentary film _Black Gold_ about Fair Trade coffee (released in early 2007), is not supportable. Some of the most judicious observers in the coffee world—guys like Price Peterson, who serves on the board of Oxfam and cares strongly for social justice—tell me the anti-Starbucks campaign makes no sense. Still one cannot help being sympathetic. Starbucks is a very rich corporation and the Ethiopian growers are among the poorest in the world. How can it be that Starbucks, and to be fair, the small roasters I am traveling with, benefit so generously from the great coffee grown in Ethiopia, and the growers benefit so little? This is a profoundly significant question that anyone visiting coffee farms in Ethiopia must ask. That I will ask throughout this trip, seeking to understand a Byzantine system of buying and selling.

"This is a question that representatives of the Ethiopian government, Ethiopian exporters, Starbucks, and other smaller roasting companies certainly should address while sitting across from one another at a negotiating table," says Rick Peyser, director of social advocacy and coffee community outreach for Green Mountain Coffee, who serves on the board of the international Fair Trade umbrella group, Fairtrade Labelling Organizations (FLO) International, sometime later. But this was not the question that was addressed in this lawsuit.

Instead Ethiopia and Starbucks were arguing about Ethiopia's desire to trademark the name of certain geographical areas. There are massive problems with such designations and, in general, U.S. trademark law does not allow place names to be trademarked. For one thing, it is not generally possible to prove that a coffee or any product comes from a particular area, and the temptation to cheat is vast. If coffee from the small town of Yirgacheffe gets a premium simply by reason of location—and that's what the trademark issue is about—how do you stop unethical traders from tacking a Yirgacheffe label onto their coffee? And how does the Ethiopian government ensure that coffee sold as Yirgacheffe is actually from Yirgacheffe and not neighboring areas? This is precisely what happened in Jamaica with its Blue Mountain coffee and in Hawaii with Kona. Fakes were marketed as the real thing, undermining the reputation of the originals, and these practices are still going on. The $88 million specified in the lawsuit represents the sum Oxfam alleged Ethiopian farmers would have earned had the trademark been in place and Starbucks required to pay a fee for using Ethiopian place names.

In Addis, during the EAFCA conference, a compromise between Starbucks and Ethiopia was announced. That agreement later fell apart. Eventually the two sides did manage to get together. Ethiopia softened its stance, and Starbucks agreed to sit down and talk about ways that Ethiopia's greatest "appellations" could benefit not from trademarks but from licensing agreements. All this took months and did inestimable damage to the whole idea of specialty coffee. Or at least that's what Peter Giuliano tells me. He's worried that Oxfam's big campus-oriented anti-Starbucks campaign has planted an idea in the minds of college kids that the specialty coffee industry is made up of "a bunch of greedy capitalists out to screw the poor." Peter finds this idea painful personally as well as professionally. "Here we are working our butts off to create an industry based on fairness," he says. Then he adds that he knows his industry is not blameless and that terrible injustices exist. Still, he says, he believes the high end of the specialty coffee industry is full of people trying to do the right thing.

Peter's assertions are confirmed by one of the most respected numbers guys in the world of sustainable agriculture:

Daniele Giovannucci, a former food company executive and senior consultant to the World Bank Group. "I love these young coffee guys," Daniele has told me. According to him, specialty coffee, though far from perfect, is ahead of other industries in the agricultural sector in terms of trying to do the right thing for farmers. Moreover, his research shows that improving coffee quality and selling to specialty does improve the financial situation of coffee farmers around the world.

I manage to sit across from Daniele at lunch on my first day in Addis. About a dozen of us wind up eating lunch together at a traditional Ethiopian restaurant, one of the best in the city. We lounge on chairs and sofas. The food is presented on platters resting on wicker baskets. It is Lent and we order traditional Lenten vegetarian "fasting food." Lean as a marathon runner, with a shaved head that accentuates his long nose and prominent bone structure, Daniele, forty-eight, expertly puts the situation into context.

His overriding interest is sustainable agriculture: this overused, under-comprehended term refers to agricultural, social, and economic practices that allow farm families to protect their land as a precious resource, continue farming their land, and prosper over generations. Sustainable is not another word for organic: sustainable agriculture may include organic practices, but is not limited to them. Dumping vast amounts of poisonous chemicals on the land certainly is not sustainable, but employing moderate amounts of safer chemical fertilizers may well be.

The next day, I attend Daniele's conference presentation. Daniele talks about his work as research director of an international panel linked to the United Nations, the Committee on Sustainability Assessment (COSA)—this body studies the costs and benefits of various programs that promote sustainability in coffee-producing countries. Daniele and his colleagues looked at a fundamental set of questions, seeking to discover if programs promoting sustainability such as specialty, organic, Fair Trade, Rainforest Alliance, and so forth benefit coffee farmers and coffee-growing regions financially, socially, and environmentally.

Daniele begins his talk by noting the rapid sales growth of coffees that meet various high standards. "In the United States, this segment of the coffee industry is benefiting from increases in growth ranging from 20 to 50 percent a year, depending on the category," he says. No doubt about it: there is money to be made selling coffee as specialty or with labels that read "certified organic" or certified "Fair Trade." But who benefits? Do farmers, cooperatives, and coffee-growing regions benefit in concrete ways, enjoying increases in revenues and improvements in social conditions that outstrip their increased costs? Or do all the benefits accrue elsewhere?

Many coffee drinkers do not realize that it costs growers money to sell their coffee outside normal commodity channels. There are direct and indirect costs to taking part in specialty and certification programs. For a farm or cooperative to be certified organic or Fair Trade, for example, a professional must make regular inspections and attest to the fact that the farm meets a series of requirements. Farmers and cooperatives are charged an annual certification fee, sometimes a substantial one.

Those selling their coffee as specialty do not have to pay to be certified, but they do incur extra costs. Specialty coffee costs more to produce, and yields may be smaller. If your yield is 25 percent smaller because you sell only the highest-quality cherry, and you are paid a 25 percent premium for selling higher-quality specialty coffee, you probably haven't gained a thing. Labor costs for specialty are higher too—if you don't care what color cherry you are picking, you can strip your trees quickly and send your pickers home. Specialty buyers insist on ripe red cherry, which means pickers must make repeated passes through the same area, significantly adding to the length of the harvest.

Based on their research, Daniele and his colleagues created what economists call a "tool" to help growers figure out if the costs of taking part are offset by increases in income. Their formula makes it possible for growers to plug in the numbers and accurately assess whether the various direct and indirect consequences result in a net gain. The program's creators look at sustainability broadly, helping coffee producers understand the economic impact of certification programs—do these programs increase farmers' revenue?—, as well as their environmental and social impact. Daniele calls this three-legged approach to sustainability a useful innovation.

Daniele's formula attempts to empower coffee farmers by enabling them to predict outcomes. By providing a new way of talking and thinking about specialty programs, he and his colleagues have also taken some of the rancor and emotion out of the debate.

The issue of Fair Trade is particularly contentious. The Fair Trade movement emerged in western Europe in the late 1980s as a way to protect agricultural workers in poor countries from the gross inequities of globalization. Ten years later Fair Trade came to the fore in the United States, as American consumers, too, became aware of the horrendous working conditions of laborers overseas producing coffee, chocolate, cotton, and other valuable commodities.

To participate in the Fair Trade program, coffee farmers and coffee roasters both pay large fees. TransFair USA, the American Fair Trade organization, collects a licensing fee of around ten cents for every pound of Fair Trade coffee sold in the United States, which annually adds up to approximately $2 million. TransFair spends nearly every penny of this money sustaining itself.

On the other end of the chain, coffee-growing cooperatives pay between $2,000 and $4,000 a year to be certified Fair Trade by the international Fair Trade umbrella group, FLO. FLO guarantees that labor and living conditions on member cooperatives meet Fair Trade requirements. FLO only certifies cooperatives. Independent farms small or large cannot be certified Fair Trade.

Participating in the Fair Trade program guarantees coffee cooperatives a minimum price of $1.21 a pound for green coffee—$1.41 if the coffee is also certified organic. When coffee prices sank in 1999 to around fifty cents a pound and stayed there for several years, Fair Trade was a life-saving program for farmers. "I watched cooperatives spring up in the countryside under the FT banner that provided security for small farmers who had previously been at the mercy of the local exporters," Geoff Watts wrote in a long Internet posting discussing Fair Trade. As coffee prices climbed, the Fair Trade minimum price for Arabica coffee did not keep pace, though it is scheduled to increase to $1.26 a pound in June 2009. In 2007, the organic premium and the Fair Trade premium—the so-called social premium—each increased by five cents.

Rick Peyser, director of social advocacy for Green Mountain Coffee, sits on the board of FLO. He explains that this "social premium" of ten cents a pound "is set aside to be used by the cooperative for socially beneficial projects, such as building new classrooms, roads, medical clinics, things like that. The only requirement is that the decision concerning the use of the social premium be voted on democratically," Rick says.

Rick views the Fair Trade system as "not perfect, but fair and as transparent as possible. There is an audit trail all the way back to the individual farmer to make sure that everything is on the up and up. The co-op has to maintain a set of books that can demonstrate what each farmer receives in terms of pay and benefits for his coffee."

Recently, Geoff and some other high-end specialty buyers have reconsidered their participation in the Fair Trade system. They object to the fact that the Fair Trade designation does not address quality. "Consumers buy Fair Trade coffee assuming that the FT label refers to high-quality coffee grown under humane conditions," Geoff says. "But that is not the case." Moreover, he believes that the Fair Trade movement has been more or less hijacked by multinationals. "As the program expands and aggressively solicits participation from the largest roasting companies, it finds itself in a quandary," Geoff Watts wrote in an email. "These multinational companies lobby hard against any price increases for coffee [price increases for farmers that small companies like Geoff's endorse], yet they are fast becoming some of Fair Trade's biggest buyers by overall volume. The interests of companies such as Folgers and Nestlé are not aligned with the goals of the specialty industry," Geoff says, adding that many "early adopters and some longtime FT participants are becoming disillusioned."

Geoff prefers to give the ten cents per pound that Intelligentsia previously paid TransFair USA directly to the farmers to improve infrastructure and quality of life. Although some Intelligentsia coffees continue to come from farms that are certified Fair Trade, Intelligentsia no longer pays Fair Trade licensing fees. Stumptown has considered withdrawing, but has not. Both of these companies and Counter Culture routinely pay at least 25 percent above the Fair Trade price for coffee.

Rick Peyser scoffs at the idea that assessing quality should be the job of Fair Trade or any certification program. "I don't know a single coffee buyer who would entrust a buying decision to a certification system's 'seal of approval.' Every coffee buyer I know bases the buying decision on the careful evaluation of the quality in the cup, as discerned by his or her own palate," he says.

The rising cost of coffee further confuses the Fair Trade issue. In January 2008, commodity-quality coffee was trading on the C-market above the Fair Trade price. "It's easy to criticize Fair Trade in a high market like we are in now," Rick says. "Farmers don't see any benefit when prices are high. But I have been on the FLO board, and I have seen what happens. Fair Trade operates like an insurance policy when prices plummet, as they periodically do. Ten years ago when prices collapsed and farmers couldn't feed their families, we saw six hundred thousand farmers in Latin America migrate to the United States. That's when everyone wants to be in a Fair Trade cooperative. I think we need Fair Trade to guarantee a level of sustainability. It's not a magic bullet, but in my opinion it is the best protection farmers have."

Guys like Rick and Geoff and Peter debate Fair Trade as colleagues and friends who disagree, but respect one another's motives. Their civility, however, is not always the norm. Which brings us back to the EAFCA conference and the Daniele Giovannucci talk concerning sustainability and its costs. Having been present at coffee events where the Fair Trade debate elicited rabid emotions, Daniele and his colleague brought reason and quantifiable criteria into the discussion.

I have another reason to be grateful to Daniele later that evening. There is a big EAFCA banquet and close to one thousand people descend on the Addis Sheraton. When I show up, I see no one I know. I work the room during the cocktail hour, doing my reporter's gig. Then we are told to go into the ballroom for dinner. I circle the vast ballroom looking for a table. I bump into Daniele, who is sitting at the head table.

"I will find someone interesting for you to eat dinner with," he tells me. As we circuit the room, he says, "no, these guys are dull"…"no" and "no." And then we come to a table where a number of gentlemen with little beards and small embroidered skullcaps are sitting. Daniele says, "This is where you should sit." He introduces me to a guy in a turban named Shabbir Ezzi. Ezzi is a Muslim trader, an Ismaili—the Aga Khan is the Ismaili spiritual leader. There are one million Ismailis worldwide and they are famous for never taking sides in sectarian disputes. They trade with everyone: Israel, Egypt, China, Afghanistan. My dinner partner is the patriarch of a family of paper traders who had lived prosperously and peacefully in India for five hundred years. He tells me that the Yemeni government approached him and asked if he would help them market their coffee. Yemen, a country where you can buy a Kalashnikov rifle in the market almost as readily as you can buy a loaf of bread, has a few public relations and marketing problems. So Ezzi has moved his family there and he is trying to learn everything he can about Yemen's coffee trade, established five hundred years ago—Yemen's port city, Al Mokha, provided coffee with its nickname, Moka.

Ezzi and I chat all through dinner. As far as he is concerned coffee didn't originate in Ethiopia. It originated in Yemen. To prove this point, he refers to the goat-jumping Kefa myth, which he tells me comes from *The Arabian Nights*. "The Ethiopian word for coffee is *buna*," Ezzi tells me. "*Kefa* or *kafa* is the Arab word for coffee, not the Ethiopian word." Proof positive in his mind that coffee originated in Yemen, not Ethiopia, though most experts think coffee originated in Ethiopia, evolved in Ethiopia, and was later transported to Yemen, where it was cultivated fifteen hundred years ago. Either way, the sun-dried coffee of Yemen has been highly prized for centuries, though in recent decades its quality has suffered.

After the dinner at the Sheraton, I wind up hanging out at the bar in the Hilton with Peter and a bunch of coffee people. War stories are being told. There's this macho thing in specialty coffee among male and females alike. Libby Evans, lean and athletic with an angelic scrubbed face, works for the coffee importer David Griswold, and is talking about swimming in Lake Tanganyika, even though, in her words, "it's full of stuff that can kill you. It's just one of those things you have to do."

The subject turns to scary airplane rides. There's a story about a pilot for Air Malawi who shows up drunk and shouts back at the passengers during takeoff, "Come on, people, let's rock and roll." It turns out that each of the five coffee folks sitting with me has recently been on one of those flights—where the small plane is tossed around during a thunderstorm like a dinghy riding out a hurricane, or where the pilots overshoot the runway of their mountain landing strips.

The talk strikes me as a kind of exorcism. The fact of the matter is that traveling in coffee-producing countries can be dangerous. Peter, Geoff, and Duane buy coffee in the hills of Colombia, where a drug war and a civil war have dragged on for decades and people are kidnapped all the time. Coffee grows in those treacherous hills. Some years it's safe to venture by foot or by donkey into terrain controlled by drug dealers and insurgents to buy coffee, and some years—well, better not. But how do you know? How do you know that this year won't be the year you miscalculate and wind up with a bullet between the eyes? The coffee guys talk about these things with a certain amused fatalism, but scratch the surface, and you know it's sometimes as scary as hell.

They tell stories about Geoff, who they say is infamous for drinking and partying. "It's gotten better this year. Last year I was afraid he might flame out and become our Jim Morrison," Peter tells me.

This talk is more than idle gossip, though there's plenty of that. Geoff is loved and he is envied. There's something so damn compelling about the guy. I saw this on our first night in Addis, when Peter, Geoff, Tim, and a bunch of other coffee guys had dinner at a traditional Ethiopian restaurant. The place was decorated with rugs and baskets, silver fixings, brass trays—all the embellishments you'd find inside the tent of a nomadic chieftain or rich camel herder. Three or four hundred people were crowded into the club, lounging on wicker stools and divans. During the performance, one of the dancers had to choose a guy from the audience to teach the exotic, snakelike head-and-shoulder movements of her dance. So whom does she chose? A wealthy Ethiopian merchant? A smooth-looking tourist? No, she picks Geoff, despite the fact that he's in ratty clothes and drunk on Tej, the local honey wine. She doesn't choose him because he looks like a big spender. My sense is that he must have been aiming his topaz eyes straight at her, like headlights.

There's some recognition in the specialty coffee community that the intensity and fearlessness that Geoff brings to his work and life is the very quality that might kill him. Every movement seems to have a tragic hero, and Geoff may be ours, Ric Rhinehart from Groundwork Coffee in Los Angeles later tells me.

The EAFCA conference is, well, a conference. I learn a lot. I meet a lot of people, but by the end of the second day, I start to get itchy. It seems crazy to be in Ethiopia and not see a coffee farm, not visit Yirgacheffe, but these things aren't on our schedule. In a few days, Peter and Geoff and I will all go our separate ways. Until then, Peter and Geoff are wedded to the idea of staying in Addis Ababa and cupping a lot of coffees.

So the next morning after breakfast I stop by the table of Lindsey Bolger. She is the director of coffee sourcing and relationships for Vermont's Green Mountain Coffee Roasters, a $250 million publicly traded roasting company. I had met Lindsey only once before, briefly, but I know Peter and Geoff consider her a star—a roaster and coffee cupper who possesses an unusually discerning palate and has made big contributions to the industry, teaching cupping all over the world.

"By any chance are you traveling to origin?" I ask.

She looks at me, considers my question for a moment, and then says, "I am leaving for a two-night trip to Sidamo [five or six hours away] and Yirgacheffe with a group of buyers in an hour." She tells me that if I can get ready that fast, I can join them.

By midmorning I find myself riding in a two-truck caravan that includes Lindsey as well as Shirin Moayyad, Peet's newly hired director of coffee purchasing; the sweet-faced Libby Evans, twenty-two, from the socially conscious import company, Sustainable Harvest, located in Portland, Oregon; Kim Cook, a wild woman—as in wild women don't sing the blues—photographer in her late 30s based in Colorado on assignment for Sustainable Harvest; Rick Peyser; and Jason Long, a former finance guy in his early thirties who is a principal of Minneapolis-based Café Imports. Leading the expedition is Menno Simons, the young Dutch trader who directs Trabocca, an Amsterdam-based trading company that "sources" organic coffees in Africa—meaning that it locates high-quality beans and then works in partnership with farmers and licensed exporters who sell to importers who represent buyers such as Peter, Geoff, and Duane. The system is pretty complex, but that's how it works in Ethiopia and a lot of coffee-growing countries.

Menno founded Trabocca in 2004, and he owns 35 percent of the company. He has been working in Ethiopia for a decade. In 1998 he introduced the first organic coffee certification program into the country. Many of the best coffees exported from Ethiopia to Europe, the United States, and Japan are sourced by him. Counter Culture, Intelligentsia, Stumptown, Peet's, Sustainable

Harvest, and Green Mountain depend on Menno to help them source their coffees. Geoff, Peter, and Duane all love the guy. Duane, in fact, dreams of going into business with Menno in Amsterdam, opening Stumptown-style coffee shops in a city where Duane says it is currently easier to buy (legal) marijuana at the corner café than a memorable cappuccino.

On the first leg of our journey, I'm in a truck with Lindsey, Shirin, and Rick Peyser. None of us has yet been out into the countryside and we eagerly look out the windows. Here and there villages are splayed out on either side of the paved, two-lane road that heads south through the Rift Valley and then up into the mountains. There aren't too many roads in Ethiopia and this is the same route that Peter and Geoff took to Yirgacheffe two years earlier when they visited for the first time. As we pass through towns, we share the road with horse-drawn wagons topped with bright orange canopies that protect the drivers from the sun, bicyclists, pedestrians, men pulling donkey carts, schoolchildren in brightly colored uniforms, schoolgirls walking hand in hand, schoolboys walking hand in hand—adults of the same sex also hold hands in Ethiopia—and women wearing white diaphanous wraps that protect them from the sun and dust. Fat, humped cattle cross the road at will. Everywhere we smell eucalyptus and charred coffee. Squash and potatoes are for sale along the side of the road. As we slow down to let a donkey pass in front of us, a little girl holds out her hand and says "money money money money"—a pro forma plea to strangers that we will hear often in the coming few days.

Further out in the countryside, we see thatched huts, herds of cows, women bent over carrying big bundles of laundry, and surprisingly, Ping-Pong tables set up on the side of the road. We wonder why people would choose to play adjacent to the highway.

We pass few private cars but many trucks and vans. Almost all are Toyotas. It's rare to see an American car.

It's hot. Bright sun pours unobstructed into the car, and there is no air conditioning. Shirin, Peet's buyer, sits in the front seat; she commandeers the front because of a tendency to become carsick. Pale and blond despite Persian origin through her father, she has an English accent and an education, from elite American schools. She is in her early forties and although she has lived all over the world—Singapore for eight years, Papua New Guinea, one of the hottest places on earth, before that—the heat still bothers her and she periodically sprays water on her face from a small aerosol can that she offers to the rest of us. She has only been working for Peet's for a few months. Based in San Francisco, she finds Americans crass and living in the United States something of a trial.

I've been talking with Rick Peyser about Green Mountain's programs to aid farmers in Latin America and Africa. Fifty-six-year-old Rick's a "side of the angels" fair-minded guy with a young-looking face and white hair—his liberal impulses are combined with judiciousness—so it's not surprising that he sits on many boards. Thinking about our conversation and the passionate concern Peter, Geoff, and Duane express for coffee farmers, I idly ask if everyone in "coffee world" is a "leftist."

"What do you mean?" Shirin asks.

"You know, do-gooders," I say. "People who identify with the downtrodden."

"I believe in business as the way to draw people out of poverty," Shirin answers tartly. It seems she has been offended by my question, so I let the subject drop and turn my attention to Lindsey.

No matter how hot it gets, Lindsey, trim and athletic, in her late thirties, with long dark hair, assertive black brows, and blue-green eyes, looks composed—she never seems to wilt. Lindsey is a coffee guy's coffee guy. A star who wears stardom lightly. Coffee reviewer Kenneth Davids wrote about her in his online site Coffee Review, saying Lindsey "is greatly admired by her colleagues for her honesty, her genuine understanding and sympathy for coffee growers and their challenges and achievements, and for the sort of deeply original personal engagement with coffee that transcends profession and approaches art." Her company, Green Mountain, sells a small amount of specialty coffee online; it's known best, however, for roasting and selling high-quality mass-market beans to supermarkets, gas stations, and other middle-of-the-road customers, which means that few outside the specialty coffee business know Lindsey. She doesn't get the press coverage that Peter, Geoff, and Duane regularly garner. On the other hand, she has stock options, works for a highly respected, stable company, and lives in Vermont, where she and Rick Peyser and a lot of her coworkers find the living pretty good. Of the five women present on the journey, Lindsey and I are the only ones who are married and the only ones with children—her son is seven. Her husband, a tech guy, works from home, which makes handling her career a lot easier than it might otherwise be. Not that traveling six months a year is ever easy.

Lindsey says, "I have always cared totally about the taste and smell of things. I guess I found my lost tribe in this business." She grew up outside of Rochester in what she calls "a fragrant house." Her father was an architectural historian, an expert in historic restorations. Her mother was a passionate gardener. "My house smelled of books, herbs, old carpets. I have always loved to smell stuff. I can't buy anything without smelling it first."

In 1987, as a college student at the Washington State University in Olympia, Washington, Lindsey started to work for Batdorf and Bronson Coffee Roasters. She loved coffee, and she was attracted to coffee roasting as a nontraditional job for a woman. "I was the perfect customer who became a roaster and then a roast master."

The legendary Alfred Peet, who died in 2007 at the age of eighty-seven, was her mentor and helped her take her innate talent as a taster to a higher level. Peet was Dutch—his father owned a small coffee roastery. He had immigrated to the States and started Peet's Coffee & Tea in Berkeley in 1966. His knowledge of coffee was encyclopedic. In addition to a sensitive palate, he had a talent for translating what he tasted in the cup into words, which made him a particularly valuable teacher. Lindsey met Peet in 1989 at one of his seminars. "I had this raw enthusiasm, and Alfred wound up giving me a forty-eight-hour tutorial." They stayed close for many years. "It was a paternal relationship. I learned a lot from him."

It's almost 6:00 p.m. We started out at 11:00 a.m. an hour behind schedule, and bad roads and a long lunch delayed us more. It is getting dark when we arrive at the washing station of Shoye Dada co-op, representing forty-five hundred farmers in five different locations in the Sidamo region. Each farmer works just half a hectare of land—about an acre. The land is leased; under Ethiopian law there is little private land ownership. Farmers cannot mortgage, sell, or develop property. In addition to coffee, most farmers grow vegetables to feed their families. To the dismay of the Ethiopian government, millions also grow khat, a plant that produces an amphetamine-like high when its leaves and twigs are chewed. Khat turns users' teeth green, a common sight in rural Ethiopia. When coffee prices decline, khat production inevitably increases, as it did in the first years of the new century.

Representatives of the Sidamo farmers' union have been waiting for us for hours.

Libby Evans—quite resourceful—is carrying a GPS device. "We are facing north," she reports. The altitude is 1,994 meters— over six thousand feet. Oddly, many coffee growers don't know how high their farms are. They just repeat some number their grandfathers or their neighbors told them. (A coffee grower in Panama told me that in Latin America growers deliberately exaggerate when asked the altitude of their coffee farms, the way men exaggerate when you ask them how many women they have had. It's a guy thing.)

Rain threatens and the air on the mountain is cool and breezy. Menno, Shirin, Lindsey, Libby, Jason, Rick, and I are ushered into little wooden chairs that have been set up in a circle alongside a storage warehouse in a clearing overlooking a steep green valley and another tree-covered mountain on the other side.

In a green T-shirt, cargo pants, and black running shoes, Menno runs the meeting. Quick-witted and blond with small, sharp features, Menno, through his company Trabocca, has been working with farmers in Sidamo and Yirgacheffe to upgrade the quality of their organic coffee. As part of a public/private partnership launched in 2005, Trabocca is purchasing new pulping machines, washing equipment, dry hullers, drying tables, cupping room equipment, and power generators for thirty organic coffee cooperatives, depending on their most urgent needs. This venture was funded for two years with provisions to extend it for another eight. Trabocca invested approximately $375,000 of its own money, and the Dutch government provided a grant of $600,000.

Seventeen growers, dressed in worn shirts and pants and scuffed leather shoes, sit and stand opposite Menno and the buyers, all of whom identify themselves in a formal, businesslike way. The farmers and co-op representatives view the buyers intently. Many of the farmers have sculpted faces and rail-thin bodies. Others are rounder and look African or Asiatic. All are weather-beaten, with skin tones that range from light brown to dark. It's been a tremendously difficult time for these farmers. In the past few years, prices have rebounded from the collapse that hit in 1999, but unpredictable weather and the lack of infrastructure have worked against these farmers.

Most of the coffee growers represented by the Sidamo Union still live in communities without electricity or running water—despite abundant supplies of water. In fact, the region has suffered from too much water, and coffee crops have been damaged by the worst rains in decades. The elected head of the Shoye

Dada cooperative is also the president of the board of the entire Sidamo Union, which encompasses thirty-six large cooperatives like this one—some 150,000 farmers or more.

Large unions like Sidamo have the legal right to sell coffee and operate as exporters. The unions mill coffee or see that it is milled. They cup it or taste it at Addis's central liquoring (an archaic term for cupping or tasting) facility and then oversee its sale at auction. In this complicated global environment, many of these unions have begun to adopt the practices of commodity traders—trying to protect themselves by buying and selling on margin. This effort to play the international finance game can be perilous. The former head of the Sidamo Union is in jail, accused of embezzling hundreds of thousands of dollars. These charges may or may not be trumped up; they may or may not relate to an effort to protect the position of the union on the international market. Everywhere we go Ethiopians and non-Ethiopians are discussing these matters, but no one seems to possess definitive information. What is known without question: the Sidamo Union is in danger of losing its Fair Trade certification, and no one can tell us exactly why. It all adds up to a big mess.

In previous years, the Shoye Dada cooperative has sold thirteen containers of coffee—almost half a million pounds—per year. This year the cooperative will have only half as much coffee to sell. Menno doesn't know why volume has decreased so drastically. Are the "blood-sucking" privates getting in early and spiriting the coffee away? Or is there an agronomic explanation to this mystery? Although Menno spends a great deal of time in Ethiopia, and has a full-time Ethiopian employee based in Addis (far from the co-ops), he finds it extremely difficult to understand precisely what is going on within the cooperatives.

Menno bases his business on the conviction that Ethiopian growers, with the right help, can grow great coffee consistently.

But right now consistency and profitability are elusive. Menno is spending time and resources in Ethiopia, traveling widely in search of the cooperatives growing the best-tasting coffee and then working with them, upgrading their infrastructure, improving their agronomic practices, paying for them to be certified organic, and helping them market their beans. Some people think Menno has bitten off way more than he can chew, but they admire what he is trying to accomplish. There aren't many outsiders who are willing to throw themselves body and soul into the effort to lift Ethiopian farmers into the specialty market.

The day we visit, Menno wants to know what has caused Shoye Dada production to decline so dramatically and what he can do to help boost the coming year's production. Translating back and forth from English to Amharic is Abraham Begashaw, an Ethiopian coffee guy and former government official who works for Menno at Trabocca's Addis office. Questioned about declining productivity, the farmers talk among themselves before answering. They mention the rain. How difficult it was to dry the cherry. Financing has been a problem too.

The head of the cooperative says, "The bank doesn't release money to the farmers on time, so the farmers have to sell their coffee to the privates." Perpetually burdened with debt, the farmers depend on "pre-financing" to pay for preplanting expenses. If this money doesn't arrive early, farmers are forced to borrow money at disadvantageous terms and then, pressed to repay, they wind up selling their coffee to itinerant local buyers who may take advantage of their desperation. These buyers—called coyotes in Latin America—sell to whomever they please for whatever amount they please. Some independents are fair, but others are rapacious.

Lindsey asks, "Is the problem that the cooperative is not preparing the prefinancing documentation properly for the bank? This is a problem we often see in Latin America." As she speaks, a large, honking bird flies overhead. Birdlife is abundant at the cooperative, and as twilight falls, birdsong rings from the treetops.

The problem, however, seems to run much more deeply than preparing paperwork. The local representatives cannot say precisely what happens to their prefinancing, but they appear to believe that the bank releases the money to the union in Addis Ababa, where it gets lost.

As twilight falls and the meeting continues, all that can be determined is that cash isn't moving properly through the pipeline from Addis Ababa, to Sidamo, to local growers who are spread out in five separate areas. But no one is able to pinpoint the source of the difficulty. The lack of electricity, the dearth of communications, the long distance between Addis and Sidamo, plus the large number of players certainly feed the confusion. A few co-op officials have cell phones, but other than that, the farmers are completely cut off from their representatives in Addis.

A small rainbow shoots across the sky. A few raindrops splash on our faces.

At last, Menno is told that although he has been providing funds for prefinancing to the union, his money was never received by the local guys. He is at a loss. Where did all this money go? he asks. He worries that the union may be playing favorites, funneling money to some cooperatives while withholding it from others. Is the problem corruption? Incompetence? The lack of infrastructure? All of the above? None of the above?

"Things have to change in the union," Menno says. "It can't go on like this."

Menno wonders if he would be able to deposit money directly into the bank account of the local cooperative. It appears this might be possible if permission is given by the national bank—likely not so easy. The farmers say that if the prefinancing money arrives in a timely fashion, they believe they could produce seventeen containers of washed coffee in two years' time.

Thunder rolls around the mountains as the farmers take Menno and the buyers on a tour of their facility. Menno asks if there is enough drying space to process all the coffee. In the distance, we hear the sound of children laughing and playing, though we cannot see the village.

Lindsey wants to know how many women belong to the growing group. The answer is 127. Less than 1 percent. Most of these are widows. Women, by law or by custom, don't seem to function independently as farmers in Ethiopia.

Menno tells the farmers he will be back in a couple of months. He's going to try to have their financing by July, when coffee starts to ripen and the farmers need money to plan for the harvest. I walk back to the truck with Menno. He's lost in thought.

I ask him if he is making any money in Ethiopia.

"I don't know," he answers. "I sold millions of pounds of Ethiopian coffee last year, and I could be selling more, but we need to get control of quality. It's a matter of investing the time. Being here enough to build up trust. You can make a difference working with these people. I prefer that to the usual kind of trading. I guess I like dancing where one wall is missing," he says, meaning that he is a risk taker, unfearful of walls caving in on him.

The co-op guys swing open a large wooden gate so we can leave. Waiting to enter is the organic certifier, the guy hired by Trabocca to certify that the cooperative's coffee meets organic standards. This cooperative is certified Fair Trade as well.

It is completely dark when we leave the cooperative heading for Yirgalem, an hour and a half away, where we will spend the night at a pretty country hotel before visiting Yirgacheffe in the morning. The mountain road is treacherous—the rains have done their work and the ruts cutting into the red-clay dirt road are deep and wide. Then our truck's headlights go out. The lights are dead. We're like a bunch of skiers caught on the top of a black diamond ski slope in a blizzard. Despite the rain, the road ruts, and the danger of going down this steep mountain in the dark, there's no alternative. Our driver inches toward the other car in our caravan, trying to take advantage of the first car's headlights. I close my eyes and wait for the descent to be over.

It is after 9:00 p.m. when we arrive at our destination, an eco-tourist hotel called the Aregash Lodge, which is built deep in the forest to resemble a traditional Sidamo village with individual huts to accommodate the guests. We wake before sunrise to the distant sound of Christian prayer—it's Coptic Lent—and the faithful in a nearby village have gathered outdoors to chant before dawn. A few minutes later we hear Muslim prayer, from a different village. When we exit our huts, wrapping sweaters around ourselves, we smell the frankincense and Queen of the Night growing wild around our little thatched dwellings. It occurs to me that I have never been in a place that smells so good before. And has so many birds. Maybe Peter and Geoff weren't overly romanticizing Yirgacheffe when they called it Eden.

The morning air is chilly, but we eat breakfast outdoors. White-faced colobus monkeys with comically long, white tails hiding high up in the distant trees try to catch a glimpse of us as we try to get a glimpse of them. Lindsey claps her hands and shouts to the maids serving breakfast, "Buna. Buna, buna."

"This is a crazy place," Kim says. "I felt huge spirits last night in our hut. I thought lightning had hit us. I thought I'd been electrocuted. I heard animals—all this energy being stirred up..."

"Jackals and hyenas come out at night," Shirin says.

It's like there's a hallucinogenic up here, someone says.

"I felt a pulsation of energy in the air," says Lindsey.

The guys have gone walking in the forest. It's just the girls who seem to be going Druid—Lindsey, Libby, Kim, and Shirin, but not me. I am not much into this moon goddess stuff, but maybe I spend too much time in Washington, D.C.

I look at the other women. Shirin is on the short side, but the other three are tall and spare. I can't help wondering if there is some sort of self-selection going on, whether the kind of women who are attracted to the coffee trade tend to be like this—lean and leggy. All of them are athletes. Shirin is a horsewoman and polo player. In Singapore, she rode horseback every morning. In the afternoon she played polo, and she wears a "stick chick" T-shirt. Shirin says she had her final job interview with Peet's on her cell phone while on horseback. Kim, the photographer, with her wide smile, wild hair, and rangy body, hikes and skis and bikes—if it's dangerous, she's into it. Libby, the daughter of two forest rangers, was an Olympic-caliber equestrian until she broke her back riding. "I loved the competition, but I hated the snootiness of the horse world, so upper class. Now I just ride my bike," she says. Lindsey was a competitive rower in college, also with Olympic aspirations. She got pretty close to that goal and then discovered that she didn't have a killer instinct.

"The day I quit rowing was the happiest day of my life. I didn't want to attack my teammates for spots on the national team. That's what you have to do to make it into the Olympics. Beat out your teammates. I didn't have it in me. I'm still pretty competitive, though. My husband and I can't use the rowing machines at the gym without racing each other."

Leggy, hyperkinetic Kim is on assignment and is feeling desperate to take more photographs, so on our way to the Yirgacheffe washing station we stop at a village with a small Coptic church. We pull over and she jumps out and heads back down the road to a house we just passed. We park in front of a forty-foot-long wall of shiny green foliage and dazzling red poinsettias. They grow wild around here. They're everywhere. Village children surround us, laughing and pointing at our digital cameras. We take pictures of them in front of their houses and then show them the shot, which sends them into fits of laughter. We shoot more pictures of the children, this time with their mothers. Kim comes racing down the road, thrilled that she has a shot of an old man and his many wives.

"He's all wrinkly and gnarly," Kim says. "Must be eighty years old. He lives in that compound over there with three or four wives. There's a baby son toddling around. Can't be more than three. The old guy was shy at first. Didn't want his picture taken."

We credit his virility to the coffee. Kim has traveled a lot, and has an eye for what's really going on. Later we stop on the road at another village.

We all jump out of the van and look around. The village is surrounded by lush vegetation. The women and girls wear their hair braided and swept up in the back. One little girl is wearing a T-shirt proclaiming "The United Colors of Benetton."

Kim sniffs the air and runs off. When she comes back she says that she had smelled marijuana—or it might have been marijuana cut with khat—khat plants and khat use are endemic in coffee-growing regions. Following the scent, Kim had walked into a house to take pictures and she saw a couple smoking what she called "big old fatties."

"It was a girl and a guy. They ran off when they saw me," she says. I marvel at her fearlessness.

Kim has traveled with Geoff Watts, and she knows that I have too. She looks at me. "I bet Geoff would have found that pot," she says with a laugh.

We stop at the washing station where coffee is depulped, demucilaged, and fermented. Menno has just paid for a new Pinhalense machine from Brazil that ferments the beans in just three hours and separates the heavy, ripe red cherry from the lighter weight green.

"The local people call this machine evil," Menno explains, because it rejects green cherry, improving the coffee but lowering their pay. The farmers are paid by weight.

The warehouse contains jute bags full of coffee.

"I cupped this coffee on Monday," Lindsey says. "It was beautiful."

Menno hands out T-shirts to the farmers. Lindsey pastes iridescent fish stickers on the hands of the kids who surround us and promises to send pictures of our visit. The children all want our empty water bottles. (Wherever we go they want our empty bottles, and I never do find out what they do with them. No one seems to know, but one thing is for certain: this is an area where materials are scarce.)

At the next co-op, Menno, Abraham, and a bunch of local guys huddle for a long time.

"It's always the same story," Menno says, disgusted. "I paid the union thousands of dollars to prefinance this coffee. The union took the money, but the farmers never collected."

The farmers have no idea what's going on. "They're always kept in the dark," Menno says. "The information flows one way. There is no trust. These guys are really angry."

He seems angry too. He's made a huge investment and has nothing to show for it. No coffee to sell. No deepening relationship with farmers who see that he is able to deliver what he promises.

We stop again for Menno to huddle with another group of farmers.

Kim gets out to shoot, then jumps back into the truck. "Hey, that kid tried to steal my lens case." She's shocked. This is a traditional society and thievery is not common. The thwarted theft puts a pall on our mood. It's hot. We get sick of sitting in the truck going nowhere. Menno's meeting goes on and on. Soon we are surrounded by a group of children with their hands outstretched, chanting, "You you you you you you you…"

"Do you ever feel 'overworldly'?" Libby asks. "Like you know too much about the world [in comparison to people who don't travel]. People who know me don't ask anything about where I go or what I have seen. It's like they don't want to know."

"How about when you say you've been to Addis Ababa and they say, 'Where's that?' and you know they don't want to know," Shirin responds.

"The other mothers look at me like I am nuts to leave my son. I come home from a long trip. I walk into a birthday party or something else and no one even asks. I just jump right back in as if I have never been gone," Lindsey says.

Menno comes back to the truck. "I am going to increase my price and pay directly to the cooperative. I'm not going to deal with this union any longer. I think we are at a critical state, and I need to help these guys."

The next day farmers from this cooperative make the long trip to Addis Ababa to deliver signed papers to Menno, designating him, rather than the union, their legal representative.

PANAMA

MENTION YOU ARE TRAVELING TO BOQUETE, PANAMA, AND
specialty coffee guys get a dreamy look in their eyes. Boquete is the
center of Panama's small coffee industry and the birthplace of the
mythical Geisha, the coffee that "sang sirens, sirens to Odysseus,"
in the memorable words of Don Holly. Even without Geisha,
Boquete, a flower-strewn coffee Camelot perched on the eastern
slope of the eleven-thousand-foot Baru Volcano, attracts travelers.
The sun shines, the humidity is low, the locals are friendly, and the
hills echo with birdsong. No wonder the editors of *Fortune* named
this town of fifteen thousand one of the five best places in the
world to retire.

So it is easy to understand why twenty-five specialty coffee
professionals answered "yes" when asked to spend close to an
entire week as judges at the annual Best of Panama coffee competition in April 2007. I had come to Boquete not only to attend the
competition but also to learn more about Geisha coffee. Among
the best-known members of the panel were two Dutch guys with a

lot of Geisha-related projects in the works: Menno Simons, the coffee "sourcer" who led the visit to Yirgacheffe in Ethiopia, and Willem Boot, the consultant who organized that infamous, muddy trek to Gesha in November 2006. Willem is growing Geisha on the coffee farm near Boquete that he bought a few years back. Menno is trying to create a model coffee farm in Ethiopia where he hopes to grow high-quality Ethiopian varietals, including Geisha. Another of the judges is Joseph Brodsky, a founder of the tiny Novo Coffee based in Colorado that imports coffees from Ethiopia and Panama with cupping scores over 90. Serving as head judge: Ric Rhinehart from Groundwork Coffee in Los Angeles. (Peter and Geoff were last-minute no-shows at the competition: Geoff traveled to Nicaragua for another showdown with Cecocafen, and Peter spent all his spare hours that spring poring over SCAA financials following an employee embezzlement.)

The Panamanian contest offered coffee guys the chance to preview many great coffees in addition to Geisha, or more accurately, in addition to the Geishas—currently there were three farms in Panama with Geisha trees mature enough to harvest. Two of these—Esmeralda Special and a mystery Geisha from a grower who entered without revealing his name—were going up against each other in the Best of Panama competition.

Not entered was the grandfather of all Boquete Geishas grown by Francisco Serracin on one of the area's top farms, Don Pachi Estate. Serracin's father, Francisco Senior, was responsible for setting the whole Geisha craze in motion back in the 1960s. In his official capacity as an employee of the Ministry of Agriculture searching for disease-resistant plants, Francisco Senior had imported Geisha seeds from Costa Rica and shared them with his neighbors. The resulting trees, with their low yield and mediocre taste, were considered a flop. Not much Geisha was ever planted. This happened decades before Daniel Peterson of Hacienda La

Esmeralda discovered that Geisha turned into the sex goddess of coffees when grown at high altitude.

Instead of entering their Geisha in the competition to sell in the auction, the Serracin family sold the crop while the cherry was still on the tree to Stumptown's Duane Sorenson. Duane moves fast and pays top dollar. Stumptown's coffee buyer, the brash and talented Aleco Chigounis, thirty, visited Boquete the week before the 2007 competition. All the competition coffees were ready and he managed to cup them all, including the Serracin and Peterson Geishas.

Writing on the Stumptown Web site, Aleco said, "I don't know of any coffee buyer in the world who wouldn't salivate at the thought of an auction lot table with coffees from Elida Estate, Finca Lerida, Don Pachi, Don Pepe Estate, San Benito, Dona Berta, and Los Lajones and others.…With flavors ranging from lemon zest to tangerine to cantaloupe to baker's chocolate," the Panamanian coffees compose "a table that is easily one of the world's finest displays of stellar quality."

Describing the two Geishas, Aleco sounds like a young man in love. He refers to Hacienda La Esmeralda's Geisha as a woman: "The Esmeralda looks beautiful…and as always, she sparkles like a precious gemstone in the cup. The fragrance is like papaya drenched in maple syrup, fresh-cut sugarcane and jasmine. The up-front flavors are just like they're supposed to be—complex—citrus, mango, papaya, and intense bergamot. The Petersons seem to be perfecting their craft each year."

As for the qualities of the Don Pachi Geisha? "This coffee is much more berried and sweet than its La Esmeralda counterpart, although it doesn't have the same tealike and citrus flavors. I think I am leaning toward Pachi as being ever-so-slightly superior to La Esmeralda this year.

"Pachi is the heavyweight Geisha this year," Aleco writes, a judgment, he admits, that might be colored by the fact that it's a Stumptown exclusive. Aleco proudly notes that Stumptown is the only roaster to offer multiple Geishas—these two, plus the Geisha Duane Sorenson discovered on his pit stop in Costa Rica.

Aleco is not the only buyer to sing the praises of Panamanian coffee. Though these growers compose less than 1 percent of the world's coffee farmers, their coffees often place in the top ten coffees in the world at the Cupping Pavilion Competition at the SCAA's annual convention. In 2007 judges named Hacienda La Esmeralda Special from Boquete number one and the coffee from Carmen Estate in Volcan, on the other side of the Baru Volcano, number seven. In 2006, Hacienda La Esmeralda ranked first and Duncan Estate, an organic coffee from Café Kotowa in Boquete, ranked fourth.

After the international coffee agreement lapsed in the early 1990s and the price of coffee dropped like a skydiver without a rip-cord, growers in Panama realized that to survive they had to upgrade their product and sell quality. This they did, with some success. Then as they were beginning to breathe easier, Vietnam flooded the market with a glut of cheap coffee, cutting world prices in half.

"We arrive at 1997," industry leader Maria Ruiz, whose family owns Boquete's largest coffee business, tells me, "and the industry collapses once again. We thought quality would always be valued. In 1995, when I went to Germany, a package of coffee cost seven marks. In 2000 that package cost 3.5 marks. The price was slashed in half. Quality was not the point because consumers were accepting lower quality. Also, Germany had a new industrial process for treating robusta, making it taste better.

"So we had to rebuild again," says Maria. She and the other growers realized they had to get out of mass market entirely and into the specialty market. None of the growers were earning any money. "The bank owns our property. We went to the bank to see if they would restructure our loan," recalls Maria.

Then in 1999 another blow came. "Some magazine [*Fortune*] decided Boquete was one of the five best places to retire. Suddenly the bank wants us to sell to gringos. If our land is so valuable, why not restructure our loans, we say."

The growers quickly understood that they would have to reach out to experts outside the country to help them. "We had organized the Specialty Coffee Association of Panama (SCAP), and we started going to SCAA meetings in the United States," recalls Hacienda La Esmeralda's Price Peterson.

"We would stand up at meetings and say, 'I'm a grower from Panama.' At the next session another one of our guys would stand up and say, 'I'm a grower from Panama...' And people in the industry would go, 'My God, another grower from Panama.' We got ourselves known by the buyers and other people in the industry."

"SCAA gave us a forum to have direct contact with buyers," Maria recalls. "We become our own middleman and started dealing direct with buyers we meet at SCAA meetings."

Putting themselves out there, the Panamanians learned how the specialty game was played from the buyers' side. They realized that "all the brokers know each other. If you sell one bad batch of coffee, you can ruin your reputation and kill your business," adds Peterson. They used their growers' association, SCAP, to support each other's efforts to improve quality. Well before Geisha appeared, the reputation of their coffees was rising. When Geisha took the specialty world by storm in 2004, these growers were able to capitalize on all the attention this one coffee received to benefit their entire industry.

The Panamanian coffee industry is centered in Boquete and Volcan. The two towns, perched on different sides of the Baru Volcano, share many natural advantages—rich volcanic soil, altitude, and many distinct microclimates that help to individuate their coffees. Panamanian farmers possess man-made advantages as well. Shipping is easy. A huge portion of the world's trade travels through the Panama Canal, and Panama is the world's second most active banking center, after Switzerland. Although the median income in Panama is low, the infrastructure is world class. Moreover, the growers have a cadre of forward-looking leaders who are well educated, and many of them speak English. Ricardo Koyner of Kotowa Coffee, Wilford Lamastus of Elida Estate, and Johnny Collins of Finca Lerida all lived and studied in North America during the Noriega years. Price Peterson, from Esmeralda, is a former professor of neurochemistry at the University of Pennsylvania. Mario Serracin, a specialist in organic agriculture, is a PhD agronomist. Maria Ruiz and her three siblings studied in the United States and speak English. Maria, who oversees quality and other aspects of the Ruiz business, has a PhD in organizational behavior from Case Western Reserve University in Cleveland. And the list goes on.

Peter Giuliano sees the Panamanian coffee industry as a hybrid, mixing traditional farming know-how and very advanced technical skill. "When I am feeling cynical," he tells me, "I can't help thinking it takes an educated guy like Price Peterson to grow the best of the best of the best coffee." Peter has logged a lot of miles visiting coffee farmers in places far less comfortable than Boquete based on his conviction that farmers in every corner of the globe are capable of elevating the quality of their coffee. Still, he has moments of extreme frustration. Encouraging farmers who are not trained to look at the world scientifically to make systemic changes on their farms is a Sisyphean task. Year after year you teach the same lesson, but as soon as you go home, farmers resume doing what they have always done. The truth is, most human beings resist change, and none resist change more vigorously than those whose lives are steeped in local traditions. The receptivity of the growers in Panama to new ideas and new ways of operating sets them apart from most other coffee farmers in the world.

Being the kind of people that they are, it's not surprising that the leaders of the Panamanian coffee industry run their own coffee competition, rather than taking part in the Cup of Excellence. This decision has an upside—they control their own show—and a downside: they have to do the logistical work that Cup of Excellence takes care of in other countries. Staging a coffee competition is a little like organizing a fancy wedding that lasts for a week with many out-of-town guests who must be fed and feted and shepherded around. Managing the complicated logistics of the competition itself is another challenging task. There are hundreds of samples that have to be perfectly roasted to highlight the intrinsic qualities of each coffee—if you over-roast or under-roast, a coffee's taste profile is lost. There are scores of workers and volunteers whose efforts must be coordinated. The sites. The cupping tables, electric kettles, and other high- and low-tech equipment. The discussion room, the chairs, the recording equipment, the blue cupping aprons with each judge's name embroidered on the front, the endless platters of fruit and bottles of water to help the cuppers clear their palates.

I arrive in Panama a few days before the competition, eager to soak up the local color and meet the owners of Hacienda La Esmeralda. I immediately fall in love with Boquete. Downtown isn't much, just a couple of streets vaguely reminiscent of the Old West—lots of bars and taverns—but the town itself and its mountainous environs are dazzling. Everywhere I look, I see bright-colored impatiens, hibiscus, jacaranda, coral-colored trumpet flowers, poinsettia, and audaciously red Christmas lilies growing wild. In mid-April, the place smells of flowering coffee blossoms, lemongrass, and sweet guava.

I stay at an inn on the grounds of Finca Lerida, a high mountain coffee farm producing prize-winning coffee. My room is artfully rustic. Plenty of hot water pours from the showerhead. There's a patio with a bench where I watch the mist clear over the mountaintop in the morning and the fog descend in the afternoon. Behind my cabin, a path shoots into the mountains: each morning birders with binoculars around their necks slip by at dawn in search of the 950 species that visit Panama each year, including the resplendent quetzal, an iridescent green freedom lover with an outrageously long tail that has been known to kill itself rather than live in captivity.

Johnny Collins, opinionated, but fundamentally kind, built this inn to produce revenue to support his coffee enterprise. Johnny is an engineer by training, and the grounds and outbuildings at Finca Lerida reflect his perfectionism—his two hundred and forty thousand coffee trees are planted in rows so precise, they would fit in a formal garden.

Johnny is a history buff, and he explains to me how the history of coffee in Panama is intertwined with the history of the Panama Canal. Many of Panama's first coffee growers were engineers and managers from Europe who emigrated to Panama to work on the canal, which was completed in 1917. Finca Lerida, for example, was built and run by an engineer of Norwegian descent named Tollef Bache Monniche, who designed the emergency dams at the Panama Canal. When his work on the canal was complete, Monniche and his wife escaped the miserable heat and humidity of Panama City for the cool beauty of Boquete, where he applied his technical skills to creating a modern coffee plantation high in the hills—Johnny is in the process of restoring Monniche's processing plant and turning it into a museum. He and his wife Zoraida live in the house Monniche built for himself and his wife one hundred years ago.

Eating breakfast my first morning at Lerida, I see Zoraida and three other women working in the small kitchen. They are talking and laughing companionably. Johnny's in the open-air dining room with a pair of well-behaved, shiny-coated dogs who accompany him everywhere. Even the dogs in Boquete look happy. The farm is so manicured, yet welcoming, I am reminded of that famous quip by George S. Kaufman when he visited his pal Moss Hart's vast estate in Bucks County, Pennsylvania. Contemplating all the improvements Moss Hart had made, Kaufman commented that he was seeing "what God would have done if He had the money."

I couldn't help wondering if Johnny had the money to support this huge operation—he had mentioned in passing that building the inn cost hundreds of thousands of dollars, and he has told me that he intends to plant another sixty thousand coffee trees on his land. I asked Johnny if any of his four children were interested in running Finca Lerida. "Well, one son finds the business appealing, but he doesn't want to go through the financial hard times that I have experienced," Johnny says.

Like many of the growers in Boquete, Johnny has made significant financial sacrifices to stay in the coffee business. These growers love coffee, and they love the way of life in Boquete, which provides them with a sense of place and a sense of the continuity between past and present that few North Americans possess. They are hopeful that, in the long run, prices for specialty coffee will stabilize at a high enough level to make coffee profitable. They have little to say about what will happen when coffee prices fall.

"How else but through coffee do we keep what we have not only for ourselves, but for the future?" asks Maria Ruiz when I meet with her in her small office looking out over the production area at her family's coffee business. "Coffee farms allow generations to maintain the land, and coffee farming is an activity that can hold our valley together; otherwise we will lose all that we have here: our history, our past, our homes and way of life. If we sell to the developers who come calling every day, what then?"

The Ruiz family has been growing coffee in Boquete for nearly one hundred years—one of Maria's grandfathers was a picker. Today the family processes seventy to eighty containers of high-quality coffee a year—close to three million pounds. They grow coffee on their own land and they buy coffee from independent growers with whom they partner. They own a café and they also roast coffee for domestic and overseas markets. Theirs is the very model of a quality-driven vertically integrated business.

Small and intense, with a heart-shaped face and dark hair and brows, Maria, forty-six, understands the coffee business in a way that runs deep and casts a light. Her PhD dissertation focused on creating social change. She says, "My subject was, how do you create change at the country level?" She undertook her work knowing that the Panama Canal would be nationalized in 2000. "I wanted to know how you take advantage of the change at the canal to set processes in motion that would benefit the entire society. I devised a theory of change that was sustainable," she says. In other words, her theory could be applied broadly, helping the government, coffee growers' groups, individual farmers, and businesspeople understand what steps to take to promote positive economic and social growth and development.

Maria believes that change can be facilitated. "You can create change if you observe and if you view events from a certain perspective. The main thing I learned was the role of language—how important the way we tell the story is." To explain what she means, she points to Martin Luther King's use of the language and stories of the Old Testament in encouraging African Americans, with their tradition of Bible reading and churchgoing, to rise up against oppression.

"Change has to come out of what people know," Maria says. "What you are comes out of the past. If that past is understood it is possible to see potentialities for the future. If it is not known, you can spend a lot of time spinning your wheels." While her words sound abstract, the kind of social change she promotes and her strategies for creating change are concrete and quantifiable.

An illustration of how Maria has put her theoretical understanding into action comes from the model program she designed to help a group of Ngobe Bugle Indians obtain organic certification for the coffee they grow on tribal lands. Maria hopes that this program will eventually be self replicating, with one member of the Ngobe community teaching others.

The Ngobe are central to Panama's coffee industry. Tens of thousands of them work as pickers and laborers in Panama and Costa Rica. Many live itinerant lives, moving back and forth between their own remote communities and the medium- and large-size farms where they earn cash wages.

The Ngobe speak Ngoberie. Many cannot speak Spanish or are not fluent in Spanish. Farming was not a large part of the tribe's traditional migratory way of life, and they do not pass farming know-how from one generation to the next. This lack of knowledge is a problem for their own coffee enterprises and for their growers who employ them. As a result of a series of lawsuits in the 1980s, the Ngobe tribe controls 100,000 acres of land on their own reservation, or comarca, high up in the mountains.

The Ngobe grow coffee on the comarca, but the quality is poor, says Maria. "They would bring this coffee down from the mountains, and they couldn't sell it. Some years, hundreds of thousands of pounds of it was thrown out." Early efforts staged by the Peace Corps and other development agencies to help the Ngobe improve coffee quality were pretty much a disaster. "It did no good to give them coffee trees that had been successfully grown in other regions where farmers use fertilizer that they didn't have and couldn't afford," Maria tells me. One such project "wasted time and energy for a decade before anyone realized the varietal the Ngobe were trying to grow was wrong for the area."

Maria used her understanding of how change happens to create a strategy for helping the Ngobe that avoids this kind of "tone-deaf" mistake. The first step was understanding the people she was trying to help. "You have to pay attention," she says. "When you are trying to bring about social change, one size definitely does not fit all." For example, "in a family system like the Ngobes, where everyone works, you have to make sure that every family member has a place in the plan you devise, including the youngest and the very oldest."

The Ngobe's farming practices were already organic by default. But to win organic certification they needed to be able to document that their agricultural practices conform to organic standards.

"They have no written language, so I had to figure out how we could get them to create some sort of permanent record of farming practices relating to the organic system so that they can apply for organic certification. We decided to use digital cameras that recorded the date of pictured events," Maria says. But she couldn't just deliver a speech, hand out a bunch of digital cameras, and expect Ngobe farmers to begin documenting their agricultural practices.

First Maria had to teach the teachers. Maria created a seminar for the Peace Corps and other volunteers who work with the Ngobe, designed to help them understand the worldview, history, and mentality of the Ngobe. Most of the volunteers didn't understand her approach the first time she presented it. So she presented the same seminar three times. Only when the volunteers understood how the Ngobe experience the world could they become effective trainers.

Gregory Landrigan, a Peace Corps volunteer who lived for two years in a Ngobe village that is a two-hour walk from the nearest town, attended Maria's seminars. The first time he heard her talk about the Ngoberie, he found what she was saying incomprehensible. After he attended her seminar a second time, he started to get her point. "Language issues are bigger than people think," Greg tells me, when I ask him what he learned. "It's not just the words people don't understand. It's the concepts and the whole approach. The Ngobe are not used to learning by words. Their system of learning is kinesthetic. They learn by copying body moves. They learn by doing. It took me a long time to understand this," Greg admits.

Once the Peace Corps volunteers were on board, the program to help the Ngobe gain organic accreditation was able to proceed. "The participants take a series of pictures that are dated. They can look at these pictures and see how change happens over time," Maria says. The pictures document the Ngobes' process for organic certifiers, and they also show Ngobe farmers the impact of certain agricultural practices. "They can see with their own eyes how the plants grow over time, how pruning, for example, is done and how it benefits coffee plants. They can see what red cherry looks like." Furthermore, the cameras are not expensive.

"The underlying attitude of my approach," says Maria, is respect. "You have to accept, and not just on a theoretical level, that each person and group has their own worldview that is legitimate." And then you have to find a way into their system that is both respectful and effective.

Maria's theory is applicable to the central problem I saw played out time and again during my year traveling to origin.

Everywhere I went, the question was the same: how do you encourage smallholders and laborers to change how they pick and process cherry in order to produce coffee that deserves the specialty label? This is the same problem that Geoff is struggling with in Nicaragua with the growers from Las Brumas, that Menno is struggling with all over Ethiopia, and that Peter confronted in San Ramon. It's the central issue in virtually every coffee-growing locale. Outsiders come in making suggestions about how coffee should be grown, but they do not necessarily understand how their message is received.

Talking with Maria about her work broadened my understanding of the specialty coffee business, and my understanding of the problem the coffee guys are facing. Maybe the problem isn't the recalcitrance of tradition-bound farmers and laborers. Maybe a part of the problem resides with the specialty buyers themselves. According to Maria, to help a farmer grow better coffee and earn a better living, you need to understand how he understands the past, how he perceives himself, and how he perceives you as an outsider. Without that comprehension, you can't impact his behavior.

It was time to find out more about Geisha at the source. I had never met the Petersons or even seen a real Geisha plant up close, so I was extremely pleased when owner Price Peterson invited me to have lunch with his family at Palmira, the idyllic dairy farm where he and his wife Susan live. Rachel Peterson, who markets the Petersons' coffee, is in town for the competition. She lives in Puerto Rico with her two children—it is spring break—and all three are staying at Palmira. Daniel Peterson, the family farmer, is married and lives with his wife on the other side of town; he joins us for lunch too.

I drive up to Palmira with an old friend of the Petersons, David Roche from the Coffee Quality Institute. David has spent a lot of time in Panama. I pepper him with questions that seem to drive him crazy. At one point when I ask about the per capita income of Panama, he yells at me that he is an agronomist, not an economist. Though I don't like being yelled at, I can see his point about all the questions, and I have to admit he maneuvers his rental car, a sprung Corolla, like a master as we traverse the endless, winding, pothole-riddled dirt road to the Peterson manse.

Soon after we arrive, Rachel, David, and Daniel go off to cup coffee in the Petersons' luxe wood-paneled cupping room, a top-floor addition to the sprawling white frame farmhouse, where, on clear days, you can see all the way to the Pacific, an hour's car ride away.

Price, who is tall and elegant with white hair and an easy sense of authority, leads me on a tour of his Mendel's garden. Here, perched on a high meadow facing the mountains, he is experimentally growing coffees that are genetically related to Geisha. "It's only recently, in the past fifteen years or so," he explains to me, that research into the genetics of coffee has been undertaken, "because up until then, we had so little genetic material to work with."

Price and Susan have lived at Palmira for more than thirty years. Both, in Price's words, grew up as "city kids" who knew nothing about farming. Price's father, a banker, bought Palmira in the 1960s, thinking he would retire there. But it turned out that he hated retirement and cared little for farming. In the early 1970s Price was a tenured professor at the University of Pennsylvania, but he and Susan had wanderlust.

"We came down here several summers and really enjoyed the place. My father's frustration with the farm was growing." Price and Susan decided to make a break with the past and take up farming. "When I told the chairman of my department at Penn that I was resigning and moving to Panama, he said, 'We'll hold your job for a year; I am sure you will be back.'

"We had no experience as farmers, which turned out to be the biggest plus because we didn't come here and try to do things the way they were done in the States. We had the sense to learn from our neighbors here." At first, the couple raised cattle and grew vegetables. They switched to dairy farming, a business that proved to be lucrative, and twenty-five years ago they started growing coffee as well. The dairy operation still supports their coffee enterprise, despite Geisha's huge success, though the coffee business has been inching toward profitability since 2005.

Price points out the three dozen or so carefully labeled coffee varieties growing in his experimental garden, urging me to look at one with reddish bronze-tipped leaves. Then he tells me something that blows the dust balls in my brain out my ears: it is Price's belief—his theory—that the Geisha that has made Hacienda La Esmeralda famous is not the same plant as the Geisha that is described in the early historical record. In other words, there are two Geishas, not one.

Price explains this two-Geisha theory, noting that "an early botanical description referred to the cultivar from Gesha as having bronze-colored new leaves, a poor liquor (inferior taste in the cup), and considerable fungal resistance. The Panama Geisha has green-colored new leaves, a very good taste in the cup, and is resistant to leaf rust, but not Ojo de Gallo (rooster's eye) fungus, the killer Costa Rican and Panamanian coffee farmers most dread."

The old Geisha and the new one do not resemble one another, but no one knows when or how one tree replaced the other. What Price calls "a good chain of custody" traces Geisha's possible path out of Ethiopia and around the world to Panama. "But only a detailed DNA analysis will reveal the truth of this mysterious paternity case," says Price.

The research all indicates that the Geisha story began in 1931 with a British consul entering the forest near Gesha in southwest Ethiopia and collecting coffee seeds or beans. Apparently some of these seeds were sent from Ethiopia to Kenya in 1932. In 1936 in Lyamungo, in Tanzania, there is reference to a Geisha tree, apparently from the consul's batch of seeds that is identified as VC496. It looks like someone sent seeds from VC496 to Costa Rica in 1956, where a new generation of Geisha trees was grown. Sometime in the 1960s, Geisha seeds were sent to Panama.

A French biologist named Jean-Pierre Labouisse, who worked at the Ethiopian Institute of Agricultural Research in Jimma, Ethiopia, from 2004 to 2006, checked official records there and came up with this "chain of custody."

It was Labouisse who discovered that there are three different towns in southwest Ethiopia where Geisha might have evolved. There is Gesha in the province of Kaffa, district of Kefa. There is a second Gesha in the province of Kaffa, district of Maji and Goldiya. And there is a third town, Gecha, in the province of Illubabor.

Labouisse's most startling discovery, however, concerns how the original Geisha seeds were gathered. In a February 2006 email to Price, he wrote that the British consul who went out into the forest collecting coffee seeds in 1931 "probably collected them in bulk from different trees." Meaning that from the very beginning, seeds from different trees were bulked together and labeled "Gesha."

Price picks up the story. "I looked up the British consul to this part of Ethiopia. He turned out to have been quite a character and swashbuckler. His colleagues accused him of stirring up the natives and always wanting drama. Thus," continues Price, "the consul's notion of collecting seeds 'in bulk' probably consisted of getting seeds from numerous trees in the area of the village. From what I understand of coffee in Ethiopia, it is very unlikely that many trees would have been from the same cultivar, so he probably collected at least several cultivars and mixed the seeds together." Which would provide an explanation for how two trees with different traits and characteristics that followed the same route from Africa to the New World both came to be called Geisha.

Genetic science is beginning to provide at least partial answers to some of the identity questions Hacienda La Esmeralda's lovely little Geisha bean raises. Thanks to an advance made in plant genetics, it is possible to determine how the plant evolved. Using a genetic technique called amplified fragment length poly-morphism, biologists in France and Costa Rica wrote in a paper published in 2002 that they had created an evolutionary tree for coffee that enabled them to tell how different coffee cultivars evolved and where one split off from another.

The team of scientists created their tree using some thirty-five to forty coffee cultivars, including the two—Bourbon and Typica—from which all coffee in the New World is descended. Most of the varieties on their tree came from Ethiopia.

Trying to explain how this works, Price says, "Imagine a tree with fifty branches spread out from left to right. Way over on the left you have the New World coffee varieties. Bourbon, Typica, and all hybrids bred from them. These coffees are all very closely related and all evolved within the past couple of thousand years.

"Then you have the rest of the Ethiopians spread out left to right. These coffees evolved tens of thousands of years ago at the minimum, and probably far longer ago than that. When you go two-thirds of the way to the right on this tree where the coffees from Ethiopia are located, you see Geisha and around Geisha you see half a dozen interesting-looking coffees that are genetically similar."

These are the coffees Price is growing in his experimental garden. "We obtained the seeds for them from Costa Rica's Tropical Agricultural Research and Higher Education Center

[CATIE]. We have germinated them, transplanted them, and now we are growing them in a field. The point is to find coffees that taste even better than Geisha, or that are genetically similar, taste just as good, but have larger yields. Maybe we will discover that all of these coffees are genetic losers and we will discover that Geisha is a genetic oddball," says Price. Or maybe they will hit pay dirt.

"So far we have only had the chance to work with around thirty-five varieties. What we are hoping to do next is extend the AFLP analysis from thirty-five to all eight hundred Ethiopian cultivars in the CATIE collection." To do so, Price will need to forge a relationship with a research laboratory or university. It is not clear how such work would be funded, and to date Price has not been able to move forward.

As he finishes speaking, Price turns to show me one of his sample coffee plants—E-238, from the evolutionary tree. "This one is interesting," Price says, showing me a row of green and shiny plants twice as tall and bushy as those in adjacent rows. "This one just took off like a bat out of hell, growing like mad. Could be it turns out to be a winner. Or maybe not. We won't know anything for a couple of years, until it matures and we can harvest its cherry and cup the result."

Price and I go into the house for lunch. Sitting at the Petersons' large round table, David Roche remarks that Geisha has completely changed the nature of genetic research in coffee. Up until now, he says, coffee research was about finding varieties that were resistant to disease and that had higher yields, such as Catimore, which was created in Brazil's research lab, and RuiRui11, the hybrid it took researchers in Kenya twenty years to create. "These two coffees are disease resistant, but less than optimal in the cup, although it is controversial to say so"—the Kenyans are very sensitive on the subject of RuiRui11, insisting that this high-yielding plant tastes as good as traditional Kenyan varieties, but few coffee guys agree. "Now, because of Geisha, the focus of genetic research is turning to taste," David says.

One of the subjects of great interest to David is the relationship of terroir to variety. Would Geisha grown in Kenya or Guatemala taste like Geisha grown in Panama? To date no one knows, although David is taking steps to remedy that lack, creating a research protocol that would have cuppers evaluate ten different varietals grown in ten different environments.

Price listens to David and then says, "I sometimes wonder, if we were producing this coffee in Ethiopia, would people think it was so unusual? Some people say that Geisha has the clean, brightly floral taste of a washed Yirgacheffe, but I am not so sure. Willem Boot told me that he has given Geisha to Ethiopians to cup and they have been surprised. They felt they had never cupped anything like it from their own country. I really don't understand," Price says. And that's the thing: no one understands. Not yet.

A few days later I join a group of judges from the Best of Panama competition on a tour of Jaramillo Farm led by Daniel Peterson. The distance from Palmira to Jaramillo is five miles as the crow flies—but when driving you have to go down one mountain and up another and it takes close to half an hour. The Geisha trees are planted on a hillside as steep as a ski slope.

After all the buildup, I find the look of the trees disappointing. Tall and rangy, their appearance strikes me as totally at odds with the gorgeous language cuppers use to describe the coffee. It is as if the world's most luscious peach, a fruit so succulent its fragrance could make you mad, with juice that flows lasciviously down your naked arm, grew on a tall skinny pine tree among a lot of other tall skinny pine trees. When I say something to this effect to Daniel, who is tall, fair, and big-boned, he looks startled and a little hurt, as if I had said his firstborn had rickets. "The plant looks different from other coffee trees, that's for sure," Daniel says. "It's long and slender, and so are its beans." To make sure I didn't miss the point, he says, "This is a very special tree. It thrives where other plants just wither and die. For two or three weeks in January winds gusting up to sixty or seventy miles an hour smack these trees without harming them."

Geishas grow twelve or fifteen feet high, but in order for sunlight to penetrate, they require more space between them than other coffee plants. Their height and the steep hillsides on which they grow make them hard to care for. Pruning is a nightmare—the tall trees require ladders, but ladders don't hold steady on steep hillsides. On Geisha branches there are three-inch gaps between the nodules where cherries appear. It all adds up to a tree that produces maybe 50 percent as much coffee as a hybrid.

Some people call Daniel's discovery of Geisha an accident, but there was more talent, persistence, and work than luck involved. When Price purchased Jaramillo Farm, Daniel undertook a systematic study of all the plantation's coffee trees. He discovered Geisha at fourteen hundred meters—forty-five hundred feet—growing in a field with several other low-yielding varieties he thought might thrive at higher elevations. He cupped them all. "At fourteen hundred meters Geisha's flavor didn't show up consistently. Sometimes it was good and sometimes it was bitter. We had four varieties to choose from. Geisha won our hearts. I had high hopes on the basis of cupping. We harvested eight different locations over two years. The result wasn't consistent until we hit the right altitude. When we harvested it in this microclimate, we knew: wow, this is good."

At first Daniel pruned his Geisha plants by lopping off the top—that struck him as the easiest way to go—but it didn't work out. Now he is pruning selectively, using labor-intensive methods. "We are still learning about this plant."

Daniel uses synthetic fertilizers on the Geisha trees, but no insecticides. Fungicides, used selectively, are a must because the microclimate where Geisha grows is very wet. He adds chicken manure to improve the soil texture. Hacienda La Esmeralda is Rainforest Alliance—a certification that allows farmers to use some synthetic fertilizers, but not the twenty or so toxic chemicals, including DDT, on the "dirty dozen list." "Luckily in coffee we don't have to use insecticides," Daniel says.

Geisha is sun-dried on a patio, and then it is demucilaged without fermenting, a method Daniel reports that "is used in most of Panama and is now being adopted elsewhere because it is safer than fermenting.

"Fermenting is risky. If it's 2:00 a.m., the coffee is fully fermented and it's time for it to be washed [washing away the mucilage], but your foreman decides to wait until morning because he doesn't want to stick his hands in the ice-cold water. Basically there is nothing you can do. Your coffee is ruined and you are screwed," Daniel explains.

"The nonfermenting technology we're using to get rid of the mucilage is ten years old. For the longest time our buyers would not accept processing without fermenting. Then we did a blind cupping and coffee that had been demucilaged without fermenting cupped better."

Not everyone agrees with Daniel and the other Panamanian growers that fermentation contributes little or nothing to the taste of high-quality coffee. When I ask Peter Giuliano the to-ferment-or-not-to-ferment question, he tells me he believes that "done properly, fermentation adds a beautiful dimension to coffee." In his opinion, skipping this step gives Panamanian coffees, even Geisha, a "neutral" quality. Fermentation can add depth and interest to coffee, though he admits there is a down side. "If the tank is dirty or the fermentation process goes on too long, it can make coffee taste like Dumpster juice."

Not fermenting uses less labor than fermenting, and labor costs are definitely an issue in Panama, where the minimum wage is ninety-four cents an hour and rising. Rachel later tells me that, in the height of harvest season, which runs from November through March, one thousand laborers and their families, most of them Ngobe Indians, live on the family's two coffee farms in Jaramillo and Palmira.

The Petersons, like other growers, provide housing, kitchen facilities, bathrooms, health care, and an extensive list of social programs, plus food. Pregnant or nursing moms can eat at the day-care center, where parents can safely leave babies and small children while they work. The day care center is staffed with certified teachers. Conditions in mountains where the Ngobe live are extremely tough by anyone's standards, and they can get medical treatment at the Petersons' farms.

"We also have a program where some Jesuits come and stay up here as part of their training, and that's helpful too. Pickers earn upwards of $1.75 for picking thirty pounds of ripe cherry; laborers picking Geisha get two or three times that to encourage them to pick only the ripest fruit and to compensate them for Geisha's low yield. For pruning, maintenance, and other work, workers earn 10 or 15 percent above the minimum wage."

To put these labor costs into context: Geisha accounts for only 4 percent of the family's coffee production. While the auction lot of Geisha sold for $130 a pound in 2007, most Geisha that year sold for $12.50 a pound—this relatively low price was set before the auction. In 2007, the Petersons sold their other high-quality specialty line—Diamond Mountain—with cupping scores that ran from 84 to 88 (on a scale of 100) for around $2 a pound. Most of their third line of specialty coffee, with cupping scores in the 82–83 range, was sold to Starbucks for a price above Fair Trade.

Selling coffee in this lower range, Rachel tells me, "often doesn't cover the cost of our production and our social programs. The teachers we pay, the food, the medical costs, scholarships to kids with passing grades, plus extra payments called bonuses that growers are required to provide twice a year. When buyers fight us for pennies, they never think that they're taking money from our pickers. But they are. There's just not enough to go around. If producers don't cover costs, you know social programs go first," she says. Her words underline what Geisha, with its alluring promise of dollars pouring into growers' coffers, means to the residents of this resource-rich, income-challenged community.

The Best of Panama Competition begins officially at 9:00 a.m. on Wednesday and runs through Saturday afternoon. The Panamanian growers are big-hearted hosts. At midday on Wednesday, Thursday, and Friday, they truck two dozen visiting judges, ten or twenty locals, and me up and down the mountains for outings and lunches at farms or natural wonders. Every evening there is a party. On Thursday Johnny Collins and Zoraida host a buffet dinner at Finca Lerida. Cocktails and hors d'oeuvres are served on the flagstone patio overlooking the mountains. As the evening grows cool, we move inside for dinner. I fill my plate and find a place on a couch next to Rachel. We talk about ourselves, our families, the challenge of raising sons. I had watched Rachel during the cuppings on Wednesday and Thursday. She's a Q Cupper, meaning she has passed a very rigorous series of sensory and cupping skills tests, and the Panamanian growers and the members of the international judges' panel seemed to take her comments seriously. She strikes me as smart and friendly, but guarded. Sitting and talking, some of that guardedness falls away.

The next evening, another party. This one is at the superglam home of grower/entrepreneur/coffee industry leader Ricardo Koyner, who owns several coffee farms, a small chain of cafés, a commuter airline, and a bus line. High in the hills, with a broad verandah, sweeping vistas, and burnished surfaces, the house glitters and gleams. There's live music. Impeccable service. Abundant food and drink. I stand in front of the buffet table tasting this and that and chatting with Wendy de Jong, a small, slim woman in a gauzy white shirt who is cutting a swath through the food. Wendy is director of coffee for Tony's Coffees, and she's based in Bellingham, Washington.

Wendy tells me she was the only female coffee professional who took part in Willem Boot's expedition to the three Geshas in Ethiopia. She had traveled there to attend a coffee conference organized by Willem for U.S. AID that introduced Ethiopian coffee professionals to Western buyers.

Across the room we see Menno Simons, the Ethiopian "sourcer," also serving as a judge in Panama.

"I traveled with him in Ethiopia. He's a good guy," I say.

"He's a good guy, all right, but I want my coffee, and I can't seem to get a straight answer from him about when it might arrive," Wendy says, not hiding her annoyance. She bought a lot of coffee from Menno through Royal Imports. "Organic and Fair Trade. I don't have any idea when I might see this coffee," she says, adding that she has been planning to use these coffees in her blends.

"What do you mean?" I ask.

"Well, I ordered coffee from him in February when the harvest was already complete. It's mid-April, and the coffee hasn't arrived. So far as I know it hasn't even been shipped."

Ric Rhinehart, from Groundwork in Los Angeles, joins us. He's the head judge in Panama.

"Me too," Ric says, responding to Wendy's comments. "I want my damned coffee. I ordered natural and washed Yirgacheffes from Menno. I need that coffee."

Turns out Wendy and Ric aren't the only roasters waiting for Menno's coffees. I later learn that Peter, Geoff, and Duane all ordered containers of Ethiopian coffee from Menno in February, and in the middle of April none of the orders have been shipped.

You'd think the woman who markets the most expensive coffee in the world would enjoy a competition that three years in a row has brought her family fame and fortune. But she does not. During the Best of Panama Competition, Rachel confides that she's filled with the unpleasant premonition that this year her family's coffee is going to lose.

Hacienda La Esmeralda's Geisha had come in first for the past three years, selling at auction in 2006 for $50 a pound green, which is another way of saying wholesale—forty times the going price for specialty. Since Esmeralda appeared on the scene, the coffee world has been counting the Petersons' "riches"; few paid much attention to the fact that only the auction lot—approximately one thousand pounds in 2006—had sold for $50 a pound. Thirty percent—$15,000—of the $50,000 the top Geisha microlot earned was returned to the Specialty Coffee Association of Panama to defray the costs of staging the auction.

This year, 2007, Rachel is pretty sure Hacienda La Esmeralda's Special Geisha will be dethroned by the other Geisha grower, the one who didn't put his name on his coffee, because, in her words, his plan is to "jump out of the box and shout 'gotcha!'"

Boquete is a small place, and most coffee people have a pretty good idea who this farmer is. At least they think they do. He is a guy who had come to Boquete from Spain with less than nothing and scratched his way to the top—not the most popular fellow in town, though he has his friends and supporters.

Rachel, forty, tall and fit with blond hair pulled back in a ponytail and small gold hoops in her ears, looks like the kind of well-born person one would expect to go home with the trophy. Rachel has been marketing the family's coffee for just one year, during which she raised prices 40 percent. She's gutsy, but her courage must come at a cost because when the subject is coffee, her family's coffee, her anxiety is palpable.

Rachel plays soccer three times a week in a league, so she has an athlete's familiarity with winning and losing. Intellectually, she is fine with losing. "You have to lose sometime," she tells me, adding, "My father and brother desperately want to win this year, but I don't see it like that." But as the week progresses, and the two Geishas on the table battle it out for the judges' affections, Rachel looks increasingly tense. Money, international attention, publicity, status, and pride are at stake.

During the competition, thirty-one coffees are judged by the international panel. As in the Cup of Excellence in Nicaragua, competition coffees in Panama are cupped blind; coffees are assigned numerical codes so no one will know who grew what coffee. But skilled cuppers—and Rachel is a very skilled cupper—don't need a nametag to identify their own coffee or that of their neighbors. And when the coffee in question has the distinct flavor profile of Geisha, even an amateur like me can pick it on the cupping table. It's not so easy, however, to differentiate one Geisha from another.

The first Geisha that appears on the cupping table on the first day of the national competition blows the panel away. Ric turns to the judges sitting at the table at the SCAP headquarters upstairs from the cupping room. He asks for the judges' comments on the coffee and then goes around the table. Judges give it a numerical score and then describe what they have tasted: "Anise, ouzo, syrupy, black pepper, gorgeous gardenia/peppery, raspberry, honeydew melon, apple, like Yirgacheffe, natural Ethiopian, strawberry jelly, apricot, pineapple, basket of fruit."

The scores: 93, 95, 92, 93, 94, 95, 99.25, 95, 92, 90, 90, 93, 93.5, 94, 96, 95, 92, 91.5, 95, 92.5. One judge gives it an 89.

Ric later tells me that the coffee tasted like the finest unwashed Yirgacheffe. He didn't think that first Geisha was Rachel's.

The next afternoon, when the other Geisha comes up for consideration, it earns twenty-five scores above 90, but the numbers aren't quite as high or the compliments quite as over the top.

The coffee is described as silky, floral, crystalline. Clearly it is a superlative coffee, but it seems to have less of the old comic book *pow*! than the first Geisha.

Rachel agrees with Ric that the first Geisha probably belongs to the other grower. She's not sure, though. Part of the confusion stems from the shortcomings of the Petersons' home roasting machine. It isn't very good, and no matter how often Rachel and Daniel roasted and tasted Esmeralda samples before the competition, they weren't happy with the results. Geisha, like most specialty coffees, is very roast sensitive. In the competition, all the coffees are roasted on small high-quality Probat roasters. Rachel and Daniel had no idea how their Geisha would taste when it was optimally roasted.

Daniel shares Rachel's worries. "I think we have been out-Geisha'd," he comments.

The competition finals take place on Friday and Saturday, during which the sixteen coffees with the highest scores are recupped. On Saturday afternoon, the eight coffees with the highest scores are cupped one last time to determine which coffee will come in first, second, and so forth. These are the coffees that will be sold during the online auction. A huge crowd shows up at SCAP headquarters to hear the judges discuss the top contenders. The scuttlebutt indicates that the two highest-ranking coffees are the two Geishas—some of the judges think a third high-scoring coffee is a Geisha blend, but Johnny Collins tells me this is not so. Everyone seems confounded by the mystery of the two Geishas.

"How are you doing?" I ask Rachel before the judges begin their final discussion.

"Only so-so," she answers.

During the final round of judging, the two Geishas seem to have changed places. The first Geisha on Saturday afternoon is the less dramatic one, the one that Rachel, Daniel, and Ric have identified as probably belonging to Hacienda La Esmeralda.

The scores are excellent: 90, 95, 92, 92, 91, 92, 96, 91, 93, 94, 93, 94, 93, 91, 90, 93, 92, 96—that high score belonging to Ric.

"Good Geisha," someone says.

"Was this the first Geisha or the second Geisha?" another judge asks.

No one knows. The judges, too, are confused about the Geishas.

"Lovely coffee, bright, clean, acidic. Needs a little more fragrance and body, but really, really wonderful..."

And then comes the discussion of the Geisha with out-of-the-ballpark scores: 94, 95, 94, 96, 97, 96, 95, 96, 93, 93, 95, 98—that from Willem Boot—94, 96, 94, 92, 100. 100! You don't see that very often.

"Syrupy and sublime."

"Big fat juicy, grapey, love it, fabulous, more body, more ripe berry..."

Once again, for the judges, God has appeared in a cup of coffee.

The Panamanians start handing out beers to the judges. The competition is over. If you are a grower, there is nothing to do but go home and wait until the banquet later that night to find out the names of the winners.

At the banquet that evening, Rachel takes a seat beside me. "We've had a good run. We can win next year," she says, sitting down next to me. Dressed in black silk pants and a beaded top, Rachel asks if it is okay if she hides out at our table, far from the podium. "If they call our name for second place, I refuse to go up and receive the plaque. Daniel can do it," she says, smiling wickedly. So much for her being okay with losing.

We eat dinner. We drink wine. We wait for the chairmen of the event to thank each resident of Boquete—fifteen thousand people—personally. That's what it seems like, anyway. Finally the winners are called to the podium, in reverse order as in the Miss America pageant.

Number Fourteen. Number Thirteen...Number Three.

Number Two. The second-place winner is...NOT the Petersons.

They've done it again. The first-place winner is Hacienda La Esmeralda's Special Geisha. Rachel shouts. Daniel shouts and throws up his arms. They've won four out of four.

A month later at the closed online auction for wholesale buyers, Hacienda La Esmeralda's Special Geisha sells for $130 a pound green. Wholesale. The price is simply unheard of. But people in the specialty business understand that the Petersons' run won't last forever.

In two years, grower Graciano Cruz had told me when I was in Panama, "everything will totally change. There will be five more Geishas in the auction. After that, fifteen Geishas, maybe twenty. When we get them all together it will be a fire test of microclimates."

Talking on the telephone a few weeks later with Geoff Watts, he says, "Everyone in Panama is planting Geisha. It reminds me of the classic fight scene in the movie *Star Wars*...where all these clones come out to fight. I wonder what will happen to this market."

PORTLAND, OREGON

ASK AMERICAN COFFEE LOVERS TO NAME THE SPECIALTY coffee capital of the United States and many will answer Seattle, the city that introduced Americans to the delights of espresso and is the birthplace of Starbucks, the commercial mother ship of specialty. Ask hard-core coffee geeks the same question and the cognoscenti may well name a Pacific Northwest city somewhat to the south of Seattle: Portland, Oregon, home to Stumptown Coffee, the specialty roaster and retailer that claims to possess the world's most expensive supply of coffees. Portland is also home to Sustainable Harvest, the socially conscious specialty importer, four print magazines that closely follow the specialty coffee industry—*Barista*, *Roast*, *Fresh Cup*, and *Imbibe*—and Bellissimo Coffee, the coffee consultants and trainers who teach specialty coffee wannabes from around the world the arts of café ownership and espresso making.

In Portland, specialty coffee is embedded in a lively culinary culture that celebrates all things local—microbrew beer; fine wines from the Willamette Valley vineyards; a cornucopia of fruits, vegetables, cheese, fish, and grass-fed meat from nearby farms;

and locally roasted coffee. Support for these local products crosses economic and generational divides. Hipsters and haute bourgeoisie are equally enthusiastic about Portland's burgeoning reputation as a culinary center. This sense of local ownership results in a Portland coffee culture that is enthusiastically embraced by local residents to a degree that is unimaginable in other cities. Where else, for example, would dinners pairing locally roasted specialty coffees with locally sourced delicacies be sold-out events two evenings in a row? These "pairing" dinners took place at Navarre, one of Portland's most highly rated restaurants, in August 2006. Navarre's chef and Stumptown owner Duane Sorenson planned the menu, which also included wine. At the dinner, Hacienda La Esmeralda Special Geisha Reserve from Panama was paired with *pain épices* (gingerbread) and goose pâté, Ethiopian Yirgacheffe was matched with foie gras and a terrine of serrano ham, and so on through a seven-course meal that joined Nicaragua's Los Delirios with candied beets and concluded with Ethiopian Sidamo served with hickory-smoked chocolate mousse. More recently a local Portland chef, another Stumptown customer, made a steak rub using ground Esmeralda. Matt Lounsbury, the company's operating chief, tells me, "Stumptown Coffee is completely intertwined with the city's 'eat local' foodie ethic."

People say the sun never shines in Portland, but when I visited in early May 2007 the weather was sunny and breezy, around 60 to 65 degrees—close to perfection. With all of Portland's charms, I figure it is a good thing the sun makes itself scarce eight or nine months a year. Otherwise Portland wouldn't be Portland. It would be L.A.

I arrive in time to drop my stuff at the Ace Hotel in the fast-gentrifying, funky downtown area locals call the Vaseline district (use your imagination). The Ace caters to run-of-the-mill business travelers like me committed to private bathrooms and to kids in ripped jeans and Chuck Taylors who share dorm-style digs. I peruse my room—spiffy clean, claw-foot bathtub, nice view of raffish street scene eight floors below—then dash off to meet Stumptown's boy wonder of espresso training, Stephen Vick, of the clever repartee, endless number of friends, and single diamond earring. I had met Stephen the year before in Nicaragua. A former barista champion from Seattle, Stephen, not yet thirty, is one of those alert and connected types who always know what's going on—a perfect tour guide.

I hand Stephen the keys to my rented red Camaro to begin a Stumptown tour of Portland, stopping at Stumptown's roastery and four out of five of its cafés—the fifth is located inside the Ace Hotel where I am staying. (Stumptown and the Ace fit together like puzzle pieces, and it is hard to tell where one company ends and the other begins.) Stephen serves up a constant, clever line of patter about all things Portland and Stumptown, explaining Portland's "urban growth boundary" that encourages the central city to grow up instead of out and the role Stumptown has played since its founding in 1999 in the city's redeveloped strategy that focuses on local business districts.

Even though the sun is still shining, it's dinnertime in the East and I am hungry. We head over to Rocket, a new restaurant that has been generating a lot of buzz. We eat on the rooftop patio overlooking the city's new aerial tramway, ordering a series of small plates. The first is a salad of tiny balls of avocado nestled in a constructed basket of shrimp—the dish, by ignoring the cliché of shrimp served in an avocado half, inverts expectations, which I soon realize is a Portland trademark. In this town, you get points for approaching subjects with a humorously contrarian eye, naming a restaurant Noble Rot, a coffee company Stumptown (paying homage to Portland's logging past), and an espresso blend Hairbender, after the former beauty parlor where it was first sold.

Eco-consciousness is big in Portland. Bikes are big too. Portlanders proudly tell you their city has more miles of bike paths than any other city in the country. Bikes also figure prominently in the coffee-centric hipster culture that thrives in Portland and elsewhere—I learn this when Stephen describes the bicycle-powered espresso machine at the annual Burning Man festival held in the Black Rock Desert in Nevada, where the espresso bar is 125 feet long.

After dinner we stop off at the Stumptown Café located in the downtown business district. This store is pretty swish with a huge glass art installation filling the long wall across from the bar that serves wine and beer as well as coffee. We share a Rodenback fermented sour Belgian ale. I think I could get into this Portland lifestyle, pairing civic virtue with fine food and drink.

The next morning at the Ace, room service delivers Stumptown coffee to my room in a carafe on a tray with a scone and a little card reading, "Rwanda Musasa—Pineapple juice. Meyer lemon. A lush floral character." The Ace Café is located right off the lobby where half a dozen twentysomethings take advantage of the Wi-Fi night and day. Luxuriously paneled in dark wood, Stumptown's Ace Café is outfitted with four Clover brewing machines. These nifty one-cup-at-a-time machines cost $11,000 each. With the high-tech Clover, the barista can customize all the operations related to brewing. Installing four of these stainless steel beauties in one café is the act of a showman—to date no other café in the country has four Clovers. It's Duane's equivalent of Tarzan's jungle cry.

The Clover, which hit the market in 2006, was designed by three young guys from California—recent graduates of Stanford. As of early 2008, two hundred Clovers had been sold worldwide. The pricey machine has developed something of a cult following. Certain fans have greeted it with the enthusiasm of the devout contemplating The Rapture. After millennia, they say, brewed coffee has its rightful due—a brewing system that is as sexy and arcane as the beloved La Marzocco espresso machine handcrafted in Florence.

Made of stainless steel with curved edges, the Clover is well designed but not earth-shattering—it resembles a Saab more than a Maserati. The size of a small television with a built-in computer that allows the user to program time, turbulence, and temperature, the Clover sits on the counter facing the barista. On its top is a round aperture, six inches across. Ground coffee lands in this opening and is sprayed with hot water. Then the wet grinds are sucked down into a vacuum chamber—the force of the vacuum propels the coffee through a filter and out the bottom of the machine into a cup. The whole operation takes about a minute.

Duane has championed the Clover because in his opinion, it does a better job than other brewing methods of highlighting the subtleties in each coffee, particularly single-origin microlots. With the Clover, he says, "you get more of the delicate and floral flavors, the subtle sweetness, the notes of perfume and citrus."

Stumptown's operations and marketing guy Matt Lounsbury reports that the Clover has "helped to lure customers to drip coffee away from espresso." Matt sees the Clover's one-cup-at-a-time feature as a huge plus because it forces Stumptown customers to choose among different coffees. "We don't have a coffee-of-the-day brewed up and waiting in a carafe or thermos. Customers have to decide which of our thirty-five coffees—many of these from small microlots—they want to try. That gives us a chance to talk about our coffees. They pick one, and we brew a single cup just for them," he says, adding that the ritual of choosing and waiting for the coffee encourages customers to really pay attention to the taste of what is in the cup.

Jeff Jassmond runs Stumptown's open-to-the-public cupping room—the Annex—where customers wanting to buy whole-bean coffee are invited to come in and try different offerings.

"At the Annex we use the Clover to replicate as true an experience of the coffee as you get in a formal cupping. That's the benchmark," Jeff says. When Stumptown bought its first Clovers, Jeff continues, "baristas were wary, calling it a coffee robot, but it's not that at all. It's just a very precise tool that users can make good coffee with or mediocre, depending on how well they are trained."

Jeff has been surprised, though, by how difficult it has been to get the right Clover recipes to highlight each coffee. For some Stumptown coffees, it has taken him "fifty or one hundred permutations working with the grind, the extraction time and the dosage" to figure out what parameters deliver the optimal taste.

"Some people have complained you have to use a lot of coffee," Jeff says. "Every new coffee that comes in we tend to dose on the lower side, sometimes using as little as twenty-two grams for an eight-ounce cup. We do this because we don't want to waste coffee and out of respect for where the beans come from and for all the labor involved in growing it."

Regarding the Clover, he says, "We are learning as we go. We have been implementing changes to see how customers respond to different recipes. We want to find out if the age of the green coffee affects taste as well."

I was curious to hear what Peter would say about Jeff trying fifty to one hundred times to get the right Clover recipes for different coffees, so I called him up and asked. "You know how coffee guys are," Peter told me. "We love fiddling with brewing parameters. It's in our hardwiring. The Clover puts the controls right in front of you, so of course baristas will start fiddling and they get obsessed." Not that you need a Clover to go crazy, he adds. "You can go nuts fiddling with the variables for a French press too."

Still, Peter is a fan of the Clover. Great coffees, he says, should be brewed one at a time. "It isn't consistent with the specialty coffee aesthetic to pre-brew and store coffee in the kind of thermoses you see in gas stations, hotel lobbies, or bullshit coffee shops where they sell French Vanilla."

"The nice thing about Clover or the French press or that $20,000 halogen-powered siphon from Japan that they are using at the Blue Bottle Café in San Francisco—these brewing methods disorient the consumer. That's important because if we don't give the consumer a shock, then he or she just blindly walks into the coffee shop expecting the same old, same old. We've got to do something dramatic to alert them to the fact that this is a different kind of coffee shop selling a different kind of coffee. That's what the Clover does beautifully."

And in case this needs to be confirmed, the Clover makes a damn good cup of coffee. I usually drink my morning coffee with milk, but the Clover-made Rwanda Musasa delivered to my room at the Ace on a silver tray is too lively and delicious to adulterate. I don't get the flavor of pineapple that is promised on the little card, but the lemon and the florals come through with lovely clarity. The scone's not bad either—high-quality coffee retailers, all of them, obsess about the quality of their pastries, even the best of which lose freshness within a few hours, faster even than coffee.

After breakfast I walk over to the Pearl District, the downtown area adjacent to my hotel where the Fair Trade organic import company Sustainable Harvest is located in a beautifully renovated historical building known as the Eco Trust Building—the tenants are all ecologically minded. There I meet with Sustainable Harvest founder David Griswold, in his mid-forties, who is quick to unleash a rush of information: Sustainable Harvest is a for-profit importing company that sells almost ten million pounds of Fair Trade organic coffee a year, with gross revenues of $17 million and an operating budget of $1 million. The company spends roughly half what it earns—or about half a million dollars a year—on producer training and overseas offices to help farmers meet the standards of the specialty roasters. From his $1 million annual budget, Dave supports twenty-four employees in four offices across the world, including five agronomists in Latin America and East Africa who teach growers how to boost the quality of their coffee.

Dave talks in the excited coffee-mad manner of many young coffee guys. At first he seems a little full of himself, but his willingness to lift the veil on every financial detail related to the specialty trade is a positive and much more compelling trait. Using sophisticated software of his own devising, he has redefined transparency: all of his company's financial and importing data are on the Web. A farmer in Mexico who sells his coffee to an elite roaster such as Intelligentsia or Counter Culture, for example—with Dave as the importer—can follow the money trail online to see exactly who earns what as the coffee moves through the system from the farm to the mill in Mexico to the Mexican trucker to the Mexican warehouse to the container shipper to the port of New York to the warehouse in New Jersey and eventually to Counter Culture's roasting machine in Durham or Intelligentsia's in Chicago, and then out the door to wholesale customers who might pay $6 or $7 a pound for this coffee.

In my year of talking with the principals of a dozen elite roasting companies, no one has been as willing as Dave to divulge the nitty-gritty details of the coffee business. No one else (except Ric Rhinehart from Groundwork in Los Angeles) showed me financials or told me exactly what they were paying, what they were earning. Not one of the young specialty roasters that I followed around, for example, revealed that small companies like theirs do not generally finance or warehouse their own coffee purchases. Importers like Sustainable Harvest or Volcafe Specialty Coffee, based in Petaluma, California, finance the purchase of coffee; do all the logistics, including warehousing; and then release small amounts of coffee as needed, billing the specialty guys as they burn through the supply.

Dave identifies with the passion and excitement of the Third Wave guys, and thinks highly of their business model. Small roasters like Counter Culture, Intelligentsia, and Stumptown do not nickel-and-dime him to death, he explains. Like him, they believe coffee prices at the retail level must rise: Dave is aiming to break the $12 or $13 a pound retail ceiling, a must, he says, if coffee farming is to survive in Central America and elsewhere. This buy-high-sell-high model is difficult for the publicly traded specialty companies. High-volume specialty companies—he asks me not to name them—may want to be farmer friendly, but when push comes to shove they believe themselves to be legally compelled to serve their stockholders by buying low and selling high. While these companies may be entirely ethical, "generally the conversation moves toward finding ways of lowering costs and pushing down the margins we earn," Dave says. "It is the challenge of our current economic system, where buyers are pinned between the short-term pressures of Wall Street and their long-term interest in sustaining the poor farmers.

"This 'race to the bottom' makes it hard to compete, when our costs are compared to the big multinational import-export firms that don't provide the same direct relationship-based service. We are doing extensive training at the farm level and sending videographers to digitally photograph the work that goes on at origin. Our buyers can use this photography in-store to educate their retail customers, showing them where their coffee comes from and how it is grown"—telling a story that would help customers understand why high-quality coffee costs more, a position championed by small elite roasters but less common among larger ones. "The corporate buyers say, 'Yeah, yeah, Dave, you are great, but we need this price to come in close to the multinationals.'"

Where Dave takes issue with the elite specialty companies is in their attitude toward the cooperatives that represent groups of small farmers. He recognizes that the co-ops can be difficult to work with: "No one wants a story that has tones of gray," he says ruefully. Still, he believes the co-ops must be supported, rather than circumvented or eliminated, because they "provide twelve months of services to farmers in the areas of health, education, coffee agronomy, milling, and more. Cooperatives provide the social services in remote regions where government agencies often don't reach. If you close down the co-ops, farmers end up being sharecroppers instead of stakeholders," he says. In other words, when farmers operate as individuals and sell to private buyers who may or may not pay well, they do not have access to social benefits. As members of cooperatives, on the other hand, the growers are stakeholders in a larger entity and they can count on services being available to them in good years and especially in bad years when their needs are most desperate.

Dave believes the specialty guys have their hearts in the right place, but they don't always fully comprehend the historical and economic context at origin. He poses a question that takes on greater significance as the economy declines, transportation costs increase, and credit tightens in the months after my Portland visit. "If a specialty roaster were to go belly up, what happens to the farmers from whom he or she has contracted to buy? Sure, the roaster has promised to pay the farmers high prices in perpetuity, but what guarantee is that? Companies fail all the time, and without the benefits that a cooperative provides, what protection do the farmers have when times get tough?"

I go from global macroeconomics to Portland microeconomics, meeting up next with Matt Lounsbury, thirty, Stumptown's smooth-shaven operations and marketing chief, a self-described "former coat-and-tie guy" with an MBA. Matt's square-jawed, clean-cut good looks and pink shirt set him apart from all the skinny musicians with tattoos and multiple piercings who work at Stumptown during the day to support their "music jones."

Matt wants me to see one of Stumptown's wholesale customers, so we get together at Crema, a spacious, high-ceilinged, window-lined café and bakery located in the up-and-coming Burnside business and retail district.

He emphasizes Stumptown's connection to the local community, noting that independent cafés like Crema that sell Stumptown coffee, and the five Stumptown owned-and-operated cafés have helped to promote high-quality, people-friendly economic development in neighborhoods all over the city. Moreover, Stumptown promotes from within and it pays employees full benefits and a decent wage. "Our baristas are buying houses in the city and having babies."

As to the coffee, "We broke the record in seven countries for what we paid for coffee at auction." Stumptown, Matt is certain, roasts and sells coffee that is superior to anyone else's, but the company has no plans to go national. Growing too large is not the Portland way, he says.

"Our customers keep close tabs on us," Matt says. "If we get too big they'll gripe about our 'empire' expanding." In keeping with local preferences, Stumptown doesn't chase business and doesn't market. In fact, to hear Matt tell the story, Stumptown "antimarkets."

"We interview potential retail customers," he says, such as restaurants and coffee shops that brew and serve coffee. "We turn 'em down if they won't execute up to our standards, investing in equipment and training. We roast and deliver every day and insist that customers use our coffee within seven to ten days."

We stop by the Stumptown sales office located adjacent to the roastery. The roastery is spiffy. The office is a closet. One of the account people, Shari Bagwell, sporting elephant tattoos on her arms, approaches Matt with a problem.

Some bagel joint in Jackson Hole, Wyoming, a high end resort area in the mountains, wants to order fifty pounds of coffee. "They're bagel purists in the Stumptown sense," Shari says. "They don't have toasters. They want their bagels eaten on the day they are baked. They're willing to pay to overnight air freight the coffee."

"No go," says Matt. "I'm not shipping a random fifty pounds of coffee to people we don't know."

"I talked to these guys. They sound legit," Shari says.

"Okay," says Matt. "I will call them."

We climb back into the car and sit there as Matt dials Pearl Street Bagels in Jackson Hole. Matt is wearing a headset. I can only hear his side of the conversation.

"We don't do wholesale programs out of state," Matt says. "I suggest you call Zoka in Seattle…If you just do drip I am more inclined to sell to you.…Drip coffee showcase? Two stores. Fifty pounds of coffee in one week? French roast is our only dark roast.…What about your cleaning protocol? Wash down equipment after brewing?…Clean airpot? I don't mean offense, but we insist on seven-to-ten-day freshness. Awesome! We have broken the ceiling of what we paid to farmers in Guatemala. Finca El Injerto in Huehuetenango…The coffee's amazing. The grower is visiting us right now from Guatemala. I'll send you some information.…I would like to talk more. Keep me on your hot list. It goes out by 3:00 p.m.…You're the kind of guys we want to do business with."

In plain English, here's what Matt was saying: He started off this conversation doubting that a pair of bagel stores in Jackson Hole, Wyoming, could brew and sell fifty pounds of coffee in one week. Stumptown expects its customers to use its coffee fast—no storing coffee in a back room for months on end where it grows stale and will taste dreary.

When Matt learns that the café does not sell espresso, and that it features brewed coffee from a different elite roaster each week—that's the "drip coffee showcase" he mentions—he begins to believe the stores could use fifty pounds in one week, and his antipathy begins to wane.

Matt then asks about the café's cleaning protocol not only for its coffee-making equipment, but also for the airpots—the thermoses or carafes where brewed coffee is (briefly) stored before serving. Such containers keep the coffee hot without cooking it, unlike old-fashioned systems where the coffee was boiled to death on a hotplate. Matt later tells me, "Cleanliness is something we deal with every day. No matter how good the coffee, if the brewing system and the airpots aren't washed regularly with special cleaning products, you don't taste coffee; you just taste skuzzy airpot."

When Matt is satisfied that the Jackson Hole bagel store lives up to Stumptown standards, he changes his tune and becomes enthusiastic about selling coffee to them. "Keep me on your hot list" means he wants to be on their list of active suppliers. He is satisfied that it is a worthy customer who will do right by the coffee.

That evening at a party hosted by Stumptown at the Ace, I meet the farmers from Finca El Injerto who grew the fifty pounds of coffee Stumptown has just sent off to Jackson Hole. They are Arturo Aguirre Sr. and Jr.—the younger Aguirre, in his thirties, speaks English. His father does not. The father and son are in the United States for the annual SCAA convention that took place the previous week in Los Angeles. Afterward they flew up to Portland to visit one of their most important customers. When growers visit, Stumptown and the other high-end roasters often host informal get-togethers to enable their employees and best wholesale customers to meet them.

Daniel Peterson from Hacienda La Esmeralda, who visited Stumptown a few weeks after me, told me how helpful it was for him as a farmer to meet the end users of his product. "As a grower you are so removed from this end of the coffee chain. You have no idea how your coffee is being brewed and sold, who is buying it, what it means—you're really in the dark," said Daniel.

Arturo Jr. and Daniel are about the same age. After talking with them, it occurred to me that specialty coffee's Third Wave may encompass more than coffee buyers—maybe it also encompasses a generation of thirtysomething specialty growers who speak English and are coming to view their coffee not as a commodity but as a valuable artisan product.

Arturo tells me how grateful he is to Duane for giving him the opportunity to earn more for his coffee. "He taught us about cupping; now we have a cupping lab," Arturo says. "Our employees are learning how to cup....Duane keeps on pushing us to do more. Now we separate our 100 percent Bourbon from the other coffee varietals on our farm."

The reception room is crowded and noisy. Standing by the buffet, Shari Bagwell and I are talking with Arturo. Then someone pulls Arturo away, and Shari, who is small, spicy, and smart, puts Arturo's comments in context. Coffee has to be a profession because farms need capital to modernize. Coffee is labor intensive, but the labor supply is decreasing with people coming to the U.S....Many farmers in Guatemala are planting sugar for ethanol because it is easier to grow and sugar prices are increasing. If we can't increase what the farmers earn, there won't be any coffee farms left in Central America."

Mingling in the crowded Ace party room that evening was George Howell of Terroir Coffee in Acton, Massachusetts. George, one of the best known Second Wave guys, was a founder of Cup of Excellence. I had met him in Nicaragua, and I had visited his roasting plant in Acton. George and several other people had flown to Portland after the SCAA convention in Los Angeles—all these visits illustrating Stumptown's status as an important specialty coffee destination. George and Duane could not be more different in style or background. George, the Yale-trained New Englander, dreams of someday opening a café in Paris. Duane is the rock-and-roll bad boy of coffee. But these attributes hadn't kept these two who care so much about getting the details exactly right from striking up a friendship. Duane has taken George out to his favorite winemaker in the valley. Now George, who is old enough to be Duane's father, is willing to consider that the Clover coffeemaker that he has previously disdained might possibly have something to offer the specialty world.

Menno Simons is also in Portland, and he too is at the party drinking beer and hanging out. Menno still has not been able to get the Ethiopian coffees that were ordered months earlier by Stumptown, Counter Culture, Intelligentsia, Groundwork, and many other small roasters out of Ethiopia. But that doesn't put a crimp in his friendship with the Stumptown gang.

The party breaks up. The evening is mild and a group of coffee guys stand on the sidewalk in front of the Ace. I am talking with George and some other people, including a nerdy-looking guy in his thirties from Portland. He's a coffee aficionado, a coffee groupie, like a baseball Annie—without the sex. This guy studies specialty coffee like jazz lovers study the discographies of Miles Davis and Charlie Parker. He refers to all the coffee guys by name.

Peter. Geoff. Duane. Duane. Duane.

"Duane is God," he says.

The next morning I prepare myself for coffee roasting 101 with Joel Pollack, Stumptown's senior roaster, a minority stockholder who has since been bought out and is no longer with Stumptown. He says mass-market coffee companies roast coffee several hundred pounds at a time on automated machines that require little human intervention. Stumptown and the other high-end companies prefer to roast the old-fashioned way, roasting small batches by hand in refurbished cast-iron machines imported from Europe.

Stumptown's roasting machines are Probats from Germany that have been restored inside and out with the obsessive spit-and-polish that car enthusiasts lavish on antique roadsters. Probat tried to buy one of Stumptown's roasters—an antique from 1919—for its museum, but Duane wasn't selling. Stumptown's large machine, the one at the roasting plant, roasts coffee in lots up to one hundred pounds. The company also fires up a miniature Probat in a reinforced corner of its homey Division Street café for microlots of twenty-six pounds or less.

Specialty roasting is risky business. Get it wrong, and a lot of very expensive coffee goes up in smoke.

Coffee guys usually describe their roasters as resembling industrial-sized clothes dryers—only the coffee enters from the top and exits from a front hatch. All roasting machines have large drums where the coffee beans are tossed around in the heat. Most specialty roasters are dual fuel, meaning many of their functions are electric powered, but they "cook" with a gas flame that is easy to control and can be turned off instantly. Air inside the center drum is heated by gas to temperatures that may climb to 450°F; a set of electric-powered interior paddles tosses the coffee beans around to ensure even roasting.

Practitioners compare roasting coffee to popping corn. Green coffee, like unpopped corn, is full of water—between 9.5 and 13.5 percent of its weight is plain old H_2O. As heat drives the water out of the coffee beans, they do what kernels of corn do in a popper: they swell and expand. Pressure builds up along the groove that runs lengthwise down the coffee bean, and the bean, just like a kernel of corn, pops as it cracks open. The coffee does not explode, but it does burst its seam, providing roasters with the all-important "first pop." Papery detritus called chaff floats out of the bean as it pops. If the roasting is stopped there, it's considered a light roast. This showcases the flavors of floral coffees such as Geisha, which is generally roasted on the lighter side. Coffees for cuppings are also roasted lightly because darker roasting obliterates some of a coffee's innate characteristics.

After the first pop, the roasting process accelerates quickly and if the roaster does not pay close attention, he or she can easily ruin a batch of coffee. To monitor the process, the roaster pushes a long, narrow ladle into the body of the roaster and removes a spoonful of beans. He checks these for color and quickly shoves them back into the machine, repeating this procedure over and over while jockeying the controls to get the precise effect he seeks. A special device called an Agtron produces a constant reading of the roast intensity. As the coffee "cooks," it continues to expand. If left in the roaster, the beans will pop again—that's the second crack. Some specialty coffees are removed from the roaster before they crack a second time. Darker roasts require longer roasting time and undergo that second split.

Joel is roasting orders that will be delivered later in the day. "It's all about the curve of time and temperature," he says as he gracefully handles the small 1959 Probat. "As you approach the second crack you start to lose some of the citrus and floral flavors, so you have to step the temperature down, but you don't want to jolt it. If the temperature drops precipitously, we'll lose complexity.

"What we do is establish the large parameter with the first crack and the fine parameter with the second. We're looking for that balance between body and sweetness. In the high end near the first crack is the citrus and in the finish, a winey, syrupy sweetness" that is paired with the good acidity roasters value highly. Joel continues, "The point is to reveal the coffee's innate qualities....Roast too long and the coffee becomes generically chocolatey and sweet, loses acidity, and the complexity is reduced. It will taste like a cup of brownie for breakfast."

Between the first and second cracks, "you want the temperature to cascade gently down. You want it to smell sweet and complex. If it doesn't, something is weird in the lot, and then we have to cup it out to see what's going on. The beans expand as they roast. Steam marks the last bit of caramelizing going on inside the bean. Without that browning of the sugars the coffee will be underdeveloped in sweetness. You want to stretch the first and second crack out to extract different flavors.

"In the old days, we would never talk about roasting technique," Joel adds, somewhat surprised by his own openness, as if he is giving away state secrets.

Later Matt Lounsbury tells me there is another reason Stumptown doesn't broadcast too much information about its roasting recipes and techniques. "What we are after is the best results for each coffee. We try not to get sidetracked talking too much about our blends and how we roast them because coffees change all the time. We roast what is in season, and we are constantly changing, searching for the right roast profile for whatever green coffee is available that day or that week. People are always saying, 'Hey, the blend changed.' Of course it changed. I read stuff on the blogs where people go on and on about our blends and our roasting, extrapolating as if they knew what they were talking about. Basically, we would just rather not go there."

Back at the small roaster, Joel has finished roasting another batch of coffee. Coffee beans pour out of the drum onto the empty tray that he has cleaned with a small brush. "If you don't wipe it off carefully between roasting, it's like dumping fresh food into a dirty pan. You have to clean the tray very gently; you can't use anything smelly, anything that leaves residue." The beans go from the tray into a clean bucket. During the roasting process, they will have lost between 15 and 22 percent of their weight, a combination of moisture loss, the loss of volatile compounds, and a variety of chemical reactions, some of which, like sugar caramelizing, produce water and carbon dioxide as by-products.

"You need to use your senses to roast coffee," Joel says as he prepares another batch. "It's like fine baking or wine making. It is all in the feel and smell. You have to think about the cup, what effect you are you going for. A Sumatra, say—you want a chewier, full-bodied flavor. You roast for that."

More beans pour into the hot drum of the roaster. My nose wrinkles. The smell of green unroasted coffee is unpleasant.

"It smells like buttered popcorn made with slightly rancid butter," I say.

"No," Joel corrects me, "it smells like the burning silk of corn." He's nailed it.

"Sumatra," he adds, showing off by getting even more specific about coffee's unroasted odor, "smells like fish sauce steam coming out of the kernels."

We're almost at the first crack. Joel checks the coffee after eight and a half minutes, and he keeps checking it, removing a ladleful that he studies and shoots back into the machine. "You have to make sure the coffee is roasting, not baking. If it bakes, it will develop too slowly. It will take the acidity and aromas and send them up the chimney. Like sautéing onions. You want them caramelized, not burned or stewing."

I ask Joel why he doesn't check the machine's temperature readout.

"You have to learn to use your senses," he repeats.

"We never want to take what we do for granted. We have a meeting at Stumptown once a week to discuss roasting," he says. He describes the taste of different coffees. He enjoys giving me the example that Lake Tawar from Indonesia tastes like cannabis.

Actually, quite a number of people at Stumptown tell me with a smirk that Lake Tawar tastes like cannabis. Pot certainly seems to be a preoccupation around here.

The pot-coffee connection confounds me for at first. Conventional wisdom would say that pot is a slacker's drug. But the Stumptown people are focused, work long hours, and work really intently. They seem to be completely and insanely in love with what they do.

"It's about calibrating the uppers and the downers, balancing the caffeine with pot, isn't it," I ask Joel.

"There's a piece you've left out," Joel replies. "The beer. Portland has a really active microbrew scene. It's caffeine and pot and beer. Everyone in the Northwest is depressed. We get no sun all winter. We all suffer from seasonal affective disorder. Winter melancholy. The whole town is self-medicating."

Jim Kelso, Stumptown's "chief Liquorer"—its chief cupper—amends Joel's formula when we talk. "The balance is between caffeine, beer, exercise, cupping, and atomizing a six-foot bong."

Later that afternoon, I hang out with Stephen Vick in Stumptown's training kitchen, where he is teaching the owner and two senior people from the waitstaff of a soon-to-be-opened bistro how to make espresso and cappuccino. Learning to use the La Marzocco is like mastering the guitar. It's difficult, requiring superb hand–to-eye coordination, skill, knowledge, practice, and an ear for the "music" it makes. The servers get the basics fairly quickly. Like race car drivers, they start to become one with the machine. The bistro owner, though, is another story. He a bearish guy, grizzled, maybe sixty, and he describes himself as "a born klutz." You just hope he is never called upon to pull your espresso—the likelihood that he or someone like him will make your next restaurant cappuccino underscores why a lot of specialty guys think a busy restaurant is no place for an espresso machine.

Stephen talks about how important it is to wipe down the milk wand on the machine after frothing the milk. He talks about stretching the milk to incorporate air, describing what he calls its "jiggle and flow." During the training, the baristas-to-be make one cappuccino after another, using organic milk and beans from the world's most expensive coffee supply. The discarded drinks go right down the sink.

Next on the menu is beer. I am to meet Aleco Chigounis, Stumptown's green buyer at Stumptown's favorite hangout, the Horse Brass Pub, a legendary Portland joint on South Belmont. Stumptown has a lot of history with this crowded, wood-paneled bar that specializes in local brews. Horse Brass owner Don Younger gave Duane the money to start his company, and every Friday afternoon the entire Stumptown staff meets there for a "mandatory meeting." Duane picks up the tab for everybody's beers. It's a thing with Duane. He always picks up the tab.

By the time I make it to the Horse Brass it's close to 6:00 p.m. and the bar is jammed and noisy. Aleco, who turned thirty that week, is fair and of medium height with reddish thinning hair—in the specialty world, he's a rising star. Aleco is relentless and Duane affectionately calls him "a little bag of hammers," adding that "Aleco is excited to be the coffee buyer for the most spectacular coffee-roasting company in the world." (Coffee consultant Ann Ottaway once described Duane's confidence—or possibly his ego—as "something new in the universe; a thing to behold.")

Duane's comments about Aleco indirectly address the controversial matter of Aleco's hiring. Duane hired the young green buyer away from Ric Rhinehart at Groundwork in L.A. Ric, who has a knack for identifying talent, spotted Aleco in Costa Rica—brought him up from the minors, you might say. Knowing Intelligentsia was preparing to open a café and a roastery in Los Angeles—Groundwork's home base—and eager to strengthen his coffee program in order to compete better, Ric trained Aleco to be his coffee buyer and run his coffee program. Less than a year later, Duane hired him away. Ric is bitter about losing his top coffee guy at a time when Intelligentsia, the powerhouse of the high-end specialty world, is moving in on his territory. Aleco is abashed. "I love and respect the guy," he says of Ric, "but there was no way I was going to say no to Stumptown."

I had met Aleco briefly in Ethiopia, but we'd never really talked. I sit down on a barstool next to him, order a local brew, and ask a question or two. He's a talker. "Famous for being outspoken," he says, a trait that sometimes gets him into trouble. He moved to Portland three or four months ago. "Already I have more friends here than I have anywhere else I have worked. We drink together. Party together. This company is family."

Aleco grew up in Philadelphia. His father, a Greek immigrant, owned a successful coffee-roasting company. He learned the ropes working for his father's business. He lugged bags, painted walls, did sales. He learned to cup when he was fifteen. His father is a brilliant businessman, Aleco says, but his business is "very commercial. Price sensitive. A commodity business. Not that fun."

After college, Aleco moved to Costa Rica, where for four years he worked on the producer side of the table as an exporter. As part of his job he spent seven or eight months a year visiting farms and mills—his Spanish is fluent. (He also speaks Greek and some French.) "That's where my real coffee training began. I thought I had known about cupping coffee, but I knew nothing. I learned about defect. I learned how to pick up smaller nuances in coffee. To be really solid as a cupper, you need five years experience at least. I learn a new flavor in coffee all the time.

"There is a right and wrong in cupping," he tells me. "People say coffee cupping is subjective. It is not. Coffee is very objective. There is floral or not. Acidity or not. Sweetness or not. Coffee has body or it doesn't," Aleco says. "Some people get it, and some people don't."

"How do you stand the loneliness of being on the road so many months a year?" I ask.

"The allure for me is getting off a plane in Burundi or Peru and feeling energized, knowing I am going to go out and spend the next ten hours in a car or truck, stay at the crappiest place you have ever seen and eat guinea pig for breakfast, knowing I am going to have the opportunity to impact an entire community by making their product more valuable. It is an incredibly empowering thing. I can have an impact on a world stage," Aleco says.

We talk a little bit about Ethiopia, how confusing it is.

"I need to learn Amharic," Aleco says. "So I can understand what's going on. The industry is run by the government. The system is incredibly corrupt," he adds.

"Do we know that it is corrupt and not just inept?" I ask.

"They are taking money, and they are also fucked up," Aleco says. "Every coffee gets sold before it is cupped. They eventually get cupped before they leave."

"You mean Stumptown is buying coffee blind?" I ask.

"Everyone is buying coffee blind. We were just at the auction. There are six licensed exporters in Ethiopia who do all the buying at the auction," he says. "The relationships are set up ahead of time. You know what you are going to buy before the auction."

"If the coffees haven't been cupped, how do you know you are getting the right ones?"

"You don't," Aleco says. "The whole thing is a crapshoot."

"What role does Menno play in all this?" I ask.

"He is sourcing the best quality, and he is the one able to find it, but the reality is last year his coffees showed up two months late. This year it is already three months late, and the coffees are not here. I love him as a friend and respect him as coffee guy, but he is working in Malawi, Costa Rica, and Panama, and Ethiopia is such a huge beast in itself. He seems to have bitten off way more than he can handle."

"How do the coffees taste when they arrive?"

"Hopefully, they are not too faded. This year's coffee is still in country, every day it sits there absorbing more humidity."

We talk about other people in the specialty industry. "Peter and Geoff are like my brothers," he says, noting that they have traveled together, hung out together, done cupping training together, cut loose together. There's a lot of professional respect among them, he says, and a lot of caring.

Like brothers, "we are really competitive. If the opportunity comes up to take the other out, to take first place ahead of them, to contract for a coffee we all want, I will do it. They will do the same," he says. "Well, maybe not Peter. He is less cutthroat."

"Me and Peter are old buddies. Duane and Peter are old buddies too, but there are differences there," Aleco says, referring to a rift stemming from their competition over a coffee from Honduras. Aleco adds, "As the world gets smaller and markets get more condensed, the competition will grow more bitter, and the gloves will be off." It's a thought other specialty buyers have expressed: as demand for specialty coffees increases, the competition for the best coffees will get ugly.

"From Stumptown's point of view," says Aleco, "we have to have the best coffees. We have to be first, and we will do what it takes to get the best coffees first. We will pay more. Cup first. Whatever it takes.

"Peter to me is the greatest student of coffee ever and the greatest speaker. He is overwhelmingly articulate and passionate, and he buys some great coffees," Aleco continues. "But in a business sense, it's more difficult for him because he [and Counter Culture] is strictly wholesale."

It's easier when you are in retail, Aleco explains, because retail provides you with a platform. "People come into our cafés and they fall in love with the coffee. They fall in love with the whole Stumptown thing." Moreover, the margin is bigger in retail, providing more cash with which to buy coffee and grow a business. "Counter Culture is more cost conscious. It has to be," says Aleco.

Duane echoes Aleco's opinion, saying, "I am not inspired by Counter Culture. I don't necessarily think they are doing anything cutting edge. Intelligentsia," he adds, "is doing a fantastic job."

I ask Aleco about Intelligentsia and about Geoff. "Geoff Watts," he says, "is the ultimate rock star in the specialty world. But," says Aleco, echoing comments from many of Geoff's fans and friends, "we all worry about Geoff. We are all concerned. It's his lifestyle. He does crazy things. We have a roaster here from Nicaragua named Javier. The first night we took him out to a bar. He was kind of scared, and he wanted to know, are there gangs in the bars? Because in Nicaragua at night when it gets late the gangs show up at the bars and there is all this violence. This is the kind of thing you can't help worrying about with Geoff. You worry that one of these days, he is going to get himself stabbed in a bar. He is living with reckless abandon. He will drive himself to the maximum and fall flat on his face and scrape himself up off the floor. I have a much more controlled version of that. You never want to settle for anything less than being the leading edge.

"Geoff is a celebrity. It is easy for him to live his life this way because he will always have ego support from people in the business. Everyone wants to be close to him. People are dying to sell coffee to him."

I later give Geoff a chance to respond to what Aleco and some others in the industry have said about him. His answer is pretty buttoned up.

"No doubt there are periods when I would describe myself as reckless; that's part of living. A lot of time people who don't take a lot of risks, don't discover that extra thing that you need to know about life," Geoff says, adding that at the age of thirty-four, he is less wild than when he was younger.

As for the part of Geoff that really cares about developing the specialty industry and pours hundreds of hours a year into doing volunteer work—Aleco doesn't see the point. "The SCAA," Aleco says. "Duane is not into it, and I am not into it either. It's a

whole bunch of bullshit. The Roasters Guild is a different story."
(Peter is former head of the Roasters Guild and Geoff is the current
head.) "But I ask myself, how much time does Roasters Guild
work take away from their businesses? At Stumptown we can't
afford to do that." Aleco's questions about the hours spent doing
SCAA and Roasters Guild work are ones that Peter and Geoff
often ask themselves. So far, however, each has decided that playing a role in building the specialty coffee industry and helping to
develop rising talent is worth the hundreds of hours it consumes.
Aleco and Duane don't agree.

"For me, it is all about coffee," Aleco says. "The majority
of my life is coffee. It's my hobby and my occupation. It's been a
detriment to girlfriends, relationships. It's been a detriment to
other things. But I love it. It's how I want to live. And now we are
moving into Seattle, the mecca of the coffee world."

Originally when Duane thought about expanding his
company, he thought he would move into San Francisco. He
found a location, invested in a lease, and then thought better of
the plan and bought himself out of the California lease. San
Francisco, 585 miles from Portland, was too far away to maintain control. Stumptown doesn't really get the San Francisco vibe
and Duane had no way of knowing if San Francisco would get
Stumptown. Seattle, just three hours away by car, seemed a much
better fit.

The move was a stretch. With two new cafés and a new
roastery, Stumptown doubled its payroll in one gulp. "Overnight
we'll have another forty people on payroll."

"Seattle baristas were underpaid before; now they will be
taken care of, get benefits, all of that," reports Matt Lounsbury,
explaining that up until now Stumptown has been able to expand
out of its cash flow. "This is the first time we've taken a business
loan. The first time we have used a real construction team instead
of building out ourselves. The first time we put project manage-

ment in other people's hands. We're doing all this for less than a million dollars. We are always creative in how we assemble financing. We have had a great community bank working with us for years, and we have aggressive plans to pay back."

While the cafés and roastery were being built, Duane created a bedroom in an elevator shaft above one of the locations and spent two or three days a week in Seattle. In his spare time, he redesigned Stumptown's coffee packaging, adding information about the coffees and the farms on which they are grown. When the Seattle cafés opened, Duane was behind the bar working as a barista.

"I am a difficult and high-expectation boss," Duane told me when I visited in May 2007, while the Seattle buildout was going on. "I come to work every day, I rarely take vacation, I have done everything in this company 100 percent. I am not going to ask anyone to do anything I haven't done. Like Aleco, I know his travel schedule is going to be fierce, but before he came on board I was traveling one week a month. I was the top roaster, the top barista. I have goals and dreams for the company. We have to be flexible because we have to make improvements. We can't do stuff at our cafés that we did four years ago—everything has to keep improving.

"Coffee preparation. The Clover. Customer service. It is easy for people to get lazy. It's tough working—there are days when people don't want to smile or make latte for one hundred customers, but you have to do it. We have to keep improving our customer service, our drink consistency, improving our café design, our cleanliness. There is nothing we can take for granted. That's why I work seven days a week. That's why Stumptown is always going to be at the top."

I ask what comes next and Duane tells me he has dreams of expanding his operations overseas. He's intrigued that pot is legal in Amsterdam and he's amazed that the coffee in Amsterdam is so poor. He and Menno Simons are talking about opening a café together there.

Duane says, "I'd like my kids to live in Europe, and Amsterdam is a lot closer than Portland to Africa. There's a flight every day to Kenya and Ethiopia. Being a man of few hobbies, I need more. There's so much more to do."

Duane has a definite fascination with Ethiopia. He would love to buy more coffee there, and his compassion is roused by the Ethiopian farmers he has visited. "These are the poorest guys I have ever seen in my life," he says.

The complexity of Duane's personality intrigues me. His kindness as a host could hardly be greater. He dotes on his children. He cares deeply about the people who work for him. Then there is the other side: the cutthroat part of his nature. After my visit I hear stories about Duane burning bridges in the business, Duane rejecting coffees that he has ordered from importers, Duane this, and Duane that.

Sarah Allen, editor and cofounder of Portland-based *Barista Magazine*, has known Duane since the beginning. "When he started out he didn't know he was going to have to incorporate—he was that naïve," she says. "Duane is a punk rocker and a skater [Rollerblades]. He doesn't make compromises. He is always true to his heart."

Making Stumptown grow has been a huge stretch for him. "I have never seen Duane in a tie….For him to have to go to the SCAA with all the suits making sales pitches, well, you can only imagine. No one taught these guys anything. They had to learn to play the game all on their own."

And now after years of being the alternative company, the anti-rich-white-guy company, lately Duane has starting saying that he has become that very thing. A rich white guy. "He keeps telling everyone that he is a rich white guy," Sarah says, sounding bewildered. "And you just kinda wonder what that's all about."

You just wonder what that's all about.

LOS ANGELES

AFTER VISITING STUMPTOWN IN EARLY MAY, I FLEW TO Los Angeles to check out Intelligentsia's westward expansion from Chicago to Tinseltown, an inspired move. The work ethic, perfectionism, and genius for marketing for which Intelligentsia (often referred to as Intelli) is known fits tidily in L.A. As does the company's spiffy new orange packaging with its stylish slate-gray winged logo. Coffee importer Tim Chapdelaine, who sells millions of dollars worth of coffee to Intelligentsia each year and knows the company intimately, thinks Intelligentsia might do even better in Los Angeles than in its hometown, Chicago, "because people in L.A. spend more conspicuously."

Tim elaborates, explaining that to the big brains behind Intelligentsia, coffee is about "being a sexy product, and their model thrives in a fat, rich, style-conscious market like L.A." In his opinion, Intelli's decision to open its first café in Silver Lake, one of L.A.'s hottest new neighborhoods, was pitch-perfect. Inspired. "I wouldn't be surprised if the guys producing *Entourage* [the HBO series about cool young dudes making it in the movie business] decide to shoot there."

In L.A., I am hoping to learn more about the espresso-based, cooler-than-cool barista subculture that Intelli has helped nurture. Founder Doug Zell's competitiveness is imprinted in Intelligentsia's DNA—and the company promotes the idea of star baristas in every way it can. Intelligentsia runs a certificate-granting barista school in Chicago that is mandatory for those working behind the bar at any of the company's three stores in that city. It also operates a boot camp for barista competitors. Not surprisingly, Intelli has produced a number of champion baristas, including former U.S. barista champion Matt Riddle and former Midwest regional champion Ellie Hudson-Matuszak.

Intelligentsia's training and hiring practices have helped to foster what Peter Giuliano calls "the culture of celebrity baristas." Celebrity baristas: young hipsters—skinny, stylish, cool—with personal followings that grow as a result of their taking part in barista competitions and having their own coffee blogs or being written about on blogs. The style and attitude of these young guys is shaping café culture all over the country, as well as in Europe and Asia. Some in the specialty world applaud these hip young dudes, asserting that baristas are as talented as chefs. Others hear the term "hipster barista" and groan, saying, "hipster barista. That's a guy who thinks he's too cool to make your cappuccino."

A few months before my Los Angeles trip, I attend my first barista championship—the western regional held in Petaluma, California. Each year there are ten regional barista competitions, scattered in every corner of the country, leading up to the national. The Specialty Coffee Association organizes and runs the barista competitions, and the national barista championship takes place during the SCAA annual convention.

In Petaluma I meet one of Intelli's new generation of barista competitors, Kyle Glanville. Only twenty-four years old, Kyle is in charge of barista training for Intelligentsia's entire California operation.

Ric Rhinehart of Groundwork Coffee, the L.A. roaster with the most to lose from Intelligentsia's move to L.A., is also in Petaluma for the regional championship. He is there to support competitor Eton Tsuno, the twenty-two-year-old director of his espresso program and a key person in Groundwork's anti-Intelli counteroffensive. Espresso, even more than brewed coffee, is a young guy's game.

Most fascinating at the competition is the mishmash of cheering, jeering, and laughing coworkers, friends, family, lovers, personal trainers, assorted industry people, vendors, and groupies who throng Petaluma Sheraton's ballroom to watch the thirty-two registered barista competitors, most from California—the Pacific Northwest hosts its own competition—strut their stuff. At key moments during the contest, as many as four hundred people fill the rows of metal folding chairs beneath a huge, suspended screen showing the activities taking place at the far end of the room, where three espresso bars have been set up. (A fourth machine in the back of the room dispenses free espressos and cappuccinos to members of the audience.) Fans come in all ages, sizes, and wealth brackets, but the geeks and the freaks in their tattered jeans, with multiple piercings and multicolored tattoos, set the tone. (According to Kyle, "Tattoos illustrate coffee people's joyful disregard for ideas about professionalism.")

Barista Lingo

BARISTA

Barista is the Italian word for the person who "pulls"—makes—your espresso shot or espresso drink. A well-trained barista makes all drinks to order and by hand.

BREW TIME (ALSO REFERRED TO AS EXTRACTION TIME)

It takes between 20 and 30 seconds for an ounce and a half of espresso to trickle into the cup from the espresso machine. To achieve this result, the machine heats water to 200°F and then forces it through the machinery at 8.5 bars (approximately 135 pounds) of atmospheric pressure.

CREMA

The reddish-brown foam topping an espresso. A generous layer of crema is the hallmark of a well-pulled shot.

DOSE

The traditional dose (amount of ground espresso) used to make a single shot of espresso is 6 to 7 grams, 12 to 14 grams for a double. Recently, cafés have increased their dose sizes to 8 to 10 grams for a single and 16 to 20 grams for a double. Changing the dose alters the intensity of the drink and the flavor.

ESPRESSO BLEND

Espresso is generally—but not always—made from a blend of several different coffees. High-quality roasters tend to be secretive about the contents of their blends. Blends change as coffees come onto the market and disappear during the year.

GRIND

Espresso is ground to order. Volatile oils inside the coffee bean are oxidized and grow stale when exposed to air, so it is important that as soon as the barista grinds the dose, he or she quickly tamps the coffee and extracts the espresso.

PORTAFILTER
The portafilter basket contains the ground espresso. The portafilter handles attach the portafilter basket to the espresso machine's metal fixings, called groupheads. The handles should be clean, hot, and ready to go. So should the china cups into which the espresso is poured.

TAMP
The tamp is the act of flattening and compressing the coffee in the portafilter before fastening the handle into the machine before brewing. The skilled barista uses a hand-tamping device and then leans his or her body weight into the basket on top of the counter to compress the coffee further.

The Specialty Coffee Association sponsors the annual regional competitions, sets the ground rules, provides technical assistance, and trains the judges. Using the single-origin espresso or espresso blend of their choice, baristas are given fifteen minutes to prepare four samples of three different drinks—a classic espresso shot, a cappuccino with or without latte art (designs on top of espresso drinks, also known as rosettas), and a "specialty" drink combining espresso with other ingredients: liquor, cream, chocolate, lemon zest, you name it. As the baristas work, they must deliver a nonstop commentary describing their coffees, their approach to espresso, and the hows and whys of their specialty drinks. A team of six judges scores each contestant—four "sensory judges" swallow (not spit, as cuppers do), and then rate the baristas based on the taste, aroma, and visual appeal of their drinks. Two nontasting technical judges score other aspects of the presentations, such as dose—the amount of espresso used in each shot—and tamping—forcefully compressing the ground espresso in the portafilter. Even napkin folding is judged. The six highest-scoring contestants compete in a final round, during which they have to repeat their performance. The first-place winner of each regional contest is guaranteed a spot at the National Barista Competition, which takes place at the SCAA annual convention, plus hotel and airfare. The winner of the national represents the United States at the World Barista Competition.

I watch Glanville Kyle compete at Petaluma. A former theater major, the slender, dark-haired, blue-eyed Kyle has a polished stage presence and an actor's understanding of the technical aspects of performance. He's set his act to instrumental hip-hop that is both accessible and high energy. He begins by whisking tangelo juice and sugar together for his specialty drink, which he calls "Lady Marmalade." He sets those ingredients on a small burner to reduce as he turns to making his four espressos, using a blend of Intelligentsia coffees that is made up of two parts Bolivian organic and one part Brazilian—most espresso blends include some Brazilian coffee. He deftly pours his shots into four small porcelain cups that he places on a tray with four water glasses. He presents these to the judges, and then he gets to work on the cappuccinos. His hands vibrate as he pours espresso and frothed milk. "I'm shaking to make the latte art, not because I am nervous," he smoothly tells the crowd. He refills the judges' water, cool as he can be, and serves the cappuccinos. Then he deftly returns to the burner, removes the reduction, adds organic cream, and then infuses lemon zest into steamed milk for a multilayered specialty drink. The rules allot each performer fifteen minutes. Kyle completes his routine in thirteen minutes and forty-nine seconds. More than a minute to spare. A masterful performance.

I talk with Kyle in the Sheraton lobby after his presentation. He tells me he has prepared for the competition by attending

Intelligentsia's barista boot camp in Chicago, but beyond that, he has been busy interviewing, hiring, and training the staff for the Silver Lake store and he really hasn't had time to practice.

Kyle grew up in Carmel Valley, California. His dad was in construction. His mom was a travel agent. The private school he attended on scholarship kicked him out when he stopped playing football. "There were socioeconomic issues," he says. The atmosphere of his high school was highly competitive. "Football was the thing that alienated me from high school. I wasn't into the freaky frat thing. Like most kids, I was smoking some weed. My parents were divorced. I was the third of four kids. My mother had surpassed her threshold and she couldn't deal with me.

"Okay, fine, I said. I'll get a job. I read a lot." Eventually he earned a high school degree doing independent studies and wound up at a small college in Seattle studying acting. "I landed in Seattle as a huge number of people were being laid off. I tried for eight months to get a job. I had no financial support from my family. I was hustling, borrowing, eating a lot of rice and hot sauce." Finally he took his resume to Victrola, an espresso bar where "the lighting was dark and the people were too cool." His coworkers at Victrola "became my posse... I was working the bar, learning my craft, pulling espresso shots all day long and loving it....

"I was intrigued by the tiny things you did at the bar—what a huge difference it made if you pulled [the levers of the machine] slightly more or less, faster or slower, the tamping, the whole preparing of espresso, which is so fragile and volatile. Espresso making is truly an *art*. It requires technical skill to serve so many good drinks. I started nagging my boss for more training. In the summer, I got the training job. I trained two people a month, at one hundred bucks per person. I was still not making twelve thousand a year, but it seemed amazing to me that I could make any money at all doing something I loved so much."

Kyle began studying espresso on his time off. He read Andrea Illy's iconic book *Espresso Coffee: The Science of Quality.* Andrea Illy, head of Illy Café. and his late father, Ernesto, are revered for infusing scientific precision into the art of espresso making. The word *espresso* in Italian means "fast" or "faster"—as in a faster way to make coffee. Espresso originated in Italy in 1903, when an impatient café owner added the element of pressure to coffee making. Throughout the twentieth century, Italy was the world's espresso capital, but recently, some specialty coffee roasters in the United States and Europe have designated Scandinavia, the region that consumes the most specialty coffee, as the world's true center of espresso culture. The 2006 world barista champion, Klaus Thomsen, is a Dane who lives and works in Copenhagen. In the opinion of Kyle and many young coffee guys, the Italians have not kept pace with the changes happening in the specialty world. They have not upgraded the quality of their coffee. Nor do they focus on freshness. Kyle dismisses Italy as an espresso leader, saying, "Italian fetishism is no longer relevant." He wouldn't dream of putting small amounts of Robusta in his espresso blend, as the Italians routinely do to enhance the crema, the red-brown foam that tops a well-made espresso.

After reading Illy, Kyle looked closer to home for espresso inspiration. In Seattle he studied the work of local espresso master David Schomer, owner of Espresso Vivace and author of *Espresso Coffee: Professional Techniques,* scores of articles, and teaching materials, as well as an online espresso archive. Along with many other technical advances, Schomer is credited with introducing latte art to U.S. baristas in 1990 after seeing baristas in Italy form rosettas on top of cappuccinos.

David Schomer describes espresso as a culinary art, analogous, say, to pastry making. In this view, the barista does more than highlight the intrinsic qualities of his ingredients—he actually combines science and art to create something new.

In a *Barista Magazine* profile, David talked about the importance of brewing techniques. His comments highlight how seriously barista's take their art. He discussed the experiments he had undertaken to determine the optimum temperature. He began "measuring the temperature of water as it arrived at the top of the packed coffee with a K-probe type thermocouple," then he switched to a Fluke digital thermometer in 1994. The results astonished him. The temperature of the water in even the best espresso machines varied within a 6°F range, and as a result, "my coffee varied from sour to bland with occasional brilliant shots. And I had a strong suspicion it was temperature variation causing this."

In 1995, working with an engineer from La Marzocco, he figured out how to limit the variation in temperature. He was able to get "within a half-degree stability on a given shot, but over the next few-minute cycle of the mechanical thermostat I had a two-degree range of error." Working in this range, his espresso shots were deep red brown, the ideal color, "with many more of them falling in the sweet zone."

David became obsessed with what he calls "the final push," that key development that would enable him to control temperature within one degree. "In 2001, on Ash Wednesday, we got there," thanks to engineering help from La Marzocco, which enabled a customized "Schomer-style" La Marzocco espresso maker to be fitted with an Omega 7000 series PID control loop feedback mechanism. "I began preparing coffee with tears streaming down my face, beautiful shots that tasted caramelly sweet and which distinctly matched the fragrance of my Dolce Blend, with a light buttery feel to the crema. Looking back, I would have to say that was the single greatest day of my career."

Kyle shares David Schomer's single-minded devotion to espresso. "I love being a barista. It's a Zen thing. I love the machine. I love the coffee. I love the pulse of the grinder. I love dragging my finger across the coffee to see if the grind is too coarse or too fine. To me it's transcendent. Romantic. There is an incredible history inside each cup of coffee, starting with the farmer." Soon after he began making espresso, he dropped out of college to work at Victrola full time.

In the spring of 2006 the SCAA annual convention was held in Seattle and "Victrola landed on the map....People came into the store saying they had heard that our espresso was really good....That week we hit our peak."

The SCAA exposure led to Kyle being courted by several coffee roasters outside of Seattle, including Intelligentsia. After spending time with Doug and Geoff, he chose Intelligentsia, and has been with the company for eight months. He loves working for Intelli. "We are the macro-micro big dog. People think we throw money at everything. That's not it. We all work our asses off. Doug rewards creativity, entrepreneurship." Competing as a barista fits perfectly with the overall Intelligentsia mission, and with the company's culture. "I am competitive. I am interested in winning and the pursuit of being the best," says Kyle. "Doug supports me every inch of the way."

Kyle's smooth performance at the western regional barista competition earned him a place among the top six finalists. Eton Tsuno of Groundwork was in the top six as well. So was a twenty-four-year-old blond barista named Heather Perry from Koffee Klatch in San Dimas, California, located in the valley about forty miles west of Los Angeles. Perry, whose performance was self-possessed and polished, had previously won both the Western Regional and the National Barista Championships. She walked away as the top winner at this competition as well. Kyle came in second, not bad for his first real competition. Heather's win was not without controversy. Few faulted her performance, except to say that she had "won on points." It was her lack of attitude that disappointed some. And her coffee. Koffee Klatch, I was told by several specialty guys, is not a cutting-edge roaster, and her espressos look good but don't taste that great. (I was a bit thrown by this last comment, as it struck me as illogical that she could win on points if the judges didn't like the taste of her espresso.) Mostly, there seemed to be a sense of letdown that a former cheerleader—Heather had done competitive cheerleading in high school—had won. It just didn't seem right to some that a girl with a blond ponytail walked off with the top barista prize.

My first day in L.A., I meet up with Kyle and some of the other members of the Intelli crew for a tour of the new café in Silver Lake. I had been told that the two construction projects—the café and the roastery—were running way over budget and far behind schedule. I understand why as soon as my tour guide, Tony Konecny, aka Tonx, the popular coffee blogger, and photographer, who no longer works for Intelli, tells me that the project architect, who had taught at Harvard, is a specialist in the semiotics of design. According to Tony, Silver Lake had been designed to avoid the "tropes of coffee shops." In English this means the architect was interested in the symbolic meaning of architectural forms and wanted to avoid coffee shop clichés.

The café, only partly finished when I am there, looks like it will be gorgeous—blue and white Nicaraguan tiles on the floor and up the counters, an inviting outdoor space seating sixty, with built-in misters to cool those who opt to sit in the great outdoors when it's hot and a romantic archway separating the two spaces. Too bad, though, that no one put thought into securing permits and meeting building codes for the café and roastery—oversights that Geoff later tells me cost Intelligentsia $900,000, not including lost revenue.

The plan at Silver Lake, when the café opens, is to sell brewed coffee for different prices. Customers could order a $2 cup of a high-quality blend, or, if it were in season, a $10 cup of Esmeralda Special. There would be no brochures. The baristas would be trained to educate customers about the coffees.

"We want the customers to talk to the baristas. We're aiming for a person-to-person experience," says Kyle. Doug Zell had figured out that in most cafés half the baristas are pretty much useless. His plan in L.A. is to hire four or five superstars—instead of eight of middling quality—train them well, and pay them extraordinarily well. With tips, the Silver Lake baristas are expected to make up to $50,000 a year—more than any other baristas in the industry. Bar backs would do the bussing.

From Silver Lake, the Intelli guys and I drive to the new roastery in an industrial area about fifteen minutes away. The roasting facility is beset by even more construction problems and code violations than the café, having been built without regard to what would happen to the gasline in case of an earthquake or other catastrophe—Intelligentsia's roaster is dual fuel, meaning it is powered by gas and by electricity. When it is operating this plant will roast, pack, and ship coffee for Silver Lake and a second café that is in the planning stage, plus wholesale and online accounts. The cupping room in the front of the roasting facility has Lucite stools and pale aqua furnishings that speak to Intelli's glam orange packaging. The 1942 Gothot roaster from Germany—gleaming metal, orange panels—is as burnished as a drill sergeant's belt buckle.

Stephen Rogers, twenty-seven, Intelligentsia's master roaster, has moved from Chicago to Los Angeles, and he is having a very hard time sitting around waiting for his job to begin. (Two months later, when he learned that it might take six months for the L.A. plant to be operational, he quit Intelligentsia and went to work roasting coffee in Seattle for Stumptown.)

Stephen, who has long, dark hair and is part Cherokee, grew up in the Southwest in a poor family. He has drive, ego, and a sense of himself as one who is unique. He says, "There was no money for college. So I set out to educate myself without paying for it. From age twelve to eighteen, I did college theater. I acted in thirty-three plays; I worked on sound, lights. I dive into whatever I do. I was a Texas state swimming champ. I played the saxophone, and I am the white, living representation of the independence of Zimbabwe, having been born on the day the Zimbabwe state was born." He pauses to make sure I am following. "Unfortunately, I am not doing well either."

Stephen compares the Gothot on which he will be roasting to the Probat roaster I saw at Stumptown. The internal drum in a Probat has a double wall that holds heat. "Our machine has a single wall," Stephen tells me, so "when I adjust the gas, the machine reacts quickly. If I move too fast decreasing the gas, the machine instantly detects that I slowed the roast down. If I step up the gas, I see the effect immediately. On the Probat, the response is not so rapid. Here we have a little more control."

I shoot the breeze for a while with Stephen, Kyle, Tony, and two other Intelli baristas. One of them is Ryan Wilbur, twenty-one, a handsome, long-faced kid from Minneapolis with a tattoo of a coffee roaster on his arm and two large metal plugs inserted in his ear lobes to stretch them. (These plugs and other forms of "tribal scarification" are practices of "the Urban Primitive Movement," adherents of which sometimes use spikes to pierce their cheeks and chests.)

Ryan grew up in the state of Washington near Vancouver in an evangelical family and considers himself an evangelical Christian. After high school he moved to Minneapolis to study music production and got a job as a barista. The coffee thing really turned him on.

Though he is still interested in music production, "spending my day in a dark studio was not me. I liked being behind the espresso bar....I guess I am an attention hog....It was very hard to be so passionate about coffee, wanting to be around it all the time, and still keep up on my homework." So he stopped going to school and devoted himself to coffee.

In 2006 Ryan took part in an independent barista competition. He got a reputation as a rising talent, which was enhanced by his own coffee blog. "With blogging comes pictures—evidence I could pour latte art." The blog led Intelligentsia to him. "Doug knew who I was. He is an Internet surfer. He lurks in the shadows of the forum and blogs, learning all he can," Ryan says.

"Doug was spying on you?" I ask.

"He likes to know what's going on," Ryan answers. "He liked the fact that I am committed and passionate." So Doug offered him a job as a barista at the Silver Lake store.

"All of a sudden a door opens, and I am offered health insurance, a 401(k), all the stuff you give up when you go into coffee," Ryan says with incredulity. He had arrived in Los Angeles two weeks before. "I am loving every minute of it." He doesn't own a car. Well, he does own a car but it is barely operable. Until he finds an apartment he is staying in the arts and crafts bungalow Doug leased near Silver Lake to help his employees transition into the expensive L.A. real estate market.

I have been complaining about the West Hollywood bed-and-breakfast where I am staying, which is straight out of *The Day of the Locusts*, and the coffee guys offer to put me up at the bungalow.

"Hey," says Tony, "we've got clean sheets and towels."

I turn down their invitation, but I can't help but appreciate their openness, energy, and overall ability to invent themselves. These are not privileged kids. No one has handed them much of anything. No fancy internships. No private colleges. No tutors, shrinks, and life-skill coaches. Still, they have done a critical thing: found what they love and devoted themselves to it. I don't entirely get the visual aesthetic, though.

There is a whole set of hipster styles and references in the barista world, a young friend who is unusually attuned to different social scenes tells me. A keen and ironic observer, he describes the hipster style as "the pretentious rejection of everything tradition-ally held to be pretentious."

In hipster culture everything perceived to be high class and high status is rejected in favor of its opposite. So in women's fash-ion, what's hip are 1930s housedresses. Guys like the Intelli baris-tas who adopt the hipster style have fashion preferences too. Retro shoes are big, as in named sneakers from earlier eras. Chuck Taylors. Converse. Throwback Nikes. Skinny jeans, tapered at the ankle, showing off how skinny you are. Fitted T-shirts, so long as you don't have muscles. The look is the opposite of traditional masculinity. Very androgynous. It's impossible to tell who is straight, who is gay—sometimes I am not even sure who is male and female—all of which seems to be the point.

The barista dudes and I hang out in the roasting room, talk-ing about coffee and coffee companies. After a while our talk veers to the subject of restaurant coffee. Coffee guys love to complain about restaurant coffee, how bad it is.

The problems are financial and cultural, Tony says. "Restaurants live or die on a very narrow margin." It is difficult and expensive for a busy restaurant to do coffee well. "Besides, they don't want people to linger. They want to turn the table."

But maybe things are changing at the high end of the restaurant world. Stephen Rogers, the Intelli roaster, points out that Thomas Keller recently announced that he would be serving Hacienda La Esmeralda Special at his famed restaurant French Laundry.

When I was in Portland, Stumptown's Matt Lounsbury had told me that he thinks a sea change is beginning in restaurant coffee in the Pacific Northwest. He attributes this to the emerging alliance between local chefs, local farmers, local cheese makers, local winemakers. In his opinion, chefs focusing on local provisions are beginning to think of locally roasted coffee as an important ingredient on their "buy local" shopping list. He names a number of restaurants in the Portland area—Higgins, Wildwood, Fife, Le Pigeon, Clark Lewis, Toro Bravo, and Country Cat—describing them as places that are serving Stumptown coffee and doing it well.

Kyle agrees that change is in the air. He, too, has the feeling that "early adapters" in the restaurant world are beginning to think about coffee as an element of the dining experience—like the wine service—that speaks to the culinary sensibility of the restaurant and the chef, rather than something to be gotten through with as quickly as possible. Intelligentsia coffee, it turns out, is served at Charlie Trotter's and some other well-known Chicago restaurants, including Alinea, Blackbird, Frontera Grill, North Pond Café, Custom House, and Green Zebra. At this last restaurant, the service is French press, which the baristas agree offers restaurants a reasonably priced, easy to clean, excellent method for serving freshly made coffee. "So long as they use a decent [burr] coffee grinder," Kyle says. "You really ruin the coffee with a crappy grinder."

A few months after my visit to Los Angeles, I talk with Doug Zell, who reports that a number of big-name Los Angeles restaurants are now brewing Intelligentsia coffees. Among them are Mozza, Osteria Mozza, Jar, Sona, and Comme ça—these last two offer French press service.

I also check in with Peter Giuliano, who tells me that on the East Coast, Counter Culture is also finding high-end restaurants receptive as never before to the importance of serving high-quality, beautifully prepared coffee. He mentions Craft and the Tasting Room in New York City. He is particularly excited about a restaurant in Baltimore called Woodbury Kitchen where the chef/owner, Spike Gjerde, has a barista making espresso drinks and preparing individual pots of brewed French press coffee that she delivers to the table with a small timer, indicating when the patrons should press the plunger and pour. Peter agrees with Matt at Stumptown that restaurants focusing on locally sourced foods seem most receptive to the idea of locally roasted coffee.

For so many restaurants, the coffee problem comes down to a money problem—chefs feel they can't afford the coffee and they don't have the extra manpower. "What we are trying to do is encourage them to make worthwhile compromises," says Kyle. "We have been pushing French press. Now we are encouraging restaurants to buy decent grinders. With a high-quality commercial coffee grinder like a Fetco and a standard drip brewer, you can get a pretty clean cup of coffee." What Kyle doesn't say, however, is that a Fetco coffee grinder costs around fourteen hundred dollars.

The guys all agree about what restaurants should not do. Unless they have the right equipment and staff, they should not serve espresso drinks. "The cappuccinos you get at most places are laughable," Steven says.

I ask the guys about an article I had read, written by coffee importer and pundit Tim Castle, questioning the whole ascendancy of espresso in the Third Wave coffee culture.

Tim had written that the "buzz about coffee lately has been really about espresso. The problem with this espresso obsession is that the roaster and the farmer get lost in the chaff as the obsessives work on perfecting their grind, tamping, group temperatures, etc. There is nothing wrong with a great cup of espresso but all the hoopla about espresso is leaving someone in the dust—and that's the farmer."

The response to Tim's espresso article had been swift and vituperative. The debate had quickly devolved into a generational scrap, with young coffee guys leading the charge against their allegedly procrustean elders. "People interpreted my article, took it very antagonistically...bulletin boards and blogs had ad hominen attacks on me. Anyone who is honest knows espresso is not the best way to represent or highlight the farmer's contribution....It highlights the craftsmanship of baristas," more than the coffee.

Espresso, even at its best, is a technology-dependent variation of the coffee experience. At its worst, well, when you add enough adulterants the coffee becomes irrelevant. The guys laugh at the mention of this article, but they agree that the coffee should always come first. The barista performance should honor the coffee. They feel certain, however, that the specialty industry benefits from the passion roused by espresso, baristas, and the whole coffee shop performance phenomenon.

Eventually we go to lunch—me and five coffee guys at a Burmese joint with whorehouse art and pretty good food. I am scheduled to interview Heather Perry, the barista champ, in a couple of days, and while we wait for our lunches, I ask why everyone puts her down.

Heather's family owns Koffee Klatch coffee roasters. No one at the table seems to know that coffee klatch is an outdated term for a group of people who gather together to drink coffee.

"Koffee Klatch," someone says. "What the hell does that mean?"

"Koffee Klatch," another guy answers, "rhymes with... [an obscene reference to a female body part]."

Sniggers erupt.

They compare her performance to a beauty queen entering pageants.

"Her mother was ironing her tablecloth, acting as if Heather were a show pony," one of the guys says.

Kyle keeps silent. He doesn't reveal that during the just-passed 2007 nationals his mother ironed his tablecloth too. "I asked her to iron my tablecloth and napkins. I am guilty of that," he later says privately.

Someone else at the table mutters the final word on Heather. Her family "owns a coffee shop in a strip mall. It's pathetic."

The meanness is shocking. At first it seems their reaction to Heather is based solely on only sexism. Later, in reading one of the coffee blogs, another explanation presents itself. Geoff Watts, the most famous specialty buyer in the world, had written a carefully reasoned exegesis spelling out his critique of the Fair Trade movement, explaining why he thought Fair Trade wasn't good for farmers. Agree with him or not, his article demonstrated encyclopedic knowledge of the issue. Many of the responses were complimentary. But a minority of the respondents ripped him to shreds in weirdly personal terms and talked about Intelligentsia as if it were a vast, uncaring corporate entity.

Geoff later commented on the backlash among some taking part in the online forums. "There's an interesting dynamic in specialty. The more antiestablishment, the more renegade you are, the more play you get on all the forums. It's weird for Doug and me. We aren't small anymore. We are a small- to medium-sized roaster. We are no longer the underdog."

If in the hipster worldview what is ugly is beautiful and a failure is a success, then what happens when you are, in fact, successful? That must make you ugly and hateful, right?

Maybe that's Heather's problem too. She has no indie street cred. She's not antiestablishment. She is a girl from the Valley. She doesn't pretend not to care about winning. That girl is just not hip.

Kyle competed again against Heather at the U.S. National Championship that took place in Los Angeles. He did well in the first round. He could feel it in his bones, and afterward the word leaked that he had scored extremely high.

After the semifinals, waiting to hear who had made it into the final six, he says, "I was exhausted." It was 10:00 p.m., and he was standing around waiting to hear if he had made it into the top six. "I realized I was in a win-win. The barista guild party would begin in a little while. If I wasn't in the finals, I could go get trashed. If I was in finals, hurray for me; it was my first year competing."

He made it into the finals. But this time he didn't make it into the top five. Heather Perry came in first. Which meant uncool Heather Perry from Koffee Klatch in San Dimas, California, would go to Tokyo in August 2007 to represent the United States in the World Barista Competition.

A few days later, I meet Heather for lunch outdoors on the patio at Le Pain Quotidien on Melrose Boulevard. Her hair, a natural-looking dark blond, is long and loose, but off her face.

She is wearing sunglasses and a scanty little top. She's built like an athlete. Large strong hands. Koffee Klatch is a family business, she tells me, with two stores, two carts, and sixteen baristas. Her father, Mike Perry, does the roasting. She does all the training. Her mother runs one of the stores. Her sister is a college student, not so interested in coffee.

"I have always liked the business," she says.

"You must be pretty disciplined," I say.

"Am I disciplined? No. Am I competitive? Yes."

In high school she played volleyball. Soccer. Did cheerleading. "I will do what it takes to win. By nature I am messy, disorganized—my car speaks to that—but when you are performing you have to think about every move before you make it. You have to figure out where to place everything, how to fold the napkins. You have to spend a lot of time figuring all the details adding to the ambience of a performance, putting it all together to make a total package.

"I have gone through hundreds of gallons of milk practicing for this competition. I have been emotionally exhausted, shed more tears from sheer frustration, but I won't stop till I have it right."

Why did she win?

"I outworked everyone else. I worked every weekend; I worked every evening after work. The competition consumed my life for three months. I was in it to win. This year I couldn't have worked more. I decided to go for it. I am happy with how my performance came out."

She will make whatever sacrifices it takes. She has a boyfriend. He's a tech guy who loves motorcycles. She doesn't see much of him when she is training.

"People say you won on points," I tell her.

"There is a mathematical aspect to competing. You have to know your score sheet," she says, "and you have to focus on the skills the score sheet demands." (Nick Cho, a regional barista champion and barista judge, later explains to me that a lot of young guys who compete care more about projecting an image when they perform than about showcasing their skills. Heather, says Nick, is a much more disciplined performer. "She drills and drills until every aspect of her performance is perfect. Her technical proficiency at dosing and tamping, honed during months of practice, earns points from the technical judges. Her skill at barista basics improves the taste of her drinks—resulting in additional points from the sensory judges." And that's not all. Her drinks look beautiful. The crema on top of her espressos is thick and viscous and springs back when pushed with a spoon. Her milk froth is made up of uniformly tiny bubbles almost invisible to the eye. Technically, too, her work is flawless. She doesn't waste coffee or milk. Her work area is clean. She always knows where she has placed her cleaning cloths.

Talented barista she may be, but not much of a talker.

"You're shy," I say.

"No," she says. "I am boring. It's the coffee that's interesting. My life is all about the coffee."

We prepare to go. She has to drive to the Valley, thirty, forty miles away. It will probably take her two hours with Los Angeles traffic being what it is.

"What about the sexism?" I ask.

"Women have done well," she says. "Coffee is a guy thing, but still women have done well. One thing I will never understand, though. I will never understand guys who say I don't care how I do. [That] I am just in the competition to have a good time. I take offense to that supercool attitude when I have devoted so much time to competing."

After visiting Intelligentsia, I spend the day at Groundwork Coffee, cupping with Ric Rhinehart and some of his team, touring Groundwork's roasting plant, which is less perfectly appointed than Intelligentsia's or Stumptown's, and visiting Groundwork's newest—decidedly upscale—café in up-and-coming downtown Los Angeles. Ric is a consummate coffee guy, and he has big plans for Groundwork.

To make all this happen, he needs control, and he is involved in complicated financial negotiations to buy out Groundwork's founder.

I thought I was going to be writing about Groundwork's competing with Intelligentsia in Los Angeles—in truth, in this huge and lucrative market there is plenty of room for both companies. But a few weeks after I got home from Los Angeles, I received an email from Ric telling me that it was he who was leaving Groundwork. He had been pushed out by the owner, whose vision for Groundwork turned out to be different from Ric's.

I wasn't entirely surprised to hear the news.

The afternoon I visited, I had gone into Ric's office to take advantage of his wireless connection. When he returned, we stood at his desk talking.

An idea had been flitting around my mind since hearing an offhand remark about specialty coffee profits and losses.

"Are you making any money?" I ask. This turns out to be a particularly apt question in the summer of 2007, as a credit crunch hits and fuel prices increase, transport costs rise, and the dollar drops.

Ric looks at me with a certain world weariness. "Is anyone in specialty making any money?"

He pauses and then goes on. "Tim Castle has a theory that the real waves in specialty coffee have to do with the waves of consolidation that happen periodically. You have these small, quality-driven companies that thrive for a while and then bigger companies come along and buy them up. Tim thinks it will happen again to the current crop of specialty companies."

"Do you think that's right?" I ask. He doesn't answer.

When I am back at my desk in Maryland, I call coffee importer Bob Fulmer, the head of Royal Coffee, one of the high-quality importing companies with which all of the coffee guys work. Bob has been in the coffee business since the 1970s and he has a long view of the specialty industry.

I ask him, "Do you think Intelligentsia and Stumptown and Counter Culture can sustain themselves as independent companies over time?"

"Progress always comes in fits and starts," Bob says. "Chances are these companies and many others will get sold to bigger companies that don't get the specialty coffee thing at all. The big companies will buy them up with the plan of cheapening their production costs and milking the brand for what it is worth for as long as it has value. And that's it. Then the cycle starts all over. Someone else sees an opportunity. Ric has seen this in L.A. I have seen it happen ten times.

"The Third Wave guys—most of them are doing a good job," Bob says. "They are trying to produce something unique and special, but the trouble with their quality-at-all-costs strategy is that eventually they will run out of capital."

Young guys get older, he says, and their priorities change. "Later in life, the money you are offered for your company starts to look pretty good. Someone offers you a few million dollars and you say, 'Gee, I paid my dues. This two million dollars. This five million dollars. I can live pretty well on this.' That's what happened to George Howell at Coffee Connection. He had a big family. Children to educate. The question at the end of the day is to whom do you owe your allegiance? To your family? To your customers? These aren't easy questions. But who knows? Maybe Duane or Doug will do something different. Maybe they will be able to pull off a Google-style IPO and retain independence," says Bob.

Bob's comments make it seem as if the projected downfall of these coffee guys is inevitable—all that gorgeous, crazy energy, all that love poured into finding and roasting the most perfect coffee can't continue forever, can it? Time will tell.

In August, Heather Perry placed second—higher than any American ever had—at the World Barista Competition in Tokyo. Her win came after a whole team of people from the industry rallied to her cause and helped her train. Her performance was broadcast on the Web. I watched. She was brilliant, smooth as always, but this time she exuded a largeness of spirit, a graciousness that had been lacking. She let her love for the coffee shine through her performance.

Now lots of people in coffee world love her.

As Geoff Watts said, "It was clear how much it meant to her and how hard she worked. That really hit people right in the heart."

DURHAM,
NORTH CAROLINA

IT IS A THURSDAY AFTERNOON IN JULY AT COUNTER CULTURE Coffee in Durham, North Carolina, and the last coffee shipment of the week to retail stores and distributors has been loaded—to prevent coffee from moldering in hot trucks all weekend, Counter Culture doesn't ship on Fridays. To mark the occasion, Peter Giuliano is getting ready to show a movie.

"On Thursdays we have this thing called continuing education," Peter explains. "Anybody can teach if they have something to share. Everyone is invited. Someone might offer a class on iced coffee or creating coffee blends. We do a lot of sensory education. Wine and chocolate tastings—that sort of thing.

"Last summer I showed an anthropology movie about Papua New Guinea called *First Contact* that I had seen in college. The film contains footage from the 1930s when Australian adventurers searching for gold unexpectedly confronted thousands of Stone Age people who had no idea that the outside world existed," Peter says, explaining that Counter Culture buys coffee from the descendants of the people seen in the film.

"I was able to show our employees this film shot in the very place where our coffee comes from. These people grow the Papua New Guinea coffee that we sell, a total coincidence that closed a circle for me. This kind of cultural exploration is a driving force in my life. It's a thrill for me to guide people so they can see the connection between the coffee we sell, coffee farmers, and coffee-farming cultures."

Showing *First Contact* is pure Giuliano. The guy is a born social scientist and teacher, and he sees every interaction in terms of its cultural meaning—from a none-too-sober party at the Roasters Guild retreat to his series of surprise encounters with a spear-toting young warrior who, for reasons unknown, followed him everywhere during his November 2007 buying trip to New Guinea. That reflective quality doesn't prevent him from having a good time—Peter is a flirt and a romantic who loves to have fun—but the brain is almost always observing, figuring things out.

In the specialty industry, Peter says, "I am looked at as the professor on *Gilligan's Island*. I am the guy who wants to do the analysis, wants to make things academic." He extends his power of analysis to all aspects of specialty coffee: agronomy, farmer relations, coffee processing, coffee roasting, brewing, the art of the barista, you name it.

In particular, Peter's understanding of cultural contexts shapes his work with coffee farmers. He tries to avoid asking things of them that are in opposition to their cultural norms and values.

He has taken a nondirective stance, for example, when dealing with the giant Nicaraguan coffee cooperative Cecocafen that serves as the miller and financial agent for the twenty-five San Ramon farmers from whom he buys coffee; both Peter and Geoff Watts from Intelligentsia have found Cecocafen managers to be obstructionist, nontransparent, and possibly dishonest. Geoff has clashed head-on with the cooperative leadership. Peter has tried to pursue a less confrontational path.

"With my Nicaraguan producers, I have to let them make their own choices—I don't want to be manipulative in any way. I don't need to live in their community, they do. Being part of a cooperative founded by the Sandinistas is part of their political reality. The Sandinista war was not that long ago. Co-op membership means something to these farmers that is difficult for me to fully understand, so I am cautious about pushing too hard," Peter says.

Instead of butting heads with Cecocafen, Peter searches for a middle way. "My farmers in San Ramon asked me to pay less for coffees, with scores of 90-plus and a little more for coffee in the 85 to 88 range. They weren't comfortable with the top farmers getting too much. They wanted to keep the competition friendly, and they were very worried about the impact if differences in pay were too large," Peter says, adding that pursuing "self-interest in the American sense is not natural in Nicaragua." Peter listened to the growers' concerns and agreed to alter his price structure.

"I am trying to build a durable, long-term way to sell great coffee," says Peter, explaining his strategy. Taking the long view when dealing with farmers, he admits, can involve occasional setbacks, but Peter says he is willing to hang in with suppliers in whom he believes. Of course, Counter Culture wants to be "the best over the long term, as well as the best at any given moment. But sometimes," Peter says, "excellence today and excellence tomorrow pull in opposite directions." Some roasters do not buy from the same farmers year after year, he says. "Their approach is love 'em and leave 'em. They want to get smitten every time, only buying this year's top Cup of Excellence winners....They run off with every girl and don't have a relationship with any of them. Cup of Excellence is their dating service, so to speak. That's not my approach. I'd rather fall in love with a farmer's work, develop a relationship with him or her, and not have to go back to dating well every year."

It is hot and humid in that soul-trying southeastern way when I fly to Durham in late June to visit Counter Culture. The company, with a 2007 growth rate in excess of 20 percent and annual sales of nearly $7 million, is located near the airport in a low-slung building in a high-tech/light industry enclave on the outskirts of Durham. Peter comes to pick me up in his silver PT Cruiser—the right car for a man who thinks about what the right car should be. (Intelligentsia's Geoff Watts drives a BMW. Stumptown's Duane Sorenson has no car although his wife has a minivan; he says he would rather buy another $11,000 Clover brewing machine.

We park the car in the lot next to another silver PT Cruiser—it's Counter Culture's company car—and walk inside. I drop my overnight bag and computer in the corner of the cupping room next to Peter's desk. Peter used to have an office, but the smells from the kitchen were wafting into the cupping room, making it hard to discern true coffee aromas. One thing led to another, space was reallocated, and Peter lost his office. He doesn't seem to mind. More than half the time, he's not in Durham anyway.

Counter Culture strikes me as spiffy, rather than glam— the space is clean; the feel, modern and industrial; the waiting room, modest. The only deluxe space is the light-filled tasting room where the public is invited to try Counter Culture coffees. The cupping room, aka Peter's office, has stylish appointments, too, with nice wood built-ins.

In the warehouse-size roasting/packing room a single red wall creates, a nice backdrop for the black cast-iron roasters— there's a Roure from Spain that roasts one-hundred-pound lots, a customized Joper/Renegade from Portugal that roasts one-hundred-and-twenty-five-pound lots, and a Sasa/Samiac from France that takes twenty-five-pound microlots.

Peter shows me the Agtron, a spectrophotometer that provides a precise reading of how thoroughly a batch of coffee has

been roasted by measuring how waves of infrared light bounce off
the "cooked" coffee—the lighter the roast, the more light it reflects
and the higher the score. "Our French roast," Peter explains, "is
roasted darker than our other coffees, and it has an Agtron score
of 40, while prized microlots like Kenyan Tegu get an Agtron 68.

"We've got parameters on every coffee we send out of
here—how long the coffee roasted, Agtron scores, internal temperatures. All sorts of data to guide our operations," explains Peter.

Counter Culture cuppers, led by head roaster Timothy
Hill, cup every batch of coffee, but there is a problem: "By the time
we taste the coffee, it is twenty-four hours after roasting and the
coffee is already out the door," Peter says. "It's a challenge to constantly ensure that we are living up to our own standards. A couple of our customers, Nick Cho at Murky in Washington, D.C., or
Nick Kirby at Ninth Street Espresso in New York, for example,
will call us when coffee comes in and tell us that it is great or else
they might say, 'Hmm, this most recent batch is off.' Because we
are not retailers—and therefore not constantly working with our
own coffee in our own shops—we rely on customer input. Weekly
cuppings also provide important information about roast quality
and coffee quality."

Counter Culture roasts two hundred different blends—all
the more reason a computerized tracking system is important. This
large number, which a purist like Duane Sorenson scoffs at because
he would never create a blend to please a customer, reflects the
demands on a predominantly wholesale company—Counter
Culture's business is 90 percent wholesale, though its online retail
segment, accounting for about 10 percent of gross sales, is growing
fast, fueled by a spate of stories in the national press identifying
Counter Culture as one of the nation's top roasters.

"We will roast special for our clients, depending on their
desires. As a result, we embrace multiple taste profiles. We are not
dogmatic," Peter says, a tactful statement that means he may not

be personally crazy about every blend that he roasts at customers' behest due to individual taste preferences and cost issues.

The specialty coffee wholesale business—this affects Intelligentsia and Stumptown too—is more price sensitive than the retail business, where Starbucks years ago acclimatized customers to shelling out four dollars for a coffee. High-end wholesale customers running coffee-centric cafés will pay top dollar. "If you increase the price of a top-of-a-line customer from $7.70 to $8.00 a pound, it is not a big deal for them," Peter says. But there are not enough of these high-end cafés to create sufficient demand to bankroll a company like Counter Culture. "We need a certain volume to be able to do our thing," Peter says. To fill in the gap that results from buying high but not always selling high, Counter Culture relies on volume generated from mid-level wholesale customers. Small groceries. Small restaurants and coffee shops. Breakfast joints. These places can't afford to pay for Cup of Excellence grade coffee. Counter Culture creates coffee blends for them using coffees that have good, solid 84-85 cupping scores. "But coffee prices are rising, milk prices are rising, energy costs are rising, and our customers are squeezed in every direction. They cannot afford to pay more for coffee, and this is a hard formula for us to stay on top of," Peter says.

Adding to coffee costs is the preference of many customers for coffee that is certified organic. The move within the specialty industry toward organic has occurred very rapidly. In Africa and Asia, where farmers can rarely afford commercial fertilizer, organic certification is very popular, and in Latin America, it is growing increasingly so. "Seventy-five percent of the coffee we buy is certified organic, and many farms are in transition, moving toward organic," Peter reports, adding that he is a believer.

"I think fertilizers—the ubiquitous nitrogen potassium phosphate (NPK) combination—fuck up the planet. Good soil needs the micronutrients you find in manure. Trace elements of selenium and chromium. This stuff makes coffee plants grow faster. The problem is we haven't figured out as an industry how to teach this stuff to poor farmers." There are other problems, too, Peter admits. He says certification is expensive, and some of the certifiers are corrupt. But these problems are fixable, he believes.

The cycle of rising costs, Peter says, explains why he is "on the warpath for the $7 espresso." He thinks prices for high-quality coffee need to be adjusted in a way that reflects the reality that to have a reasonable life, farmers should be earning $2, $3, or $4 a pound for their coffee and that prices on the consuming end will have to rise accordingly. That's the only way to make specialty coffee sustainable. "People think high-end roasters are squandering money [he means taking in gobs of cash and wasting it], but when you look at the economics, the facts don't support that opinion." Peter believes consumer awareness is the way to end this cycle. "That's why I think the Clover is so important. It offers retail customers a brilliant method for making brewed coffee. We have to deliver an experience that blows customers away. An experience for which they are willing to pay." (Some of Counter Culture's customers, such as Café Grumpy in New York City, are beginning to do as Peter suggests—regularly offering superstar coffees from named farms for between $5 and $10 a cup, while continuing to offer more moderately priced coffee to the majority of their customers.)

Counter Culture's strategy for marketing specialty coffee and coping with rapidly changing market conditions can be summed up in a single phrase: all education all the time. Counter Culture has built swank training centers in Durham, Asheville, Atlanta, and Washington, D.C., offering day-long free courses to coffee professionals and the public on beginning and intermediate espresso, coffee extraction, comparative cupping, advanced cupping, and coffee history. Other kinds of programs are offered, as well. For a three-day seminar at the Washington, D.C., training center in August 2007 on how to run a café, participants came from all over the country. One guy flew in from Japan. In addition, the centers, teach new and prospective customers how to use, clean, and maintain brewing and espresso equipment—like Stumptown and Intelligentsia, Counter Culture monitors client performance and insists that customers maintain high standards. Counter Culture's training isn't confined to the training centers. In New York City; for example, where the company is arguably the current "it girl" high-profile roaster, landing prestigious accounts in a market that is just beginning to open to specialty coffee, the company has two full-time employees, one of whom does nothing but teach wholesale customers about coffee making.

I visited Ninth Street Espresso, one of Counter Culture's New York City high-profile wholesale accounts, on a Friday in early summer. With three Manhattan locations, a hipster ethos, and a reputation for great coffee, Ninth has made waves in New York. Looking to establish a Manhattan beachhead, Intelligentsia had fought hard to win the Ninth Street account, but lost out to Counter Culture. The morning I visited Ninth Street, cupper-in-chief Nick Kirby had just taken part in one of Counter Culture's weekly tastings conducted online. Customers along the East Coast and at Counter Culture headquarters registered their judgments of cupped coffees from Kenya, Colombia, Ethiopia, and Indonesia. The company designed a spreadsheet on which participants record their responses to the week's offerings. "Everyone cups the same coffees at the same time on the same day and then we have a chat forum on them. This has become our special place for discussing coffees. Our internal blog. The forum is our community green," comments Peter, "and we depend on it."

Counter Culture is using its packaging as another teaching tool. Artful labels have been designed for each of Counter

Culture's direct trade farms. Each package describes the specific coffee inside.

The package for Finca Mauritania in Santa Ana, El Salvador, for example, identifies the coffee as a Counter Culture exclusive, with a map of El Salvador on the side and a star locating the farm. The back label describes the grower herself: "Aida Batlle, the owner and manager of Finca Mauritania, located on the slopes of El Salvador's Santa Ana Volcano, has become famous in the coffee world for her uncompromising commitment to coffee quality and dedication to progressive and sustainable farm management. We are thrilled that Aida chose Counter Culture to be the exclusive roaster of this spectacular coffee." The note is signed by Peter.

On the side of the package are "Tasting Notes" describing the coffee: "Intoxicating flavors of brown sugar, butterscotch, and sweet fruit swirl in this incredible 100 percent Bourbon varietal coffee. You'll love the perfect, sweet, and gentle aftertaste."

Peter compares the way he is showcasing his coffees to a foodie phenomenon closer to home. "In North Carolina people don't talk about barbecue in general, they say I like the barbecue of the Piedmont region or I like the barbecue from one particular place in Lexington. That's what we are doing with our packaging. We want our customers to understand we don't sell coffee from Sumatra. We sell coffee from Aceh in Sumatra. It's like French wine. Nobody buys French wine. They buy wine from a particular region or a particular chateau. For us Aceh is like Burgundy."

Counter Culture's focus on education has helped the company make inroads into one of the holiest realms of the culinary world: the Culinary Institute of America (CIA) in Hyde Park, New York. In fall 2007 Counter Culture took over the coffee education program for CIA students who are seeking a certificate in pastry making—the students receive both a general culinary education and a specialized education in certain subject areas of their own choosing. Counter Culture trainers now teach students enrolled in the pastry program coffee basics, cupping, espresso making, and the art of brewed coffee, as well as more theoretical material.

In the summer Peter had made several trips to Hyde Park to meet with the school's directors and to teach some preliminary classes. He loved talking with people who were so immersed in the nuances of taste, and he felt that the CIA program was going to have a huge impact on CIA students and in the long run on the culinary world.

It was a pleasure, he says, to teach students who "get it" so quickly. "What we are teaching totally parallels the basic wine education all students at CIA receive. Because they understand the impact of varietals on wine, that adds to their understanding of coffee," Peter says.

"Usually when I conduct a cupping, people have this insecurity. They worry that they won't be able to experience the nuance as well as a professional taster. These kids aren't like that. Their confidence is unsurpassed. They need us to help them articulate their ideas and take what they discern about coffee to the next step. For example, coffee blends are changing all the time because of availability. If a coffee shop has an espresso blend or coffee drink, the chef or manager needs someone to manage the blend. What we are hoping is that chef/owners trained by us will do this managing themselves so that the espresso blend they serve will truly reflect their culinary values. That's where coffee in restaurants can get interesting."

Like all the ingredients chefs use, Peter believes that "coffee should fit in with an overall aesthetic. Espresso is one choice. All restaurants seem to think they have to offer espresso, but often it doesn't fit in. It's great when a restaurant like Franny's in Park Slope, Brooklyn [a Counter Culture customer], makes a commitment to espresso. This is an Italian place serving fabulous pizza.

But for some restaurants it doesn't relate to what they do. It's like creating a wine list. The list makes a statement. 'I will not offer pink wines, but I will have the biggest selection of Argentine varietals.' Coffee should be one of those choices reflecting a particular chef's aesthetic, too."

Peter is eager to expand the CIA program to include all the students at the school, but he believes it makes sense to start with the pastry students. "These chefs are entrepreneurial. They start small restaurants, bakeries, coffee houses," and so they can play a huge role spreading the word about specialty coffee into the larger culinary world.

Back in North Carolina, Peter takes me on a tour of Durham and Chapel Hill, showing off his favorite local haunts—foodie and otherwise. He shares his delight that foodie consciousness has reached the Durham/Chapel Hill area, where the long growing season is a boon to farmers and a "buy local" movement is in full swing. Counter Culture, as the local coffee roaster, is part of the excitement, and some local restaurants—Rue Cler in Durham, Jibarra in Raleigh—have added locally roasted Counter Culture coffee to their menus.

Driving around town, Peter shares personal details of his life. He talks about his mother's death from cancer shortly after he moved to North Carolina and expresses his regrets that she, whose passion for language, love of travel, and profound interest in other cultures he had inherited, had died without having the chance to truly experience the role he had carved for himself as a coffee guy.

It is in the car that Peter tells me that he and his wife, Alice, are divorcing. The marriage, it seems, had died a thousand little deaths, due at least in part to Peter's constant travel and his passion for his work. Alice would get their house in Durham. Peter is thinking of buying another small house nearby, but in the meantime he and Alice are still sharing their house, though he tells me he has just rented an apartment in California near San Diego, where he is planning to spend one week a month. In California, he will be living close to his father, his brother, the ocean, surfing, all the outdoor things he loves to do, and telecommuting to work.

Peter feels certain he will be able to work as easily one week a month in California as in North Carolina. With Skype (the inexpensive online phone service that facilitates overseas telephone calling), email, and cell phones, telecommuting in the United States or overseas is easy, Peter says. "And people here in Durham are used to me being away."

In addition to the digital advances, what makes this move possible is the presence at the Durham plant of Brett Smith, Counter Culture's founder and majority owner—Peter owns 8 percent of Counter Culture. Brett is taking over the day-to-day management of the company, a job that Peter had previously done but in his opinion not that well—"I suck as a manager," he has told me more than once.

For a number of years Brett ran a second business and had more or less left Peter alone to run Counter Culture, although Peter notes it was Brett, not he, "who took the financial risks, such as mortgaging his house," to keep the company afloat when one of the original partners wanted to be bought out. For five years, Peter was the coffee buyer and everything else at Counter Culture. "Those years enabled us to push the limits in terms of coffee," Peter says. Brett's second business tanked two years ago and Brett has been carving a higher-profile role for himself within the coffee company. It was he who pushed the notion that the company must expand into new markets up and down the East Coast.

Peter admits the transition has sometimes been challenging, but adds that Brett's skills as a manager, a money guy, and someone who excels in developing talent are helping Counter Culture grow in crucial ways. "Our arrangement is very similar to a restaurant with a chef/owner who is known to the public—rarely does the chef/owner own the majority of the place," Peter says, adding that Brett has devoted himself to learning about specialty coffee and he has "taken an interest in crafting the way we operate as a business and has helped us push our limits."

The two share a fundamental belief that Counter Culture's success resides in its high standards. Together, for example, they agreed that Counter Culture is a specialty coffee company, not a supplier of coffee shops, and the two have recently decided that they will no longer sell the syrups that coffee shops use to flavor (or adulterate, depending on your point of view) coffee.

"Everyone makes assumptions when they hear that Brett is an MBA. They think decisions come from me that really come from him and vice versa. I think of myself as loving and supportive. I think most people would say I am a great person to work for, but I can be very, very hard. I have an Old World work ethic and really high expectations. When people disappoint me I don't always have a lot of patience. Brett is more like a Little League coach. He believes that you can bring people along. He loves to find what people are good at and help develop their talent. He is the guy at CC who gets the right people on the bus and helps them find their seat."

The next morning, Peter picks me up at my hotel and we walk over to the small café in the front of the restaurant Rue Cler. We drink freshly brewed Counter Culture Kenyan and eat beignets—thumb-sized French doughnuts filled with preserves. I open my laptop so I can type as Peter speaks. I am eager to hear his thoughts about some of the overseas developments in the coffee market.

First, though, we eat our beignets. Peter tells me that his wife, Alice, works next door at a graphic design firm and he excuses himself to walk over to her office to say hello. Then Alice stops by Rue Cler. She has long dark hair and is pretty and friendly; meeting her, I feel sad in the way married people do when other married people break up.

When we finally settle down to work, Peter talks to me about the issues he and other buyers are facing overseas. "It's been a very challenging year for specialty buyers. Farmers are shopping around even when they have a buyer, hoping to entice players who will pay more." The Esmeralda phenomenon has destabilized the market. "After that coffee got $130 a pound, a lot of producers reached out to me and said, 'Why not me? You said my coffee was great, so why not me?' Is that coffee really worth one hundred times what other specialty coffees are getting?" Peter asks. "I can't say that I think it is."

While suppliers are becoming balky, the market for highly ranked coffees is growing more competitive, and that competition undermines the camaraderie among buyers, Peter says. There's a sense in the marketplace that there is not enough high-quality coffee to go around. As a consequence, traveling with other buyers is no longer so much fun. Lots of sharp elbows.

"There is a new generation coming up, and these guys want to do what we do overseas," Peter explains. "Novo, Paradise Roasters in Minneapolis, Barefoot in San Francisco, Flying Goat. They are on the perimeter now wanting to do 'relationship coffee' too. Suddenly there are more mouths to feed. Some of these guys don't have much skill, but as an industry we have to see this as a positive thing. Still, it is challenging to see where and how the market will grow.

"The difficulties in the market are exacerbated by the Fair Trade system," Peter says. "Fair Trade doesn't look for high quality, it looks for fairly okay coffees. A farmer faces a choice. He can get the Fair Trade price or he can roll the dice with me and get a better price if his coffee qualifies as specialty grade. But farmers are always worrying what will happen if they get a 78 cupping score and don't make the cut. A lot of the farmers don't see themselves as craftspeople driven by the urge to make their product better and better. They live in an uncertain world, and they are afraid of risk," Peter says.

"Rumors circulate that specialty buyers like me and Geoff are just a different version of exploitation, a different kind of colonialism. Anyone who knows the specialty business knows that this is not true, but you can see how some people can misinterpret our role. I fly down to Guatemala or El Salvador or Nicaragua a few times a year and meet with the same people all the time. Other people in the community get suspicious and jealous."

Adding to the tension, "in a lot of countries yields were low this year for reasons that are not entirely clear and a lot of farmers were really, really struggling." For example, the yields of the farmers Peter works with in San Ramon went way down and "a lot of them blame the problem on going organic."

"The African market, too, was in turmoil. Yields were way down in Kenya, as was quality": this at a time when the government loosened some controls on a market that was internally corrupt and externally well run. No one knew if the whole system would improve, or if corruption would just spread to the external market. It was anyone's guess.

The emerging Rwandan market is struggling too, Peter tells me. Farmers are growing better coffee, sure, but so far there is a disheartening vacuum; local leaders are not emerging who are able to effectively, honestly, and transparently serve as their representatives, bankers, and agents. In Burundi, there was excitement about the coffee quality, for sure, with some folks predicting Burundi would surpass Rwanda as a coffee-growing region, but the politics remain volatile and dangerous.

Peter's fall trip, during which he, Geoff, and Aleco taught cupping to extremely eager locals, was cut short by an outbreak of political violence that left thirty-five Burundians dead and the capital city of Bujumbura shut down.

(There is some good news, however. In September 2007, U.S. Aid approved a $27 million grant that will fund a Rwanda-style coffee-development program in Burundi.)

And Ethiopia?

Well, that was the worst.

"I wanted to shower the East Coast with these extraordinary Ethiopian coffees this year," but "here we are in late June," Peter says. "The container of coffee I ordered from Menno Simons should have shipped ages ago." Menno seems to have no idea when or even if all his coffees will be shipped. And it isn't just Peter facing this mess. Virtually every specialty buyer in the high-end business is waiting for Ethiopian coffee from Menno.

Sitting in our window seat at the Rue Cler looking out on the sunny street, Peter describes a solid wall of confusion in Ethiopia. Menno, he says, is a classy guy who seems to be trying his hardest to treat everyone fairly—farmers, buyers, everyone in the chain. Many of the coffees he is buying come from Abdullah Bagersh, the only Ethiopian exporter who really seems to get the specialty message. But Menno travels constantly. Abdullah is in Ethiopia. Peter, Geoff, Duane, and everyone else—none of them understand Ethiopia's Byzantine rules and regulations.

"You have to be careful," explains Peter. "Menno and Bagersh are the pretty girls at the prom. You have to figure out how to push forward, without pushing too hard. These guys have more suitors than they can handle. You want to be urgent without being demanding. To be honest, I have tried with Menno and other people in Ethiopia to sweeten the pot in terms of price, adding an extra dime, fifteen cents to expedite the coffees, but it backfired on me. It's hard to do business when you don't know the rules of the game. It feels like when I was twenty-four and I took a trip to Sicily and I didn't understand how to get service in the bank. I spoke the language, but it was the culture I didn't understand. In

Sicily, if you want to get waited on, you can't just stand in line. You have to cut everyone off. It took me two and a half hours to change traveler's checks because I was being too polite. I didn't understand the system.

"It is hard in Ethiopia to get a sense culturally of what is pushing too hard, what is not pushing hard enough. You are operating blind."

In the months after I visited Peter, I kept tabs on Menno's coffees. All July and into August, roasters waited and waited for Menno's coffees to ship. The only coffees that made it out of Ethiopia were air freighted by Joseph Brodsky of Novo Coffee, to his wholesale customers, including Duane's Stumptown. Joseph had spent six months in Ethiopia and knew his way around. Air freighting added $1.00 a pound to the price of the coffee. "Hey, we don't mind," Aleco, the Stumptown buyer, said with his characteristic bravado, "we're already spending $25 a pound for some of these coffees."

In October, after Peter had returned from spending a week traveling in Ethiopia with Menno, we talk again at length about what had happened that year in Ethiopia. We have this conversation when Menno's coffee had finally been trucked overland to a ship in Djibouti. The coffees arrived in some cases five months, six months—a lifetime—late, some of them having lost much of their sparkle. In the meantime, Ethiopian farmers were starting to prepare for the 2008 harvest.

"Ten years ago, there were no unions representing coffee farmers in Ethiopia," Peter explains, and all the coffee there was sold by a handful of exporters sanctioned by the government. "Then a guy named Tedesse Meskela, who now heads the Oromia Cooperative, started organizing farmers. In Ethiopia any farmer can sell to whomever he pleases. Tedesse helped win passage of a law that determined that a group of farmers organized into a union was in a legal sense indistinguishable from a single farmer acting on his own behalf. So these unions, like corporations, won legal standing and were able to bypass the government system.

"Buyers like me saw the unions as a great thing. I thought, now I can work with farmers directly, rather than work in the weird Byzantine government system. Then Tedesse helped the unions win organic and Fair Trade certifications. Everyone thought we were entering into a whole new era with Ethiopia.

"This whole scenario appeals to specialty buyers' sense of what is right, and we all showed up and started offering farmers big money for their coffee. This is an old, sad story. Once the money starts to flow, the people who are running the organizations are not equipped, and then mismanagement and outright theft become rampant. The unions were way over their heads. All of them started doing shady stuff—this year a number of them were decertified by FLO, the international Fair Trade organization. In the last year two unions have collapsed because they couldn't pay farmers" for their coffee, although the unions themselves were paid.

"All of this should have been predictable. These guys went from nothing to trying to be big-time coffee exporters selling on margin, operating like players. Guys like me, we bear some of the responsibility for what happened. We wanted to pay more. We went into Ethiopia with our dollars. We pay $3 a pound for the best coffees. $3.50. Here's the money. We triggered a gold rush and then the market just disintegrated. What you had in Ethiopia this year was a total market collapse."

Now Menno is trying to put Humpty Dumpty back together, but he is not having an easy time of it. "Tremendous distrust of Europeans has surfaced," Peter says. "People are saying, 'Here's this Dutchman coming in like Dutch traders always do, hoping to grow rich.'

"When I was with Menno, he was going around trying to reestablish relationships. Menno is not a bleeding heart, but he is trying to do the right thing. There are big power struggles going on. Menno feels good about the progress he is making.

"He had a big setback last year. Now he is coming back—the market is coming back—based more on reality. Everyone knows now what can go wrong."

The Ethiopian specialty coffee market redefines chaos. "It's the polar opposite of Panama," Peter says in conclusion, leading right into my next question.

Geisha. What about Geisha and this crazy auction in May 2007 at which Geisha was auctioned for $130 a pound wholesale?

Peter laughs. Usually markets work to the detriment of producers, he explains, but not this time. "It takes a really smart guy like Price Peterson to manipulate scarcity in his favor. This year he only entered 250 pounds of Geisha in the auction. Five bags of fifty pounds each. He limited the supply and the price shot up. That was a conscious strategy."

He continues, "The Petersons took a gamble, assuming that Geisha would come in first again. They knew if they came in first and there were only five hundred pounds of Geisha available and more roasters than ever wanted to buy it—well, the result was predictable. The first year they offered twenty bags, and twenty roasters paid $21 a pound. Then they put ten bags in the auction. Ten of those original roasters bid against the others and the price shot up. This year, they entered five bags and more roasters than ever competed for those five bags." The specialty world went wild and drove the price up into the stratosphere.

"You can say that the roasters' hunger for these stellar coffees is just a function of marketing," Peter says, "but I think the truth runs deeper. This is the new luxury economy, and it is driven by people like Ric and Geoff and Duane and me who fall romantically in love with these coffees. There's a direct line between our palates and our hearts. We respond the same way we respond to a beautiful woman. Same irrational response. You just have to possess her. So there are all these guys competing for the affections of the ladies and the whole thing gets crazy.

"Most of the people who bid $130 a pound for Geisha had access to coffee growing right next to the auction lot that cost $12.50 a pound. Why would they pay $130 a pound?

"This is an industry where the participants have constant permission to indulge in hedonistic pursuits. We are entrusted to pursue pleasurable things, and pleasure becomes the dominating force in our lives. The culture of coffee is exactly the same as the culture of chefs: society gives us permission to be obsessed. That's what we think about all the time. I love the hedonism to a certain extent...love when we are comfortable experiencing the world through our senses, but it gets a little weird. Especially given the power structure. At origin, we are like rock stars. We are surrounded by people who want to spend time with us, who offer us every enticement imaginable. You are traveling for a long time, you are a young guy, and it is easy to get caught up in that and lose your footing.

"You've got to be off-kilter a little bit to get attracted to this business....By the time you are a little successful, you've been poor for a long time. A lot of these guys were social outcasts in the younger part of their lives...don't have equipment to deal with some of this stuff."

One of the qualities that makes Peter different in a sense is his love of words. It's not just the sensual thrill of the coffee that drives him; it's telling the story. Not, mind you, that he is unsusceptible now and then to all the forms of seduction, including the spine-chilling thrill of beating out a competitor.

"We were down in Honduras this year cupping coffee at Finca el Puente where Marysabel Caballero grows the Purple

Princess. This coffee is just as much a thoroughbred as Esmeralda. Last year Duane got one hundred bags of this coffee; he just beat me to the punch. He got on the plane faster," Peter says.

"This year, Kim, the person on my staff who helps manage our farmer relations, and I went down together. We went to the Caballero farm and spent a few days with Marysabel and her father. We were sitting around the breakfast table one morning and Marysabel's father pulled out a folder. He had collected everything that I had written on our Web site about El Puente and translated it meticulously into Spanish. They read what I had written aloud. I described the coffee's intense lavender perfume, its texture that reminds me of silk robes, regal robes in Phoenician purple. Marysabel's father was so proud. 'Peter, you are the Cervantes of coffee,' he said.

"That meant everything to me. The family got to see the worth of their coffee through my eyes. It was especially meaningful because I had recorded my thoughts in writing. They had never before had this form of outside validation. I am always reaching to find the right descriptors that capture the coffee taste so that I can change what is a solitary tasting experience into something communicated. A moment shared. Then it turns out the Caballeros were so touched by my writing that they had put a container of this coffee aside for me. A container. Two hundred fifty bags."

Riding in a truck on the way to Matagalpa, Nicaragua, shortly after I met Peter in 2006, I asked him what his life as a coffee guy meant to him. His answer made an impression on me because it was so different from what I had expected. I had one of those moments that journalists sometimes experience when someone being interviewed takes the conversation somewhere surprising.

"Fundamentally," Peter told me, "my interest in coffee is aesthetic. My family is from Sicily," he explained. "I was brought up by my grandmother, who didn't speak English. I learned from her that life is short, brutish, and cheap and that misery lies in wait for you. What interests me in coffee is the beauty of it. The beauty of the moment that coffee can create."

That stayed with me. "The beauty of the moment that coffee can create."

EPILOGUE

THROUGH THE FALL AND WINTER OF 2007-2008, I CHECK IN with the coffee guys, keeping abreast of their travels and hearing how their companies are coping with rising fuel costs, rising milk prices, contracting credit, the shrinking U.S. dollar, significant hikes in the price of coffee, and late-paying customers. For the past five years, Counter Culture, Intelligentsia, and Stumptown have been growing pretty fast, and now...the most serious economic downturn in a decade. These are young companies. All of them are carrying some debt. None of them has experience riding out a recession.

As 2008 begins, I also follow events in Nicaragua that have been coming to a head for Peter and Geoff and their companies. Since 2005, when I met Geoff at Cup of Excellence, he has been struggling with the large Nicaraguan coffee cooperative Cecocafen that represents the farmers in Las Brumas from whom he buys coffee. In two and a half years, Geoff visited Nicaragua a dozen times, seeking to guarantee that Las Brumas farmers who grew the best coffee were paid a premium for their efforts. Geoff paid the quality premiums to Cecocafen, but after that, it was any-body's guess where Intelligentsia's money went.

Peter also struggled in Nicaragua. The farmers in San Ramon with whom he worked for seven years complained bitterly to him about losses in revenue that they blamed on their switch to organic farming, although this turned out not to be the cause of their problems. The farmers told Peter they simply didn't have the yield to survive. Peter bought and paid for a great deal of coffee from San Ramon, and when it arrived, he had to throw away 20 percent. Cecocafen, in its role as the San Ramon exporter, had made serious mistakes. Instead of sending premium coffee from San Ramon, it shipped poor-quality coffee filled with quakers—immature beans that don't fully develop in the roast and ruin the taste of the coffee.

Geoff urged the Las Brumas farmers to leave the coopera-tive if they did not feel they were being well represented. Peter took a very different approach, trying not to get between the San Ramon farmers and their loyalty to the cooperative. Given their different stances, the way these two problems were resolved came as a complete surprise.

In January 2008, I talk with Peter, who has just returned from Nicaragua. "The farmers in San Ramon held a secret meeting and decided to 'wash their hands of Cecocafen,'" he tells me. They had voted to leave the cooperative.

For two years, the San Ramon farmers had not been paid for their coffee. The cooperative told the farmers that Counter Culture was to blame—that Counter Culture had withheld payment. When Peter looked into the problem, he discovered that Cecocafen simply did not pay these farmers for two years because the union got into financial trouble—not hard to do playing the futures market.

Now the farmers of San Ramon are "birds flying from the nest." And like all creatures that leave home, they face many daunting challenges. Cecocafen holds their organic certification, and it holds loans issued to the farmers. "I told the San Ramon farmers they have to go to the bank, figure out what they owe, and then tell me, and I can help them figure out how to proceed." Peter made it clear he could help only if the farmers take steps to help themselves. "These are pretty big challenges for people who have never before represented their own interests," he says.

"For me the situation is hopeful," says Peter, "because this was the first year it got through to the farmers that Counter Culture is not going anywhere. It's like that moment in personal relationships when things get rough and the other person realizes that you aren't leaving.

"In some ways it would be smarter for me to cut my losses and go somewhere else because of all the mistakes Cecocafen made. The San Ramon guys actually said to me, 'Peter, aren't you tired of this? Shouldn't you go elsewhere?'

"I told them, 'Look, man, we made a commitment to you guys, and we are going to keep it.' That's the moment it finally dawned on them that we are the real deal."

When he is not traveling for Counter Culture, Peter is living alone for the first time in his adult life. He's not a guy who enjoys being single, but the telecommuting from California when he's not traveling has worked out well. During the summer—during his weeks in California—he rose early, worked hard, and still managed to go surfing most afternoons. He tells me in January that he has reached out to old friends, and he's starting to have fun again. He has been offered a spot on the SCAA board that could lead to him serving as board president.

In December 2007, Geoff had been full of hope. Talking on the phone from Chicago after his recent trip to Nicaragua, he sounded

elated as he described a meeting with the Las Brumas farmers. He
and K. C. O'Keefe had made printouts of the Las Brumas harvest
report in Spanish and had given copies to all the farmers.

"This was a big breakthrough moment," Geoff reported.
"The farmers had never been able to see how their coffee cupped
compared to their neighbors' or friends'. I see now that the idea of
quality as we had presented it to them in the past was way too
abstract.

"At this meeting the farmers could look at their own cupping scores and compare them to those of one of the more active
farmers in their group.

"There's one guy who loves talking about quality details.
He's very curious. Very engaged....Sure enough this guy, Ernesto, he
submitted ten lots of coffee and nine of them qualified at 85 or above
and several cupped above 90. With him as a concrete example, we
could say to the other farmers, 'Look at how Ernesto scored. What
did he do that you didn't do?' Finally we had a concrete way to talk
to farmers about how they could earn the highest scores."

After that breakthrough moment, Geoff asked the farmers
to speak. What were their concerns? Instead of the usual silence,
one by one the farmers spoke up, sharing their worries, asking
questions, circling back again and again to questions about how
Cecocafen, Intelligentsia, and they the farmers could work
together. "K. C. and I could see there was a fundamental gap in the
farmers' understanding.

"I feel like there is much more unity now in Las Brumas,"
Geoff said. "We took a big step forward in establishing trust with
them. I was worried this year would be another year of scratching
and clawing. This project has a lot of consequence for me. We had
to work so hard, wade through a lot of water. I see that trust is
built in inches, not in feet. Step by step by step."

Geoff was sure that all systems now were go. But instead,
more roadblocks. While Peter's farmers took a secret vote and

decided to leave the cooperative, Geoff's farmers made no move to leave. Cecocafen did nothing. A month passed.

In mid-January, Geoff flies to Nicaragua once again and makes his peace with Cecocafen. In an email to me at the end of January, he writes, "After five trips to Nicaragua in the last year to meet with both the Brumas farmers and the Cecocafen leadership, we finally managed to come up with a model that would work and meet the criteria we've set out in our Direct Trade system, while still satisfying the requirements of Cecocafen.

"In many ways," Geoff writes, "it was a struggle over control—our system is built on the premise that all financial transactions need to be transparent all the way to the farm. The central Co-op was not used to having that kind of relationship, and I think it made them nervous."

Geoff does not reveal the details of the plan, only saying, "we did come to a reasonable solution....Our relationship with Las Brumas farmers is stronger than ever, the coffees keep getting better, and the prices keep going up. Cecocafen seems to have resigned itself to the fact that we are not going away and that our extreme focus on quality is indeed a positive thing."

Intelligentsia's Silver Lake café opened in August 2007. Geoff and Doug Zell expect that it will bring in $1.2 million a year, more than any of the three Chicago Intelligentsia cafés. A second Los Angeles café is in the works. And the Intelligentsia roastery is slated to open in 2008.

In the summer, Geoff had told me he was thinking about settling down. When I had dinner with him in Chicago in July 2007, he said that he and a longtime girlfriend in Colombia, a plant biologist, were talking about trying to be together more often. Maybe have an exclusive relationship. Geoff owns a coffee roastery and café in Colombia called Palo Alto, and he said he would like to rent an apartment in Cali to be near his girlfriend and his Colombia business. He said he was going to spend more time in Colombia.

In January 2008, he had not yet returned to Cali, and until his time-consuming tenure as head of the Roasters Guild is complete late in the summer of 2008, he says it is hard to see how he will find the time.

And Duane Sorenson's Stumptown? Its two Seattle cafés opened in the fall, and the Seattle roastery began operating in January. Matt Lounsbury reported in January that volume in Seattle and in Portland is building, after a holiday slump. The Ace hotel chain is looking to open a hotel in Herald Square in New York City in 2009 and wants Stumptown to open a café in the hotel, just like in Portland. Such a move, of course, would be a violation of everything Duane has sworn he holds dear. Being a regional roaster. Maintaining constant oversight of his product. Only entering markets where he understands the vibe. Will such a movement happen? "We are only in the talking stage," Matt Lounsbury says.

Stumptown in the meantime has continued to be its coffee-centric self. Aleco has been tracking and buying the best small lots, as well as larger supplies of Stumptown favorite Direct Trade coffees. Stumptown now offers as many as thirty-five coffees at a time—so many that they do not fit on the chalkboard. They can be found on Stumptown's Web site or at the Annex in Portland where customers buy whole beans.

To increase consumer awareness of the uniqueness of Stumptown coffees, Duane redesigned the company's packaging last fall. The Stumptown look is still understated—the coffee comes in a plain brown bag—but now the bag has a die cut to accommodate stiff cards that tell the story of each coffee—including information about the farm, the region, and the taste profile.

And what about Geisha?

Soon there will be half a dozen more growers of Geisha selling their coffee in Panama. No one has a clue how that will play out. Rachel Peterson and the rest of the Hacienda La Esmeralda family, who have successfully channeled their Geisha crop into fame and fortune, are trying to devise a new way of marketing Geisha. They are thinking of dividing Hacienda La Esmeralda's Geisha trees into twelve areas, microlots, cupping each separately and auctioning each lot off separately at an auction separate from Best of Panama. The Petersons want to be fair to their customers, and so far they haven't made a final decision.

Peter believes that Geisha isn't Geisha or Gesha and never was. He thinks there was a mix-up in one of the research laboratories. He notes that Geisha beans look like the Longberry Harars that grow in the Harar Valley. That physical resemblance suggests to Peter that the coffee everyone calls Geisha probably originated not in any of the western Ethiopian towns of Gesha, Gesha, and Gecha but on the other side of the country in the Harar Valley in the even more remote mountainous eastern corner of the country.

Doubts about Geisha haven't stopped coffee consultant and nouveau Panamanian farmer Willem Boot from dreaming of another expedition to the Ethiopian forest where he thinks Geisha might have originated and might still be growing. We talk on the telephone and he weaves a story that reminds me of King Arthur and the legend of the Once and Future King—the part where the Lady of the Lake rises up and offers some future Arthur the opportunity to grab hold of Excalibur. To arrive at the far-off Camelot, our hero will be forced to undergo life-threatening tests. Face down lions and tigers. The effort will be body-breaking, but the potential reward will be mythic. Our hero will grab samples of his heart's desire, then run like hell. And this time, Willem tells me, he won't tell anyone where he has been.

BACKGROUND

THE COFFEE CHAIN
EXPLAINED

THOSE LITTLE BLACK/BROWN BEANS THAT YOU GRIND TO make high-quality coffee are the roasted seeds of a tree called Coffea arabica. A hinged pair of seeds is nestled inside Coffea arabica's fruit, which coffee buyers call "cherry," almost always using the singular. In its natural state "cherry" grows in clusters on nodules running up and down the slender branches of coffee trees. When ripe, this fruit is bright red and looks like the cherries we buy raw at the grocery and eat by the handful, but the two come from different plant species and they do not taste alike.

Coffee trees grow in Central and South America, Africa, and Asia in mountainous areas between four thousand and six thousand feet high that span the globe along a latitudinal band that hugs the earth's center from approximately fifteen degrees north to fifteen degrees south of the equator. The climate in these disparate highlands tends to be temperate, with temperatures fluctuating most of the time between 60°F and 80°F.

In Latin America and parts of Africa, coffee trees are cultivated in rows on properties that look like Christmas tree farms;
elsewhere coffee grows wild in forests or in semiforested areas. In
general, the higher the altitude, the better the coffee. The very best
coffees tend to come from small farms with very specific weather
patterns called microclimates where they are cultivated by hand.

Coffee is a seasonal product, harvested once a year. In the
Northern Hemisphere, depending on climate and altitude, the harvest starts in September and runs until March. In the Southern
Hemisphere the harvest takes place in April and May. Buyers of
high-quality coffee travel the globe, buying fresh coffee soon after
it is picked and processed, and delivering it to consumers in a
timely fashion because as coffee loses freshness, its taste degrades.

Coffee trees need sun, but not too much, and they need
rain at specific times in their growing cycle. In very sunny terrain,
coffee trees thrive when planted under canopies of shade trees; in
cloudy microclimates, shade trees are not needed. Coffee requires
fertilizing and pruning and other forms of care during the year.
Ripe red coffee cherry produces coffee beans that are heavier and
far superior in taste to cherry that is tinged with green. Since coffee
cherry does not ripen at a uniform rate, pickers must make
repeated passes through coffee orchards—therefore, picking takes
many weeks or even months and is expensive.

Once picked, coffee cherries are often depulped mechanically to remove the skins and most of the fruit, and then they are
fermented or washed to dissolve the sticky coating called mucilage
that covers the hinged pair of coffee beans inside. Washing and
fermenting can take many days, but once the fermentation is
complete the farmer or the farm manager must act quickly
because overfermenting destroys the taste of the coffee.
Fermentation often reaches its apex during the middle of the
night when temperatures drop. If the person in charge of the

washing station falls asleep, as often happens, a farmer's entire crop can be lost. Washing stations are not very expensive to build, and villages, co-ops, and other small groups often have their own washing facilities.

Coffee that is not washed is called unwashed or naturally processed. Natural processes vary from region to region. Sometimes the outer skin, fruit, and mucilage are left intact and the entire cherry is left to dry in the sun. Unwashed coffees taste distinctly different from washed coffees.

Washed or unwashed, all coffee must be dried. Farmers around the world use a number of different drying techniques. Some spread their coffee on the ground to dry, although this method is not recommended; others dry their coffee on cement patios, special drying racks, or mechanical dryers that are wood- or gas-burning, or fired with coffee parchment. Some of these machines use coffee tree prunings as fuel. Again, this process takes days. If it rains, mold and mildew can ruin or degrade the coffee.

After drying, coffee must be milled to strip the parchment-like skin that covers the bean. Mills are large and expensive to build and operate. Farmers almost never own their own mills, though large cooperatives and large plantations sometimes do.

After milling, coffee beans must be sorted by size and quality. This sorting can be done by hand or by machine. People in the coffee industry refer to milled, sorted coffee as "green" because it has not yet been roasted. Once green coffee is sorted, it is poured into clean bags and stored in a dry place. Bag quality really matters. In 2006 the entire Cup of Excellence first-place auction lot from Honduras was ruined because it had been stored in jute bags tainted with petroleum. After the green coffee has rested for a month or two, it is ready to be prepared for "cupping"—taste-testing—by international buyers, who pay more for coffees that earn higher cupping scores.

At every step along the production process, coffee loses weight and mass; green milled coffee has approximately 20 percent of the weight of picked cherry. During the roasting process, coffee shrinks another 15 percent or so.

Coffee farmers, like most farmers, get paid once a year. To stay afloat financially, they generally require interest-bearing loans called prefinancing. Some farmers sell their cherry before it is washed; most prefer to sell after washing. When farmers are desperate for cash, they sell to "coyotes" who travel around in trucks buying cherry on the cheap. Other coffee farmers sell their washed green coffee directly to millers. The miller may sell to an exporter or function as an exporter.

Around the world, it is common for coffee farmers to band together in cooperatives and other kinds of associations. They join forces to create a social safety net for themselves, to have easier access to financing, and to help overcome the complexity of competing in the global coffee market.

It is virtually impossible for small growers and small buyers to directly access each other in the global marketplace. Growers almost always sell to exporters who sell green coffee to legally sanctioned import companies. Green buyers from companies like Counter Culture, Intelligentsia, and Stumptown buy from importers with whom they have established relationships. Although these coffee buyers say they "buy directly" from farmers, this phrase is misleading. They may interact extensively with farmers, but green buyers need the logistical and financial services offered by importers. Other middlemen such as coffee "sourcers," who locate desirable coffees, also play a part in the complex chain that stretches from the grower across the globe to the consumer.

Exporters generally truck their coffees to port, where it is loaded into containers and shipped to customers in the United States, Europe, Japan, and elsewhere. Importers receive the coffee and warehouse it for their customers, who roast it and sell it to their own retail and wholesale customers.

Every person or institution that touches the coffee after it leaves the farm—the owner of the washing station, the management of the cooperative, the miller, the sourcer, the exporter, the trucker, the shipper, the importer, the roaster, the roaster's wholesale customer—needs to earn a profit in order to stay in business. Often this leaves farmers in the unenviable position of growing a crop that provides others with a comfortable living while they struggle to survive.

COFFEE PRODUCERS
OF THE WORLD

COFFEE IS GROWN IN AND EXPORTED FROM DOZENS OF countries around the world. Below is the list of the largest producers of coffee by volume in 2007. Volume fluctuates considerably from year to year, depending on weather and other factors.

All numbers are given in bags; one bag equals 60 kilos or 132 pounds. Statistics are from the International Coffee Organization.

COUNTRY	PRODUCTION
Brazil	27.8 million bags of Arabica and Robusta
Vietnam	17.9 million bags of Robusta
Colombia	11.3 million bags of Arabica
Indonesia	4.3 million bags of Arabica and Robusta

Following is the 2007 output for countries producing Arabica coffee exclusively; the numbers are not broken down to indicate how much of each country's production is specialty coffee, but each country has a specialty sector.

COUNTRY	PRODUCTION
Colombia	11.3 million bags
Guatemala	3.7 million bags
Honduras	3.3 million bags
Peru	3.1 million bags
Mexico	2.9 million bags
Ethiopia	2.3 million bags
Costa Rica	1.4 million bags
Nicaragua	1.3 million bags
El Salvador	1.2 million bags
Kenya	736,000 bags
Burundi	292,000 bags
Rwanda	180,000 bags
Panama	101,000 bags

MAKING GREAT COFFEE
AT HOME

THE RECIPE FOR MAKING GREAT COFFEE AT HOME BEGINS
with a simple bit of advice: unplug your automated coffeemaker
and simplify: use a manually controlled coffee-making system.

Most automated home brewing systems are unable to
highlight the characteristics of great coffee because they do not
precisely control the temperature of the water when it comes in
contact with the coffee. This is a fatal flaw if your goal is to discover the full complement of flavors and aromas in high-quality
specialty beans.

That said, there are excellent, easy methods for making
coffee at home, and superb home-brewed coffee is within reach of
every coffee lover.

The Coffee
You have to begin with good coffee. Find a quality local roaster or
supermarket that sells freshly roasted beans. Take home a quarter
of a pound of a few different kinds of coffee and try them out.
Make note of how they are roasted. When you take the beans out
of the bag, smell them. Smell the coffee again after you grind them.

Even if you like your coffee with milk or cream, try a few sips without anything added. Taste it. Consider what you are tasting and smelling as you would with a glass of wine. And make sure you try coffees from different parts of the world—Latin America, Africa and Asia.

If you like a particular coffee, you might want to take a look at some of the Web sites listed below to see what the coffee guys have to say about it.

Don't buy more than a week's supply at a time. Store coffee in a dry airtight container. You need not freeze it.

One more thing about what goes into the pot: Make sure you use filtered water.

Equipment

- For home use, the coffee guys recommend low-tech coffeemakers such as French press pots that employ a finely perforated piston (or plunger), or drip brew pots, also called filter pots, where you pour water over ground coffee beans contained in a filter. The French press method requires a bit more dexterity, patience, and skill to master than systems such as Chemex or Melita that use filters. Stumptown and Counter Culture do not sell coffeemakers, though both companies' Web sites have information about making coffee at home. Intelligentsia recommends and sells coffeemakers and other coffee-making equipment on its Web site. George Howell's company, Terroir Coffee, also sells coffee-making equipment online.

  - *Note:* Four minutes is considered the optimal extraction time for French Press. If you use this method, you might want to buy a small kitchen timer.

- The coffee guys insist that the single most important investment you can make if you brew coffee at home is a burr coffee grinder that crushes whole coffee beans by moving them through a grinding wheel. The burr chops the coffee into uniformly sized pieces, which enables the water to run through it and extract evenly. You can buy a mid-range burr grinder for around $100. Capresso, Bodum, and Saeco make many different models, as do a number of other companies. The only specific home burr grinder recommended by any of the coffee guys is the Rancilio Rocky Burr Grinder that Intelligentsia sells on its Web site for $320. The best coffee grinders are made by Fetco for commercial use.

- *Note:* The blade grinders most people use at home slashes through coffee beans, producing pieces of uneven size that prevent water from running through evenly. In addition, these machines overgrind, producing heat that burns the coffee and spoils the taste.

- Use a standardized scoop. Most experts say 2 tablespoons of ground coffee per 8-ounce cup, but coffees differ and tastes differ. If you are very persnickety, buy a small digital scale, which will give you a truer reading, as coffees differ by weight and one scoop of coffee A may be denser and contain more flavor than one scoop of coffee B.

- If you make more coffee than you can use immediately, always pour it into a thermos or carafe to keep it warm. Never let coffee sit on a burner or warming device, as this will kill the taste.

- Cleanliness counts! The coffee guys recommend cleaning coffee equipment periodically with a commercial-grade cleaner such as Cleancaf.

- Read the directions that come with your coffeemaker and follow them.

Home Espresso

Different systems for making home espresso have passionate supporters and detractors, and home systems for making espresso can be very expensive. If you are interested in slipping down this particular rabbit hole, you will probably want to do some research before investing in a system.

A good place to start gathering information is the Web site home-barista.com.

Roasting Coffee at Home

If you are interested in trying your hand at roasting your own green coffee, take a look at sweetmarias.com.

Sweet Maria's sells home roasting equipment and high-quality unroasted green coffee beans on the Web. Sweet Maria's proprietor, Tom Owen, knows a great deal about coffee, and his site is a worth a visit, even if you're not planning to roast your own.

Online Resources

Other excellent sites for information about coffee and coffee-making methods are:

- coffeegeek.com
  Coffee Geek founder, Mark Prince, also hosts a podcast. This site has links to many coffee blogs, forums, and discussion groups.
- coffeed.com
  This site has links to many other coffee blogs, forums, and discussion groups.
- portafilter.net
  Here you can also access barista Nick Cho's coffee podcast.

You can order coffee beans and get lots of coffee information online from:

- counterculturecoffee.com
- intelligentsiacoffee.com
- stumptowncoffee.com
- sweetmarias.com
- taylormaidfarms.com (100 percent organic)
- terroircoffee.com

BIBLIOGRAPHY

Sources

Between 2005 and 2008, I interviewed dozens of coffee producers, buyers, roasters, importers, baristas, and experts, in person and on the telephone. Among those I interviewed were:

Arturo Aquirre; Sarah Allen; Andrew Barnett; Lindsey Bolger; Willem Boot; Joseph Brodsky; Kim Bullock; Timothy Castle; Tim Chapdelaine; Aleco Chigounis; Nick Cho; Johnny Collins; Kim Cook; Graciano Cruz; E. J. Dawson; Wendy de Jong; Libby Evans; Shanna Germain; Peter Giuliano; Brent Fortune; Bob Fulmer; Daniele Giovannucci; Kyle Glanville; Dave Griswold; Don Holly; George Howell; Ellie Hudson-Matuszak; Vincent Iatesta; Mark Inman; Jeff Jassmond; Paul Katzeff; Nick Kirby; Tony Konecny; Ricardo Koyner; John and Kerry Laird; Wilford Lamastus; Ted Lingle; Jason Long; Matt Lounsbury; Betsy McKinnon; Francisco Mena; Shirin Moayyad; K. C. O'Keefe; Anne Ottaway; Mark Overbay; Tom Owen; Heather and Mike Perry; Rachel, Daniel, and Price Peterson; Rick Peyser; Deaton Pigot; Joel Pollack; Richard Reynolds; Ric Rhinehart; David Roche; Stephen Rogers; Maria and Plinio Ruiz; Tim Schilling; Mario Serracin; Ezzi Shabbir; Menno Simons; Trish Skeie; Brett Smith; Paul Songer; Duane Sorenson; Susie Spindler; Andi Trindle; Eton Tsuno; Carmen Vellejos; Stephen Vick; Ethan Warsh; Geoff Watts; Ryan Wilbur; and Doug Zell.

Books

ALLEN, STEWART L. *The Devil's Cup: A History of the World According to Coffee.* New York: Ballantine, 2003.

CASTLE, TIMOTHY and JOAN NIELSON. *The Great Coffee Book.* Berkeley, CA: Ten Speed Press, 1999.

CASTLE, TIMOTHY. *The Perfect Cup: A Coffee Lover's Guide to Buying, Brewing, and Tasting.* Cambridge, MA: Da Capo Press, 1991.

DAVIDS, KENNETH. *Coffee: A Guide to Buying, Brewing, and Enjoying.* Fifth edition. New York: St. Martin's Griffin, 2001.

GIOVANNUCCI, DANIELE and FREEK JAN KOEKOEK. *The State of Sustainable Coffee: A Study of Twelve Major Markets.* Copyright: Daniele Giovannucci, 1006 South 9th Street, Philadelphia, PA 19147 USA, 2003.

GOUREVITCH, PHILIP. *We Wish to Inform You That Tomorrow We Will Be Killed with Our Families: Stories from Rwanda.* New York: Farrar, Straus and Giroux, 1998.

KAPUSCINSKI, RYSZARD. *The Emperor: Downfall of an Autocrat.* New York: Vintage International, 1989.

KUMMER, CORBY. *The Joy of Coffee: The Essential Guide to Buying, Brewing and Enjoying.* Revised and updated. Boston: *Houghton Mifflin,* 2003.

LINGLE, TED. *The Coffee Cupper's Handbook.* Third edition. Long Beach, CA: Specialty Coffee Association of America, 2001.

LISS, DAVID. *The Coffee Trader: A Novel.* New York: Random House, 2003.

PENDERGRAST, MARK. *Uncommon Grounds: The History of Coffee and How It Transformed Our World.* New York: Basic Books, 1999.

SCHOMER, DAVID. *Espresso Coffee: Updated Professional Techniques.* Seattle: Peanut Butter Publishing, 2004.

VIANI, RINANTONIO and ILLY, ANDREA. *Espresso Coffee, The Science of Quality.* Second edition. San Diego: Elsevier, 2004.

WILD, ANTONY. *Coffee: A Dark History.* New York: W.W. Norton, 2004.

Publications

Barista Magazine. "Big D and the Family," by Sarah Allen. April/May, 2007. (Contact: info@baristamagazine.com)

Barista Magazine. "Master Q & A: David Schomer." December/January 2007. (Contact: info@baristamagazine.com)

Roast Magazine. "A Family Album: Getting to the Roots of Coffee's Plant Heritage," research provided by David Roche and Robert Osgood. November/December 2007. (Contact: roast@roastmagazine.com)

You can read some of my articles about coffee on my Web site: michaeleweissmanwrites.com

INDEX